THE
CONFLICT
THESAURUS:

*A Writer's Guide to Obstacles,
Adversaries, and Inner Struggles*

VOLUME 1

ANGELA ACKERMAN
& BECCA PUGLISI

THE CONFLICT THESAURUS: A WRITER'S GUIDE TO OBSTA-
CLES, ADVERSARIES, AND INNER STRUGGLES. VOLUME 1.

ISBN: 978-0-9992963-9-4

Edited by Michael Dunne (www.michael-dunne.com/) and C.S. Lakin
(https://www.livewritethrive.com)
Book cover design by JD Smith Design (http://www.jdsmith-design.com)
Book formatting by JD Smith Design (http://www.jdsmith-design.com)

THE WRITERS HELPING WRITERS®
DESCRIPTIVE THESAURUS SERIES

Available in nine languages, sourced by universities, and recommended by editors and agents all over the world, this bestselling series is a writer's favorite for brainstorming fresh description and powering up storytelling.

The Emotion Thesaurus: A Writer's Guide to Character Expression (Second Edition)

The Positive Trait Thesaurus: A Writer's Guide to Character Attributes

The Negative Trait Thesaurus: A Writer's Guide to Character Flaws

The Urban Setting Thesaurus: A Writer's Guide to City Spaces

The Rural Setting Thesaurus: A Writer's Guide to Personal and Natural Places

The Emotional Wound Thesaurus: A Writer's Guide to Psychological Trauma

The Occupation Thesaurus: A Writer's Guide to Jobs, Vocations, and Careers

The Conflict Thesaurus:
A Writer's Guide to Obstacles, Adversaries, and Inner Struggles (Vol. 2)

Emotion Amplifiers: A Companion to The Emotion Thesaurus

TABLE OF CONTENTS

CONFLICT'S ROLE IN STORYTELLING: SHAPING CHARACTERS

All right, hands up: What's the one thing we can't get enough of in fiction but we avoid like a screaming toddler in real life? Conflict.

And it's no wonder. Conflict is painful. Messy. Unpredictable. It leads to scrapped plans, wasted effort, stress, and worry. It can force us into corners, prey on our worst fears, and push us past our limits both mentally and physically. No, we don't much care for conflict—or, at least, not too much of it. We'd much rather create a plan, follow it, and then prance our way to the finish line.

But fiction? Oh, that's different. As readers, we become book-gripping masochists, relishing every upset, backstab, and shove off a cliff that comes about. Let it rain fire and poison! Bring on the horrific, impossible choices! Sharpen the monster's fangs and set it loose! We can't get enough.

It seems ironic that something we try to avoid in real life is the very thing we can't get enough of in fiction. Psychologically speaking, though, it makes perfect sense. Books do not significantly trigger our fight-or-flight instincts, making it safe to experience conflict—after all, that bad stuff is happening to someone else. Yet, if the story is well written, it draws us in so we're right there with the hero or heroine, feeling some of their dread, anger, and confusion. We identify with their experiences because our own real-life ones have taught us the agony of uncertainty and fear and what it's like to feel completely outmatched.

A book gives us a front-row seat as the main character is dropped inside life's rock tumbler. Will the relentless, destructive machine crush them into oblivion? Or will they emerge, rough edges worn away, a mission thrumming in their chest to achieve their goal whatever the cost?

This second outcome is what we hope for: that they persevere. Because real life and fiction converge in one very important place: the euphoria that comes with achievement. Whether it concerns us or our characters, that heady moment of getting what is needed most can't be matched. And this is where we arrive at true irony. What makes a moment of victory so powerful, affirming, and satisfying is *knowing what it took to win:* the hard work, sacrifice, and costs. And that feeling only arises with opposition, obstacles, problems, and challenges. In other words: *conflict.* So, while we may not like adversity in real life and often try to avoid it, the act of overcoming it is what makes us feel truly alive.

In fiction, conflict is the crucible that tests, bruises, and shapes our characters. Externally, it pushes the plot onward by supplying the resistance needed to force characters to scrutinize their world, make choices, and take action to get what they want. Internally, conflict generates a tug-of-war between the character's fears, beliefs, needs, values, and desires. Ultimately, it forces them to choose between an old, antiquated way of thinking and doing, or a new, evolved way of being, because only one will help them get what they want. Story expert Michael Hauge calls this a choice between living in fear and living courageously. Can the character make the hard decisions, step out onto the ledge despite fear, and embrace change, or do they retreat? This battle between the interconnected elements of the character's belief system is why readers tune in. It is a powerful, emotional echo of their own ongoing struggles to overcome fear and achieve growth.

If all this internal talk is making you think *character arc*, you're picking up what we're laying down. Conflict, as painful a teacher as it can be, is an opportunity for characters to discover who they really are—but only if they can let go of who they were. In this way, it drives character development. It demands action, forcing the character to step up, fight, and recommit to the goal, which in turn proves their worthiness to readers. It will push the character to their limits and, in their most desperate moments, reveal who they truly are—their morals, values, and beliefs.

Whether they succeed or fail, who your character is at the start of the story will differ from who they are at the end because conflict is the harbinger of change.

THE PLOT-CONFLICT COMBO

In 2016, the University of Vermont and the University of Adelaide took on an ambitious project: analyze the emotional arcs of 1,737 works of fiction from Project Gutenberg's collection and determine how many narrative plots they consisted of.[1] The answer? Six. Each could be attributed to one of these six distinctive plot shapes that emerged over the scope of the story:

Rags to Riches: The story of a character who starts out disadvantaged in some way and goes on to overcome adversity and make it big. This story has a steady "rise" shape that takes it from failure to triumph (rise from despair).

Riches to Rags: The story of a character who has it all, then loses everything. This tragedy has a steady "fall" shape to it, a decline from start to finish (fall from grace).

Man-in-a-Hole: The story of a character enjoying a successful status quo who suffers a fall, taking him to the lowest of lows, which he then fights to pull himself out of. The shape of this story is one where two highs frame a dip or hole (fall-rise).

Icarus: The story mirrors the Greek tale of Icarus, who used wings of wax and feathers to escape his prison. But when he ignored the warnings about flying too high, the sun melted his wings and he plummeted to his death. This shape is marked by a character's rise and then his untimely fall (rise-fall).

Cinderella: This is the story of a downhearted character who gains happiness and fulfillment only to lose it and fall into despair. But rather than end there, the tale continues with the character making a comeback (rise-fall-rise).

Oedipus: This story, like the tragic Greek tale of the same name, involves a character who starts out well but quickly lands in trouble. They successfully climb out of this pit, but the rise is short-lived and they descend again to their doom (fall-rise-fall).

This is not the first such study on core plots, and it won't be the last. Like all argument-worthy topics, theories abound on how many plots should belong at the storyteller's table. Three?

---

1 LaFrance, A. (2018, November 1). *An A.I. says there are six main kinds of stories.* The Atlantic. https://www.theatlantic.com/technology/archive/2016/07/the-six-main-arcs-in-storytelling-identified-by-a-computer/490733

Seven? Thirty-six? Regardless, it messes with the brain that the millions (billions?) of tales found in Western society—fiction, film, TV, games, advertising, and on it goes—can be traced back to only a handful of plots. It doesn't seem possible. How can so many original, enthralling stories really be the same structures regurgitated over and over?

Well, mostly, it's a little thing called conflict.

A bold claim, we know. And don't get us wrong—characters also play a huge part in making each story unique. After all, they can be endlessly adapted through personality, backstory, desires, needs, and more. But no matter who a character is on the page, his story goal will steer him in a specific direction. Like a tired tourist heading to his hotel room, whether he chooses the elevator or stairs, he's going to stop at the same floor. Conflict, on the other hand, has the run of the building. Like a mischievous kid bent on causing trouble, he can hit all the elevator buttons and visit every floor, set a fire in the stairwell, or throw furniture out windows. There's no limit to the number of ways conflict can be used to freshen up a story or scene.

In storytelling, a plethora of conflict is encouraged. Great stories should offer a merry-go-round of roadblocks, obstacles, and conundrums—meaning, each story moment is made fresh by the problems being introduced. But that isn't to say that conflict lacks structure or it should be tossed in willy-nilly. Friction and opposition should serve the story, providing meaningful challenges that test the characters. Additionally, each story will contain a central struggle, and just as there are a limited number of plot shapes, there is also a set number of established literary forms for conflict.

> **Character vs. Character:** In this scenario, the protagonist goes head-to-head with another character in a battle of wills. They may be rivals (gym owners Peter and White in *Dodgeball*), competitors (the cast of *Game Night*), or enemies who have opposing needs, desires, or agendas (such as Hans Gruber and John McClane in *Die Hard*). They may also be participants in a push-and-pull relationship like a romance (Westley and Buttercup in *The Princess Bride*) or buddy dynamic (Brennan Huff and Dale Doback in *Step Brothers*). And whether characters have opposing goals or want the same thing, the friction between the two generates clashes in which one typically gains the upper hand over the other. This should not be one-sided; characters should be a good match in wits, skills, and resources, ensuring ongoing shifts in the balance of power until the story concludes and the outcome is decided.

> **Character vs. Society:** These stories feature a character who faces seemingly insurmountable challenges when taking on society or a powerful agency within their world. Mildred Hayes (*Three Billboards Outside Ebbing, Missouri*) pits herself against the police department to get justice for her murdered daughter. Katniss Everdeen leads a rebellion against the government (*The Hunger Games* trilogy). Oskar Schindler opposes a cruel Nazi regime to save as many Jewish people as possible (*Schindler's List*). This type of conflict contains high risks and personal stakes as the character is poised to lose much in their bid to hold true to their morals.

> **Character vs. Nature:** In this case, the character goes up against nature. Weather elements (*The Perfect Storm*), a challenging landscape (*Wild*, *127 Hours*), and feral animals (*The Revenant*) can provide forces that must be tamed or survived if the character is to succeed.

Character vs. Technology: This conflict will pit a character against technology or a machine, like Sarah Connor confronting the Terminator or Neo and his battle with the Matrix. Bigger threats often lead to narrow escapes and near disasters, and to overcome a technological obstacle often requires ingenuity, specialized knowledge, resources, and grit.

Character vs. Supernatural: A character facing opposition that exists (at least partially) outside their understanding falls into this form of conflict. This might be a character who is going up against a supernatural or magical force such as Danny Torrance in Stephen King's *Doctor Sleep*, a possession plotline like Johnny Blaze in *Ghost Rider*, or a demigod clashing with other gods and the fate set out for him in *Percy Jackson and the Olympians*. This form is sometimes broken down further into Character vs. God and Character vs. Fate subcategories.

Character vs. Self: Of all the conflict forms, this is the most personal (and often the most compelling) because the friction arises from within the character's belief system. Any good story will place a mirror in front of the character and show the battle within as he experiences mixed emotions over what he wants, has done, or plans to do.

Consider Jason Bourne of *The Bourne Identity,* a man with amnesia who is on the run from people seeking to neutralize him. He wants to regain his memory and be left alone, yet the more he unearths about his past, the more he realizes he doesn't deserve freedom or a fresh start. Another example is Dexter Morgan of the TV series *Dexter*, a sociopath who follows a code of conduct by only killing other murderers. He leads a double life: a functional blood-splatter analyst for the police department and someone who indulges in homicidal urges and vigilantism. As the series progresses, it's clear that Dexter's conflict is not limited to staying off the police's radar so he can keep killing; there's also a war within as his ability to fully embrace his darkness is stymied because some people are beginning to matter to him.

Practically every story will have a mix of conflicts from the groupings above, but one will be the most prominent—a **central conflict** that serves as the basis of the plot.

CONFLICT IS STRUGGLE

Every clash boils down to the same thing: a struggle between two opposing forces. And whatever scenarios you include, they'll fall somewhere along the spectrum between external and internal conflict. **External conflict** comes from the people and obstacles your character faces in the outer world, and **internal conflict** is centered in your character's emotions and belief systems. A good story will include plenty of both because the beating heart of a story *is* your protagonist, a complex being made of layered needs, beliefs, fears, and desires. Whenever external conflict requires a response, the character must make a choice about what that will be. This means the *what* of action is always attached to the *why* of motivation—the character's needs, values, and core beliefs that drive her to act.

A character's unique internal factors make her who she is, and she'll weigh them in each situation to determine the right thing to do. This isn't always an easy or intuitive process because these factors often exist in conflict. For example, the heroine in your story may **need** love but **believes** she is unworthy of it. Yet, she **desires** a romantic partner even though she **fears** rejection because of negative past experiences.

Imagine the battle that will occur if the right conflict is introduced to the right situation. Let's say your heroine, whose string of bad relationships has sworn her off romance forever, is engaging in some friendly banter with a teammate after a co-ed softball game. As they pack up their gear and head to the parking lot, laughing and joking, the chemistry between them builds. Finally, her teammate suggests the two head out for an after-game drink.

How will she respond? Will she listen to her *need* and *desire,* or her *fear* and *false beliefs*? And what if this decision is complicated by something else—say, a large age gap or the fact that he's her boss at the office? Will her moral sense of right and wrong squash the date before it happens, or will such thoughts be shoved into a closet because sparks are flying and desire has taken the wheel?

This type of internal conflict is practically part of a character's DNA because they (like us) will change with time and experience as their worldview evolves (or devolves). Each external situation will require internal weighing and measuring before action can take place, and meaningful conflict will challenge the character's belief system. This means it has the power to shape the character *internally.* One informs the other in a cycle of change and growth or anti-growth.

Character development doesn't stop there, though. The presence of external conflict also pushes the character to rally the troops, so to speak, marshaling the forces of their skill, strategy, imagination, and knowledge so they are able to meet the challenge or threat from a position of strength. And, depending on the outcome, the character will know where they stand and how prepared they are for the next conflict that comes their way.

Let's imagine a situation in which the protagonist, Melissa, is loading groceries into her car. She's approached by a woman who has lost her little boy, who wandered away as she was speaking with a friend in the parking lot.

A parent herself, Melissa jumps into action, abandoning her cart to search the area in hopes of spotting the child's mop of red hair. She peppers the woman with questions about where he was last seen and how old he is. So intent is she on finding the boy that she doesn't see the woman slip Melissa's wallet from her cart. It's only later, long after the woman rushes off to notify the store's management, that Melissa realizes the whole thing was a ruse.

Often, conflict catches a character unaware—meaning, they act the best they can in the moment. Sometimes they succeed, and other times they fail. A victory might reveal strengths to feel proud of or areas to consider for improvement. A failure might show just how outmatched the character was or expose a blind spot, such as the case just mentioned in which the character's motherly instincts were used against her.

In a perfect world, the postmortem of the event should help the character determine what comes next and how to be better prepared. But, in reality, it often causes internal conflict to bubble up, especially if self-blame is lurking, triggering fears of not measuring up, being inadequate, and failing other people. These negative responses cloud a character's judgment and may hold her back.

In this case, the character may become distrustful of her instincts and begin to doubt the motives of others, which damages her relationships. Or, the next time someone asks for help, she sends them packing because she feels gullible and doesn't want to be taken advantage of.

And if she discovers later that the person really was in need, well, that will erode her self-worth and self-esteem even further.

But negative experiences aren't the only ones that can alter the character's inner landscape. If a future situation arises in which she extends her trust to someone and is rewarded, that will help restore her self-esteem and reshape her worldview by reminding her that good people are out there too.

WITH CONFLICT, THINK QUANTITY AND QUALITY

The variety of conflict is what makes a story crackle with power—whether we're talking about macro conflicts at the heart of a plot or scene-level complications meant to pressure the character and raise the stakes. The best stories don't stick to the same type of conflict over and over, either. They pull from multiple forms that work naturally with the story's main premise to hit the character from all sides.

It's also possible to **blend conflicts** to create something original. Stephen King's *Christine* is about a 1958 Plymouth Fury that is sentient, evil, and out for blood. Each time it kills, Christine restores itself, erasing all evidence of the crime. This delivers conflict that is especially hard for characters Dennis Guilder and Leigh Talbot to navigate because it is both *supernatural* and *technological* in nature.

Another example would be the movie *Split*, in which Kevin Crumb has twenty-four distinct personalities, each darker and more dangerous than the last. Some try to help the victims imprisoned in Crumb's basement, and some delight in their capture. This raw story would be a textbook *character vs. self* tale if (spoiler alert) one of the personalities wasn't a violent creature—not fully human—with powerful abilities and strengths. This unexpected addition of *character vs. supernatural* conflict creates something new and chilling, transforming a standard premise into something fresh and unforgettable.

CONFLICT CATEGORIES

Conflict is at its finest when it's added where it can make the biggest impact. And, big or small, a conflict bomb's ground zero will always be in the vicinity of your characters, especially the protagonist. Sure, it's cool when there's a smash-y car chase or something blows up, but readers want to see how conflict is going to mess directly with a character they have come to care about. This is why we recommend taking a character-view approach when choosing obstacles and challenges. By thinking of how it will impact your character first and foremost, you can select conflict that keeps readers invested, raises the stakes, creates personal complications and internal struggles, and paves the way for epiphanies, internal growth, and achievement.

Relationship Friction

Pop quiz: How important are the relationships in your life—say, the one you have with a spouse, your child, or other cherished family and friends? What about the co-worker who never forgets your birthday, the critique partner who always makes time for your stories, or the neighbor who feeds your cat when you go out of town?

We all have relationships with people we admire, care about, and will make sacrifices for. We're also connected to a myriad of others, such as relatives who reside in the *it's complicated* zone, or people we try to avoid, wish we could avoid, and just can't stand. Oh, if only we could choose who to let into our world and who to keep out. Unfortunately, life doesn't work that way—not for us or our characters.

Healthy or dysfunctional, safe or toxic, relationships are complicated because characters are complicated. They're always doing and saying things that will test their connections to others. Characters can make each other swell with gratitude or recoil in shock. Regardless of their intentions, they may generate conflict when their fears and insecurities make them reactive and foolish.

Relationship friction can be the good kind (lighthearted teasing between siblings or an intense glance shared by two lovers), but often it's the other—the type that creates a bristly moment of silence after an argument or the sting of hurt after a secret is carelessly spilled. Conflicts that create problems in relationships result in your character's emotions being easily activated, increasing the chance they will lash out, cross a personal or professional line, or make a mistake that leads to more trouble.

Another beautiful aspect of the conflict-relationship combo is that a character's professional and private lives will contain a net of connections similar to a spider's web. Conflict that causes friction in one relationship will connect to others, triggering a host of problems. This can be useful when you need to bring your character to their lowest point by damaging their reputation, removing their closest supporters, or forcing them to choose work over family or family over their career. Giving them bumps to navigate in a relationship can also help them see themselves from another's point of view, awakening them to their own shortcomings, which can spark the desire to grow and change. And the right conflict can remind them of who and what they're fighting for … and why.

Duty and Responsibility

Another way to bring conflict to your character's doorstep is to think about how duty and responsibility can pile up and disrupt the status quo—especially when it comes to her personal and professional life. As we all know, there's often an uneasy alliance between work and home. A career is necessary to pay the bills, but it becomes a source of conflict when the demands of the job leak into family life. Long hours at the office, having to travel frequently, bringing work stress home, or needing to answer emails after the workday is done can all strain marital and family relationships. Likewise, if the paycheck can't keep up with the mortgage or one partner is carrying the biggest load at home, tensions will pile up.

When a character's home—that most sacred and safest of places—becomes a powder keg, how much additional conflict will blow her world to bits? What might happen if the heroine's elderly father falls ill and requires care, or she ends up in a car accident that leads to a costly repair and hospital bills? Suddenly her fragile ecosystem is shattered. Maybe pulling away from work to care for her father will open the door of opportunity for a professional rival. That could lead to the character losing out on a promotion and raise. What will she do when higher insurance premiums hit or the medical bill comes due? And what might happen when she has to break her promise to take the family on that beach vacation (that was supposed to smooth things over because she's been working so much)? Trouble. Consequences. Conflict.

Let's be clear: targeting your character's sense of duty and responsibility is a low blow. One of the worst feelings in the world is when a ball is dropped and others pay the price. Whether it's letting down co-workers at work or being unable to make it to a child's recital, your character's stress will go up and her self-worth will go down. Even if the inability to handle everything is caused by something outside the character's control, she'll blame herself for failing to manage.

However, because not coming through is a hive-inducing worry for your character, she'll be highly motivated to untie the knot she's become tangled in. The threat of letting others down can help her shed unnecessary commitments, let go of toxic influences and people, and force her to prioritize. Her greatest skills (or new ones yet to be learned) can help her climb out of this conflict hole.

But what if she can't figure out how to lighten her burdens, and she ends up letting down the people she loves and respects? Well, sometimes that's exactly what we want—for our characters to fall into a barrel of their own guilt, shame, and worthlessness. Some characters need their world to bottom out so they can see what everyone around them sees: that they're taking on too much, they're being taken advantage of, or it's time to make a change at home or work. If your character is on a positive arc trajectory, the ending of one thing can lead to the start of something else—something healthier that can help them find the balance and security they seek.

Failures and Mistakes
If you think back to the last big mistake you made, can you remember what it was? Not the I-burned-the-toast type of mistake, but one of the big ones: forgetting to pick a child up after school, carelessly leaving a friend's laptop on a park bench, or badmouthing the guy next door in what you thought was a private message but ended up being the neighborhood's group chat.

The moment we realize what we've done, we stiffen. Our breath locks in our chest. The world suddenly grows close and sharp as our mind relives the mistake in excruciating detail. An exhale slides out, a long, deep *"no"* coming with it. It's not denial but a fervent desire to go back in time to undo what we've done, knowing we cannot.

This moment is a mental hellscape, because we try very hard in real life to avoid failures and mistakes. Missteps shine a spotlight on just how inadequate we are, and we tend to be our own worst critics. In fiction, it's our job to make sure that when our characters fail or make a mistake, repercussions follow. Maybe a friend is hurt or an injustice occurs. Possibly an opportunity is lost, a new danger is introduced, and the end goal is now farther away. The negative fallout from a mistake usually causes the character to shoulder the blame, and when they do, their self-esteem plummets. The character feels trapped, painfully aware that they have no control, they're unable to correct what happened, and they can't escape the negative emotions that are bombarding them.

The aftermath of a failure or mistake can go one of two ways. If a character panics, their emotions go into overdrive and they become fixated on the worst-case scenario. They believe they must act immediately to prevent catastrophe, only they aren't calm or objective enough to think things through. This usually lands them into even more hot water, which is bad for them but good for you and the story because…*conflict!*

A failure or mistake is also an opportunity to learn and grow, so this is the second path characters can take. Their mistakes may give them the perspective they've been lacking: Are they acting out of passion or just coasting and doing what's expected? Do they need to learn to say no to avoid being spread too thin? Should they step back and reevaluate what they're doing and why?

Failing hurts, but it's also a checkpoint that forces characters to look at their route and make decisions. Are they on the right path, is the goal worth it, and are they up to the task? What should they do to avoid failure next time? If a character reflects on what happened and realizes they need to try again, then we know they're open to change. This becomes a powerful character arc moment. Things that may have held them back (a way of thinking, being closed-minded to help or guidance, etc.) will no longer cause them trouble because they're seeking growth.

Moral Dilemmas and Temptations

Here's where we encourage you to put on your Thanksgiving dinner sweatpants and get ready to feast, because this type of conflict will target your character's core belief system, which is central to their identity and worldview. It may just be the most important conflict you can introduce because it forces your character to wrestle with big questions about what they feel and believe. Moral conflicts can tear your character up, lead them into uncomfortable gray areas, and force them to sacrifice one belief for another. It's basically candy for writers, and, boy, does it taste good.

Moral dilemmas and temptations each torment your character in different ways. A dilemma is when a person faces a choice between two values, duties, or convictions that align with their sense of integrity. Moral temptations involve decisions that push the character to choose between right and wrong. Sounds pretty straightforward, but the temptation part makes it anything but.

In both situations, characters ideally need time to weigh their choices carefully, looking at the options from multiple angles, thinking about the risk, and making decisions that feel right. But, for story purposes, we want these moments to be as agonizing as possible. Employing conflicts that challenge personal beliefs or force a quick decision can lead to anguish and regret.

And temptations, big and small, are all about offering the character something they really want that maybe isn't the best option for them. If the chance to take revenge on someone comes along, will they seize it? If they can cheat with a co-worker on a business trip and their spouse won't find out, will they do it? If the character gives in, lines will be crossed, and their judgment becomes hazy as they seek to create paper-thin justifications about why it's okay to cross more.

The more personal a moral conflict becomes, the blurrier right and wrong become. For example, what should a character do when they are offered a chance to bribe someone on a transplant committee so their child can be bumped up on the waiting list? Is it right for them to put their child before someone else? What if that someone else is a fifty-year-old adult with no dependents? Is it fair that a person in this stage of life comes before a sixteen-year-old with so many years still ahead of them?

Mitigating factors are a great way to blend black and white into shades of gray. Use them to challenge your character's beliefs and see how close he can get to taking a path he never thought he would take. For example, in the movie *Prisoners*, Keller is a law-abiding, respectful man and loving father. But when his daughter is abducted and police are ineffective at questioning the person he believes is responsible, he faces a difficult quandary: *What am I willing to do to find my daughter?* For him, it means doing something abhorrent: kidnapping and torturing the person he suspects has knowledge of who took his child. In each torture session, Keller battles with his own humanity. Even his unshakable belief in the man's involvement does not make it easy for him to purposely inflict pain. Keller knows what he is doing is wrong, yet he believes it's the only path to rescuing his child. So, does that make it right?

Dilemmas and temptations—especially in extreme circumstances—can cause a character's values to shift. These moral gray areas can be equally fascinating and horrifying for readers because it causes them to think about what they might do in the same situation.

Moral conflicts are not only great for forcing your characters to examine who they are and what they believe, they can also reinforce a story's themes on right and wrong and personal identity. A character might experience conflict over a long-held idea or belief, or their values may place them in opposition to other people, cultures, or society at large. When something deeply moral is at stake, the character will often risk everything to adhere to their core beliefs and personal truths.

Pressure and Ticking Clocks

Remember that time you woke up and the day stretched out before you in an endless landscape of sunshine and solitude? How you had no obligations or responsibilities, no to-do list, and nothing to prioritize or juggle?

Yeah, neither do we.

Let's face it: life is busy, and for characters sitting in the hot seat, it's even busier. In the best of times, they must manage relationships and commitments, fulfill responsibilities and duties, navigate risk, and achieve milestones to get them closer to their goal. And, unfortunately for our characters, writers are far more interested in bringing about the worst of times than the best. We heap on burdens, tighten deadlines, tie characters down with red tape, and put everything they say and do under a spotlight.

Conflict that comes in the form of pressure or ticking clocks forces a character to put aside distractions and the extraneous to focus on what matters most. When the pressure is on, there's no room for error, so the character must harness his strengths and do his best work. But pressure can produce a variety of results. It's like making popcorn. Throw some kernels into the microwave for the right amount of time and you get a fluffy, fragrant snack. Put them in for too long and you end up with a bag of blackened corpses and a kitchen that reeks for days.

Whether you introduce a delay that makes the character late, trot out an ultimatum, or place him under unwanted scrutiny, the squeeze is on. Sometimes you want characters to rise to a challenge; other times you need to show what will finally break them. Pressure can help you do both. When complications and stresses mount, characters must dig deep and perform or be crushed—there is no middle ground.

A great example of this type of conflict can be found in the Netflix original series *Ozark*. When financial planner Marty Byrde's business partner is caught stealing money from a Mexican drug cartel, Marty has to do some fast talking to save his family—including a Hail Mary promise to use the tourism cover of the Ozarks to launder the cartel's money. Uprooting his family from Chicago, Marty is given the near-impossible task of laundering eight million dollars in three months. He quickly buys up businesses to help him mix dirty money with the clean, but it becomes an impossible task. Add in some family friction, altercations with local criminals, the FBI scrutinizing Marty's every move, and running afoul of a heroin producer, and the pressure never lets up. It's a constant back-and-forth from the frying pan to the fire.

Pressure is also great for creating tension for readers as they wonder whether a character can handle the new threat. How can he work past this new challenge? Can he beat the clock? This additional stress will keep readers turning pages late into the night, anxious to discover if the character can circumvent this latest development or not.

Pressure not only comes from other people and events, it also builds from within. Characters are complexly motivated and often have internal reasons for stepping up when the odds are against them. They'll be more willing to face danger, difficulty, and pain when they're driven by bigger emotions like love or fear. They may also feel compelled to prove their own value, fix a past mistake, please someone, protect a loved one, or achieve a seemingly impossible goal that will fill an aching need.

This type of conflict is excellent for raising the stakes, adding more problems, and increasing the cost of failure. Giving your character multiple problems will also pull them in different directions, forcing them to make choices that may surprise them. The way they strategize, reach out to others for help, or sacrifice secondary goals in favor of primary ones will show readers the essence of who they are.

No-Win Scenarios

Sometimes you need truly agonizing conflict—the type that forces the character to choose between bad and worse. Lose-lose situations are especially dangerous because they bog characters down in an emotional quicksand of fear, obligation, and guilt. This negative psychological spiral often results in them sacrificing their own happiness and needs.

Consider a character whose powerful husband made her out to be an unfit mother due to her anxiety (ironically caused by his emotional abuse), resulting in her losing a custody battle. She now has to cater to her toxic ex-husband's controlling demands, knowing if she doesn't, he'll turn her children against her or use his connections to sever visitations altogether. To maintain a relationship with her children, she allows her ex to dictate when she can see them, what they're allowed to do together, and how much influence she has in their lives.

Another example might be a young man who works hard to win a scholarship to study abroad. But pursuing his own dreams means his physically disabled sister will be put in the charge of their addicted and neglectful parents. So he decides in the final hours to give up the scholarship. A no-win situation feels like a trap for the character who's stuck in it. The more time he spends there, the more gnawing the void of that unmet need becomes, making it harder for him to cling to optimism and hope.

When a lose-lose scenario requires an immediate response, the character won't agonize as much over his options. On the surface, this seems merciful, but in reality it can be worse. Imagine a firefighter facing a horrific blaze. There are two children inside, but he only has time to search one of the bedrooms before the house is utterly consumed. The firefighter chooses the youngest child's room because it's closest to the main entrance and will give him the best chance of saving at least one of them. He busts down the door and searches through the haze of smoke, checking the bed and closet, calling out. The room is empty. Beams above him groan and let go, and he rushes for the exit, empty-handed. Later, he learns the children were sleeping together in the oldest child's room, and both were lost to the fire.

In the aftermath, what's more likely—that the firefighter will shake it off, standing by his choice, or he'll be consumed by the terrible outcome and relive that decision over and over? In most cases, it will be the latter. Guilt will hit him hard. Why didn't he pick the other bedroom? He could have saved both. And shouldn't he have suspected that the youngest would go to the oldest when smoke started filling the house? As a child, didn't he jump into his own sister's bed after a nightmare or when thunder shook the walls?

It won't matter that he made a logical and practical decision in the moment that gave him the best odds of saving a child. Hindsight causes him to overanalyze and question whether fear for his own life is what pushed him to the closest room, allowing a dangerous false belief to take root: that cowardice was the driving force behind his decision. The more he beats himself up, the more self-doubt about his character and his abilities will drown him, and the more certain he will become that he should have chosen differently, should have predicted the children's behavior.

Split-second lose-lose decisions are often barbed, leaving behind scars. Having to live with a decision and the resulting doubt is never easy and can drag a character into a very dark place. If the situation was particularly traumatic and painful, PTSD aftereffects (anxiety, depression, night terrors, and more) may also occur. Dealing with this, or being imprisoned by unfair emotions like guilt, shame, and self-loathing, may push your character toward self-destructive coping mechanisms.

Do no-win situations sound like emotional wounds in the making? They are. And while any negative conflict experience can lead to the formation of a wound, lose-lose scenarios are the trains most likely to stop at that painful station. The inner turmoil caused by making an impossible choice can very easily eat your character alive.

In your story, you can use a no-win situation to trigger an unresolved wound that involves an element of inadequacy. The character's misbeliefs about their decision will need to be undone if they are to overcome the past and let go of feelings of low self-worth. Eventually, the character will have to reach a point where they see the truth: that in the moment, they really had no choice. There were no better options because they were not in control, and they made the best decision they could with the information they had. This realization is key to self-forgiveness, which will pave the way for them to make peace with what happened and break the chains of guilt.

No matter what form it takes, meaningful conflict that encompasses an inner struggle will draw readers into the character's viewpoint. They'll agonize and empathize, remembering a time when they themselves had to make decisions without all the information, failed, acted rashly and hurt people, or had to live with the consequence of a wrong choice.

The beauty of conflict is that it comes in so many forms. It is a powerful way to poke at your character's soft spots, raise the stakes, and maybe encourage a specific path to self-growth. Use the conflict categories in this book to brainstorm possible impacts on the characters and the story. The second volume of *The Conflict Thesaurus* will cover even more harrowing categories, including loss of control, power struggles, losing an advantage, ego-related conflicts, and miscellaneous challenges.

A NECESSARY INGREDIENT FOR POWERFUL CONFLICT: STAKES

A foolhardy belief for writers is the idea that conflict equals reader engagement. Sure, we like fictional car chases, wedding sabotage, and homicidal maniacs at the bedroom window as much as the next person. But their presence in a story doesn't automatically mean we'll tune in. In order for us to care, we need to know *why* we should care. In other words, something meaningful has to be at stake.

Think about it this way. When bad things happen to bad people, how do you feel? Let's say a pipe bursts at a neighbor's house, the same guy who complains to the homeowner association because he doesn't like the rainbow flag flying over your deck. Or a restaurant that once gave you food poisoning is shut down by the health department. Other than a bit of schadenfreude, do you feel anything substantial? Is your day (or life) impacted in a relevant way?

Now, when bad things happen to good people, that's a different story. If your sister-in-law goes into labor far too early or your best friend is jailed because her wayward stepson is dealing drugs out of her basement, you don't just shrug and move on. You're making calls, trying to figure out what you can do, how to help. You're invested because you care about the people involved and what's happening to them.

For conflict to matter to readers, something needs to be at stake: a cost incurred if your character fails to navigate the situation successfully. If the detective doesn't catch the serial killer, multiple people will die. Or if the henpecked heroine can't stop her toxic family from running her life, she'll forever lose the man she loves. When each new problem has a serious or *else* attached to it, the character must take action. Their desire to avoid these negative consequences becomes a big part of their motivation for achieving the goal.

Stakes, like conflict, should show up in your story like a bumper crop of rotten apples, increasing tension and raising the cost of failure by the bushel. And while the goal is to create stakes so high the character can't turn back—not even when she's staring down her deepest fears—the consequences of failure are up to you and how evil you're feeling. To get you started, consider the categories below.

Far-Reaching Stakes, sometimes called public stakes, are those that include loss for others if the protagonist fails. If a bomb goes off, the protagonist may die, but so will everyone else in the building. And it goes beyond them too; loved ones standing anxiously behind the police tape will also be impacted. Maybe the city loses the distinction of being the safest in America. Maybe a cure for a disease is housed in a laboratory within the building, and it will be lost if the bomb goes off. Lots at stake.

Moral Stakes are in play when someone's beliefs are at risk. Imagine a police officer being offered a bribe to overlook a crime. If he refuses, he holds true to his moral code and identity as an officer, but the powerful person offering the payoff will be sure to end his career. If he takes the bribe, he reaps a temporary reward but sacrifices his values and his identity. Moral stakes can cut both ways and have the added benefit of revealing some of your character's deepest layers to readers.

Primal Stakes, also called death stakes, involve the death of something significant: innocence, a relationship, a career, dream, idea, belief, reputation, or a physical life. Death takes something important from the character, something that matters. And if it matters to your character—provided readers care about them—it will matter to them too.

Personal Stakes most directly affect the protagonist because, should he fail, he or the people he loves will suffer. Imagine a character named Rodney, a retired bomb expert. Let's say he had a close call that led to PTSD, and that's why he left the force. When his old boss asks him to take on one more case, Rodney starts to shake and can barely choke out the word *no* before slamming down the phone. He's done with all that. Someone else can handle this one. So, what might change Rodney's mind? What if his wife works in the building where the bomb has been stashed, or his child needs the cure from the lab on the second floor? Making the stakes personal changes everything; even Rodney's debilitating fear can't keep him from dusting off his gear and saving those he loves.

Stakes should touch your character on some level, even in the case of far-reaching stakes. If there's no reason the outcome really matters to the protagonist, he's going to look at the task and think, *Well, this isn't my problem.* We need him to believe it *is* his problem, otherwise why should he risk hardship, danger, and perhaps even death? So we give him skin in the game by making things personal and endangering something or someone important to him. Or we trigger moral stakes by threatening the values and beliefs tied to his identity.

MAKE THE READER CARE ABOUT THE CHARACTER
Impactful stakes are a necessary part of effective conflict, but another crucial piece is the reader's attachment to the character. If readers don't care, they may be curious as to whether the protagonist will succeed, but they won't be invested in the outcome.

So how do we make readers care? Well, it goes beyond making a character likeable or talented; it really comes down to their inner landscape: their morals and values, vulnerabilities and wounds, their fears and needs. By chipping through our character's tough exterior and revealing their inner thoughts, emotions, and desires, readers come to know them and identify with their struggles. They may share an insecurity. They may experience some of the same doubts. Maybe the character is torn between following a dream and pleasing others, something readers can relate to because they've been in that boat before. These moments become emotional touchstones because readers are able to connect with what the character is facing and feeling.

Ultimately, what's at risk for your character is the goal. But for writers, the risk is readers closing the book because the stakes are mismanaged or the conflict is too low. So focus on drawing readers in. Work at getting your character's situation firmly into the heads of your readers. Embed an invisible hook so every time they put the book down, they're thinking about what will happen next, how the character's going to solve the problem, and what other forces might step in to complicate matters. Make your readers so emotionally involved that they fear for the character and don't want anything to happen to them.

INTERNAL CONFLICT: A DEEPER LOOK

If you're looking for ways to make your characters' struggles meaningful to readers, look no further than internal conflict. We've touched briefly on this important form; now let's take a deeper dive into what it is, what it isn't, and why it's crucial for your story.

EXTERNAL VS. INTERNAL CONFLICT

External Conflicts are struggles between the character and outside forces. A physical attack, a snowstorm that causes an electricity outage, rejection by a love interest, or one's car breaking down are conflicts that are generated from extraneous entities and are largely beyond the character's control. They act as roadblocks and distractions to slow their progress toward the overall story goal.

Internal Conflicts live solely within the character. These *character vs. self* struggles include a certain level of **cognitive dissonance**, with him wanting things that are at odds with each other. Internal conflicts can manifest for the character in a variety of ways:

- Opposing or competing wants, needs, or desires
- Confusion about how he should feel
- Questioning his beliefs or values
- Suffering from indecision, insecurity, self-doubt, or another emotion that puts him at odds with himself
- Conflicting duties and responsibilities
- Grappling with an aspect of mental health

It should be noted that while internal conflicts happen in the character's own mind, they are often instigated by an external source. For instance, a private detective pursuing the goal of solving a crime may find himself deeply conflicted when he uncovers information that implicates his own spouse. The inner conflict that ensues—does he pursue this lead or destroy the evidence?—is strictly internal, but it was brought on by an outside force. So, while external and internal conflicts are clearly different, they're often interconnected.

This is important to note because well-told stories have a domino effect, with one problem directly leading to another. And while external conflicts can trigger some feelings of empathy because of their universality, internal conflicts are what really pull readers in.

The world is a confusing place, especially now, in this technological age with its overabundance of information. We're constantly analyzing new data and seeing how it integrates into what we already know, and this process isn't always a smooth one: *What's true? What's right? How does this fit with what I've always believed? How will this impact my relationships, my job, or the way I've chosen to live my life?*

As stressful as a traffic jam or lost phone might be, internal struggles are the ones that haunt us because their impacts ripple outward, affecting not only how we see ourselves but altering our future and often the lives of the people we care about. They carry a heft that can't easily be set aside.

Readers are just like us, wrestling with the same questions, insecurities, and uncertainties. When they see a character struggling internally, they empathize on a deeper level because they recognize the weight of that struggle. They see that the outcome will have long-lasting effects, and they want the character to make the right decision.

For this reason, it's important to include internal conflict in your story. And, whenever possible, it should be incorporated at the scene and story levels.

INTERNAL CONFLICT AT THE STORY LEVEL

If you're writing a story in which your character will need to evolve internally to achieve his goal, a cohesive and well-planned character arc is integral. This type of arc (a change arc) requires internal conflict, which will provide opportunities for your character to adapt and grow. Because most stories revolve around a character's evolution to become better and more fulfilled, we'll focus our study of internal conflict on stories containing a change arc. So, what does that look like?

At their heart, most stories boil down to a simple formula: It's a story about A (**the character**) who wants B (**goal/outer motivation**) because Y (**inner motivation**). That Y explains *why* (see what we did there?) the character so desperately wants to achieve the goal. Let's take the movie *Groundhog Day* as an example. Phil Connors (A) wants to win Rita's love (B) so he can find meaning in an utterly meaningless life (Y). This example shows how the character's outer and inner motivations work together in the story.

The **outer conflict** is the main external thing keeping the character from his goal. Phil's conflict comes in the form of the supernatural forces that have him reliving the same day over and over, making it virtually impossible to get Rita to fall in love with him.

And what **internal conflict** or struggle does Phil experience throughout the story? Or, as Michael Hauge puts it: What is standing in the way of the character achieving real self-worth as he pursues his inner motivation?[2] In Phil's case, he simply loves himself too much to love anyone else. This is why his initial attempts to win Rita's heart fail—not because of time limitations but because his motives are selfish. She sees him for the pretentious, condescending, self-absorbed prat he's always been, so he has to resort to deception and trickery to achieve his goal. And it never works.

At his core, Phil sees himself as superior to everyone else. His conflict arises from the incongruence between this core perception and the truth: that every person has worth, and purpose is found not so much in being loved but in loving and serving others. His failed attempts to connect

---

2 "Character Development." Writing Screenplays That Sell: The Complete Guide to Turning Story Concepts into Movie and Television Deals, by Michael Hauge, HarperCollins Publishers, 2011, pp. 63.

with Rita through subversive means provide internal conflict opportunities as he realizes that his ideology is flawed; until he can learn to value others and stop living solely for himself, his life will always lack meaning. Once he's able to realign his perception with the truth and change his behavior, he finds purpose through love and his internal conflict is resolved.

How Unmet Human Needs Contribute to Character Arc

Basic human needs are important to understand because they're the key to inner motivation.

In the real world, each of us is unique and distinctly different from one another. But certain elements are universal to the human experience—namely, the human needs that we require to be fulfilled. When any of these needs are unmet, subliminal warning bells start going off. And the bigger that unmet need grows, the more motivated we become to fill the void.

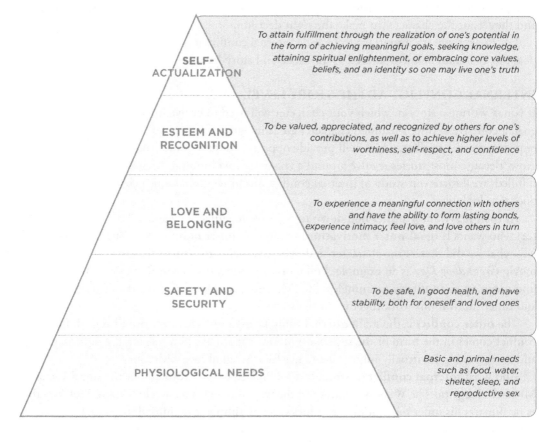

Maslow's Hierarchy of Needs

Psychologically speaking, what holds true for us should also be true for our characters. The drive to regain a missing human need will become their inner motivation—the reason they're pursuing the outer story goal.

As an example, Phil's missing human need is meaning (self-actualization), something a life spent serving himself just doesn't provide. Deep down, he's seeking that purpose and subconsciously believes he'll obtain it if he can find true love with Rita.

This is the power of an unmet need. Love, self-esteem, safety, self-actualization, physiological needs—when these are lacking, they become major motivators, driving a character's choices and pushing them to behave in very specific ways. If your character is struggling at the start of their story because a core need isn't being fulfilled (or if something happens early on to cause this), they will spend the rest of their journey trying to fill the void.

Internal Conflict Is Directly Opposed to the Inner Motivation

It's interesting to note that Phil's conflict is standing directly in the way of his inner motivation. He wants to find purpose through connecting with others, but his belief in his own superiority keeps him from being able to do that.

Whatever form the character's internal conflict takes, it usually will block their inner motivation, denying them the one thing they desperately want or need. This conundrum will provide ample opportunities for the character to search his depths and eventually understand what change needs to occur so he can be free of that inner struggle.

Internal Conflict Is Tied to Self-Esteem or Fulfillment

The strongest internal conflicts are ones that touch on the most vulnerable parts of the character's psyche: his feelings and perceptions about himself. These fundamental ideas are like the ground level of a house of cards. Poke at them and the whole thing could come crashing down.

When Phil finds himself reliving the same day over and over, he employs the modus operandi he's used all his life: he does exactly what he wants and doesn't care how his actions impact others. But as one day blends interminably into the next, self-indulgence ceases to satisfy. He's unhappy because he's been chasing the wrong goal. Until he is able to elevate others above himself, he'll continue to be conflicted and will never be at peace.

This is story-level internal conflict—the main wrestling match that your character will struggle with over the course of the story. (It differs slightly from scene-level conflict, which we'll cover in a bit.) If your character is traversing a change arc, you must know what their main internal conflict is so you'll know what they need to address before the final page. The same is true if your story contains a failed arc; the only difference here is that the character will fail to embrace the change that is necessary for them to become fully realized, and their journey will end with them in the same place (or a worse one) than when they started.

IDENTIFYING YOUR CHARACTER'S INTERNAL CONFLICT

The central internal conflict for your character won't emerge from a vacuum. We already know it will be related in some way to self-esteem or fulfillment, and it will hinder them from getting what they need most. So it's important to know their inner and outer motivations. Then it will be easier to ascertain what internal conflict will make the most sense in blocking their efforts.

Even then, internal conflict can come in various forms. To figure out exactly what it will look like for your character, consider the following possibilities.

Greatest Fear

Fears are highly motivating. The inconvenient, everyday ones? Sure, because no one makes split-second decisions better than an arachnophobe who's just stumbled into a spiderweb. (This is the voice of experience talking.) But in storytelling it's the larger fears that drive both character and story. Fear of failure, being alone, losing a loved one … these can push the character to embrace unhealthy habits or paralyze her into maintaining the status quo and resisting needed change.

Imagine, for instance, a character who is afraid of letting others down. This fear will insert itself into every situation where she's accountable to others, steering her toward doing what others want rather than what she wants, or causing her to step back instead of stepping up. She may worry that if she takes on something big, she'll screw it up, so she discards goals that could result in personal fulfillment, such as having children or leading a beloved charity group or event. This fear of disappointing others can influence her choice of career or who she marries. It can lead to her sacrificing her own joy for the happiness of others. Then, before you know it, an important human need has been compromised, leading to more problems.

Core Moral Beliefs

Nothing causes psychological turmoil quite like a challenge to one's core beliefs, and no beliefs are more central than the moral ones, because they define who we are. This is the situation Paul Edgecombe encounters in *The Green Mile*. As a death-row prison guard, experience has taught him that the men in his charge are guilty and deserve their punishment. This makes it easier for Paul to do his job and oversee their executions. But then he encounters an inmate who doesn't fit the mold, and difficult questions begin to surface. Could John Coffey, a man found guilty in a court of law, actually be innocent? If so, how can Paul execute him? And what if John is an angel, endowed with superpowers from God himself—what will killing him mean for Paul's eternal soul?

Think about what your character believes on the deepest level—his thoughts about right and wrong, good and evil. Then introduce an event that challenges those ideas. If his inner turmoil surrounding this issue or theme is what the story is really about, if it's something he could struggle with for the story's entirety, it may be a good choice for his story-level internal conflict.

Existential Ideas

Another trait particular to human beings is our curiosity, particularly about big ideas: *Who am I? What's my purpose? Is there life beyond Earth? After death?* These questions often aren't answerable, but your characters grapple with them anyway because the answers will impact and define who they are.

If your character already knows what they believe about bigger life questions, that information will become part of their core belief system. Challenging them will throw the character into an emotional and existential tailspin. If they don't have answers, the struggle to find them can lead to all kinds of internal strife. They may receive conflicting information from trusted sources, causing further indecision. Maybe a beloved mentor has a crisis of faith and changes their lifelong stance, upsetting the character's own internal apple cart. Or a natural (or supernatural) event could cause them to question what they thought they knew.

Wants and Needs

Wants are exactly what they imply: something the character desires but doesn't necessarily need. By themselves they don't generate much conflict, but when you set them in opposition to the character's missing need or a core belief, internal strife explodes onto the scene.

Dan Burns, the protagonist in *Dan in Real Life*, lost his wife many years prior and is now raising three girls on his own. He hasn't been truly happy in all that time—but then he meets Marie. Finally! His need for love and belonging is going to be filled—except … his brother is already dating her. Now his need (happiness and love) and his want (to be with Marie) are at odds, because for him to be with Marie, he would have to betray his brother. And how could he be happy doing that?

Secrets

Characters jump through all kinds of emotional and logistical hoops to keep important secrets from coming to light. They may withdraw from people, organizations, and cherished hobbies to avoid questions that hit too close to home. You can imagine the inner turmoil that develops when a character must give up an area of giftedness or a close friend in order to keep certain information from getting out. Many characters will drastically change their behavior to keep their secrets safe. Melinda Sordino in Laurie Halse Anderson's *Speak* is so determined to keep a certain event from being revealed that she stops talking altogether. After all, if you can't talk, you can't tell.

Secrets, especially those tied to past trauma or the character's shame, can cause her to fundamentally change her priorities and how she sees herself. If your character's secret is one that must be protected at all costs, it can provide compelling fodder for internal conflict.

These are just a few of the factors that can contribute to a character's inner struggles. It should be noted that many of these will stem directly from a major wounding event in the character's past, so it's a good idea to know exactly what that is and the various ways it will impact your character. For more help deciding on their internal conflict, see **Appendix B**.

INTERNAL CONFLICT AT THE SCENE LEVEL

Once you've nailed down your character's main internal conflict, you'll know what they'll be struggling with as they traverse their character arc over the course of a story. But if we put the story itself under the microscope, we see that it's made up of smaller building blocks. So let's take a closer look at scenes and how conflict—specifically internal conflict—contributes at this level.

Every Scene Has a Goal

According to David Mamet, a **scene** is a contained narrative unit that takes place within the larger narrative.[3] Each scene serves the overall story by working to advance the plot (and any subplots). Let's say your character Penny's outer motivation is to win a local weeklong baking competition. And her inner motivation, the reason she wants to achieve this goal, is to prove her worth. All of Penny's life, she endured a learning disability that caused humiliation and undermined her self-esteem, making her feel worthless. The kitchen is her safe place, and finally winning a baking contest would validate her in her own eyes and, she believes, in the eyes of others.

So every scene in this story needs to move Penny closer to her goal. It's important to know how each scene contributes to her outer motivation (or the achievement of a subplot, should you choose to include one) so you can add the right kind of conflict. Possible scenes and goals for our would-be baking champion might include the following:

---

3 MasterClass. (2021, August 31). *How to write a scene: 9 steps for short story scene writing.* MasterClass. https://www.masterclass.com/articles/how-to-write-a-compelling-scene-in-a-short-story

Scene 1: She hears about the competition and has to make a decision about entering.

Scene 2: She visits the kitchen where she'll be working so she can get the lay of the land.

Scene 3: She meets the judges on the first day and wants to make a good first impression.

Scene 4: She must get through the first round of the competition to progress to the next one …

These are just a few ideas for scenes that might figure into this kind of story. Do you see how each one is tied in some way to Penny's overall story goal of winning the competition? By identifying this connection between scene goals and the story goal, you ensure that each scene is necessary and is moving the story forward.

Every Scene Needs Conflict
Now, as we know, the path to victory isn't usually linear. A story in which the protagonist progresses directly from Point A to Point Z without any obstacles or reversals would be unrealistic and incredibly yawn-worthy. Characters should have ups and downs as they experience setbacks, get distracted, make poor choices, and are sabotaged by insecurities and fears. How do we supply those peaks and valleys?

Conflict provides valuable growth opportunities for the protagonist. Sometimes she'll respond well and surge ahead, getting closer to her goal. Other times, she'll lose ground.

Returning to the scene goals for Penny's story, let's see what conflict we can add to make things more interesting:

Scene 1: She hears about the competition and has to make a decision. Entering will require her to take a week off work, which she can't really afford (unless, of course, she wins).

Scene 2: Penny visits the kitchen at the TV studio where she'll be working so she can get the lay of the land. The digital clocks on the walls suggest timed elimination challenges. She'll have to think and act quickly—and with an audience viewing every decision and misstep.

Scene 3: She meets the judges on the first day and wants to make a good first impression. She discovers that Judge #2 is her nemesis—the person who won their last joint competition, beating Penny soundly and parlaying his win into the kind of career she's always dreamed of.

Scene 4: Penny must get through the first round of the competition to progress to the next one. As she steps up to her assigned counter and peers into the small studio audience, she sees her sister, the award-winning pastry chef with tons of advice and no respect for second place.

Now these scenes are a little more interesting. Penny has an objective in each that will lead her gradually toward her goal of winning the competition, but each scene now contains scenarios that make the goal more difficult to obtain, booby-trapping her path to victory. These additions are important not only from a scene and story structure standpoint but also because of the tension they create as readers begin to wonder if she'll be able to succeed. That tension fuels reader interest, urging them to read on to see how things turn out. Remember the importance of making the reader care about the character? An easy way to do that is to add some internal conflict.

Want Stronger Conflict? Add an Internal Element

Empathy forms when readers recognize something about themselves in the character. And while the conflict scenarios we've engineered here are universal, they're also a little superficial. That's because they're external. Financial limitations, a ticking clock, the introduction of a past rival—there is no real internal conflict in any of these scenarios, no tug-of-war within the character with far-reaching moral or personal consequences. We want to create heart-wrenching scenarios that resonate with readers, so let's see what we can do to add an internal element to the conflicts in Penny's story.

Scene 1: She hears about the competition and has to make a decision. Entering will require her to take a week off work, which she can't really afford (unless, of course, she wins). The thing Penny's really struggling with, though, is that she lost the last contest she entered, and while this is a chance for redemption, she doesn't know if she can suffer another defeat.

Scene 2: She visits the kitchen where she'll be working so she can get the lay of the land. The digital clocks on the walls suggest timed elimination challenges. She'll have to think and act quickly, but speed and efficiency have always been her downfall due to her learning disability. She can't help but worry that they'll punch a hole in her professional dreams once again.

Scene 3: Penny meets the judges on the first day and wants to make a good first impression. She discovers that Judge #2 is her nemesis—the person who won their last joint competition, beating Penny soundly and parlaying his win into the kind of career she's always dreamed of. Seeing him brings a rush of anger and shame because of the disparaging comments he made during the last contest—some of which were deliberate digs at her disability, meant to intimidate her.

Scene 4: She must get through the first round of the competition to progress to the next one. As she steps up to her assigned counter and peers into the small studio audience, she sees her sister, the award-winning pastry chef with tons of advice and no respect for second place. Just what she needs—a super-successful and hypercritical sibling to pick apart her every move and cause her to second-guess herself.

These scenarios are much more compelling, containing internal conflict in the form of needs vs. fears, undeserved feelings of shame, and finding the self-belief to stand up to her biggest critic in order to succeed. They involve undesirable emotions and will cause her to face things she may not want to deal with, such as insecurities, bad habits, and past failures. But every fall-down moment offers a chance for her to learn, to recognize the issues that are undermining her so, hopefully, she can do better next time. In short, they are opportunities for growth. Internal conflict is the crucible that transforms our insecure, conflicted, and unfulfilled protagonists into self-aware victors who can do whatever needs doing and establish their own destinies.

So, whenever possible, your scene-level conflicts should contain an internal element. If they're lacking that important piece, deepen them by following a few simple steps.

Identify the character's scene goal. It should be one that, if she succeeds, will bring her closer to either the overall goal or a subplot objective.

Identify the character's inner motivation. Why does she have that goal? What inner void does she believe will be filled if she succeeds?

Understand what's at stake. What is the cost of failure if the character doesn't achieve their scene goal? How will it complicate their situation or make the story goal harder to reach? How might it generate inner conflict?

Brainstorm conflict scenarios that make sense for the character's situation. This is where the entry portion of *The Conflict Thesaurus* can be invaluable. Look for ideas that will block your character from their scene goal and trigger some type of internal tug-of-war. If you're in the planning stage, you can build your scene around a specific conflict. If you already know how the scene will play out (which characters it involves, where it takes place, etc.), choose a conflict that fits that scene.

BONUS: Do any of the conflict scenarios specifically block the character's story-level internal motivation or highlight the void or weakness that plagues her? Remember that your character is traversing an arc, and for her to win, she'll have to resolve that internal issue or deficiency to evolve. She won't always succeed; sometimes she'll fail, so she'll need several chances to explore this area.

Now, if every conflict comes back to the same internal element, your story may begin to feel one-dimensional, so mix things up a bit and touch on varying internal conflicts. This is often where subplots are helpful. Try revisiting Maslow's Hierarchy and look for areas of strain or other missing needs that are tied to the primary one. Is there another element of internal growth the character can work on that will support their story-level arc?

IS INTERNAL CONFLICT ALWAYS NECESSARY?

Because internal conflict adds tension and often generates emotion for readers, it's a good idea to include some in most scenes. However, this doesn't mean every story moment needs to contain a deep moral struggle. Internal conflict can be a dilemma over whether to reveal a secret or the best way to proceed—especially if the character is realizing that their flawed go-to methods of solving problems aren't working. Think about how conflicting duties, goals, obligations, and ideas might generate a touch of internal back-and-forth or which biases or misconceptions might become sticking points. It's important to be mindful of pacing, of course, but if there is internal struggle, anchor it to the problems the character is facing in the scene.

There are a few specific situations in which inner conflict plays a lesser (though still important) role and should be handled as such. If your story contains a character with a static arc or a high-action scene, keep the following tips in mind.

Characters with Static Arcs
In stories that are more about the overall goal than character development, the protagonist isn't going to experience as much inner turmoil. How could he, when his focus is mainly external? But while there may be fewer opportunities for inner conflict, it doesn't mean that he still can't have his moments.

Static characters may not be on a journey of change, but they can (and should) experience doubts and struggle with insecurity. For Jack Ryan to accomplish his goals, he had to face his fear of flying. Indiana Jones mourned Marian's loss, likely feeling guilt over pulling her into his mess. Moments like these can add authenticity to mission-driven characters and a new kind of tension to flesh out scenes.

High-Action Scenes
Scenes with a lot of fast-moving action—fistfights, shoot-outs, fleeing for one's life—aren't typically going to benefit from reflection and emotional growth. Moments of self-doubt and introspection in *The Bourne Identity*'s car chase scene would've ruined it because that's not how car chases work. In life-or-death situations in which survival requires reflex and split-second thinking, there is no time for internal reflection. Action scenes are high on adrenaline and shorter on emotion, so they don't tend to contain much inner conflict.

However, that doesn't mean it can't occur in the lead-up to an action scene or in its denouement. Just before the car chase scene, Jason Bourne enters the train station to stash his stuff while Marie stays in the car, thumbing the stack of cash he's just given her. Her eyes cut to the car keys. That moment shows exactly what her inner conflict is: Do I risk my life staying with this guy or take the money and run?

Small moments of inner conflict can add emotion to high-action scenes when they occur outside of the main action. And, clearly, inner conflict isn't just for protagonists. As we see in Marie's case, other characters experience it too—especially if they're navigating their own arcs. Of course, you'll have to stay true to the viewpoint you've chosen; if you're writing in first or third person, you can't show what's happening internally for the other characters (their racing heartbeats, nausea, mental back-and-forth, and so on), but you can show external signs of the internal conflict. This might be apparent through something the viewpoint character observes (someone's gaze darting to an important object, nervous fiddling, hesitations) or through that person's dialogue, decisions, and actions.

WHAT DOES INTERNAL CONFLICT LOOK LIKE?
A character experiencing psychological turmoil is a character at odds with herself. She doesn't know what to do, questions important beliefs, or possibly is considering doing something she knows she shouldn't. To her, vacillations like these make her look weak, because strong people know their own minds. They know what to do and they do it. For this reason, the character

will often seek to hide her inner conflict. This results in external behaviors that won't match her internal feelings. This is subtext at its finest, and as authors we have to be able to clearly show this dichotomy.

Subtext can be defined as the story beneath the story, and this is essentially what we have with a character in turmoil. She'll show a strong front to other characters, acting confident and in control. But underneath, readers will see the indecision and uncertainty. They'll see the dilemma chipping away at her moral fortitude and possibly the very essence of who she is. And they'll recognize that her behaviors, speech, and visible choices are a front.

To write subtext well, we have to convey the external façade to other characters while simultaneously revealing the internal war to readers. The first step in conveying this duality is to recognize what internal conflict looks like on both levels.

Internal Goings-On

Obsessive Thoughts. Whatever's plaguing your character, he's going to be spending a lot of time thinking about it because the only way to get past the insecurity is to figure out what to do and make a decision—so his thoughts should be circling the issue. You don't want to spend too much time in his head, because too much introspection can slow the pace and diminish the reader's interest level. But the character should poke at the issue, examining it from different angles. Much of his dilemma is surrounding the consequences of various courses of action, so he'll likely be focused on those too.

Let's say we have a character named Adam whose mother is sinking into the final stages of ALS (Lou Gehrig's disease). Adam has watched her lose muscle control to the point where she can no longer walk. She has trouble swallowing and is plagued with debilitating neuropathic pain—none of which she can verbalize since she is no longer able to talk. But she says a lot with her eyes, and Adam knows that she doesn't want to live like this. No one should. But can he end her life? It's one thing to think about stopping a person's suffering, but it's another to physically make that happen. If he does decide to move forward, how can he do it without getting caught? Should that even matter? This is his mother, for crying out loud.

These are the questions that will haunt Adam's waking moments. Updates from doctors and nurses about her condition will be laid against this backdrop. Conversations with loved ones will be underscored by thoughts of how his decision could impact them. Seeing his mother will fill him with pain, because, after all, he has the ability to bring her peace.

This is an example of how whatever's going on in the character's life will bring him back to his inner conflict, and his thoughts should reflect that. Even everyday things that in other circumstances would bring joy—conversations with loved ones, family events, and memories—will pull his focus back to the decision he has to make.

Avoidance. Inner conflict is uncomfortable because it conveys an indisputable fact to the one experiencing it: *we don't have all the answers.* Like us, characters crave control and certainty, so not knowing what to do can make them feel incapable, afraid, and insecure. Depending on what the character's wrestling with and how vulnerable it makes them feel, being constantly reminded of their unsolvable problem can be emotionally painful enough for them to try to escape it.

One way to convey this is by having them slam the door on a certain train of thought. Show their mind starting to wander in that direction and them deliberately turning away from it. Maybe they get really into work as a form of distraction. They may take avoidance a step further into full-blown denial, destroying paperwork or putting away mementos that remind them of the impossible decision so they can pretend it doesn't exist. This is how you show that incongruency between what's happening on the inside and the outside.

Wavering Between Courses of Action. A dilemma is named such because the character doesn't know what to do. If we go back to Adam, his decision-making process might involve him trying on different solutions to see how they fit. He may consider for a brief time that he should do nothing. After all, she never actually brought up assisted suicide (back when she could speak). Would his mother really want him to sacrifice his future and freedom for her? Surely not. He'll consider for a while that the right thing to do is to not play God and just let events unfold naturally. But then something happens to cast doubt on that decision. Perhaps her pain increases and cannot be adequately managed through medication. This causes him to revisit the old problem, and he starts thinking of ways he might be able to end her suffering without other family members finding out.

It often takes a while for the character to figure out what action to take, and the only way he can do that is to consider the options, so indecision is a major part of internal conflict. Show the character vacillating between choices, playing out various scenarios, weighing the pros and cons. This can be a great way to show the depth of his struggle, especially when the solution requires a sacrifice.

Insecurity and Self-Doubt. Difficult decisions are daunting, especially when there are extensive consequences or moral implications. The decision may be hard because it highlights an area of weakness, a past failure, or a temptation, shining a light on a part of the character's past or personality he doesn't want to acknowledge. Even when the situation is complicated—and many internal conflict scenarios are—the character will think he should know the right thing to do and be able to take action. His inability to do so can increase his feelings of incapability. And if his indecision causes fallout for others, he'll internalize that and add guilt to the weight he carries.

In Adam's case, maybe he's always been a follower, risk averse, waiting for others to take action so he wouldn't have to be responsible. He saw his mother's condition worsening; he knew where she was headed, and he sensed that she would want to end things before reaching that point, but his fear kept him from broaching the subject. Now it's too late to know for sure, and he's forced into the same old situation of having to take action and being too afraid to do it. His mother's condition is no one's fault, but he blames himself for not being strong enough to save her from it.

Insecurities are a natural side effect of internal conflict, which is unfortunate because they further inhibit the character, making an already difficult job seemingly impossible. So consider what insecurities may be a recurring issue for your character, and show those playing a part in his predicament.

External Indicators of Internal Conflict

Over- or Under-Compensation. The character won't be happy with their own inability to make a decision or take action. If their ego becomes involved or they're the kind of person who wants to keep up pretenses, they may overcompensate by becoming forceful or pushy. Controlling external people and situations will make them feel better about their inability to control this other area of life.

Or your character could go a different direction. Plagued with indecision, they may become averse to making any choices at all. When even the smallest questions are raised, they defer to others. Letting other people take the lead ensures that the character won't make a mistake, and it will take the pressure off them for a little while.

Your character's response in this area will depend on their natural tendencies and emotional state. This is true for so many of their reactions, so be sure to explore their personality to get a feel for who they are and how they would behave.

Distraction. The human brain can only focus on so many things at once. A character whose mind is consumed with a troubling scenario isn't going to have much mental time for anything else. As a result, their efficiency and productivity at work or school could likely take a hit. They may become forgetful. Responsibilities they could always be counted on to handle may be done halfway or fall completely to the wayside. These outer indicators will be a visible sign of the chaos beneath the surface.

Emotional Volatility. We all know what it's like to be consumed by a problem we can't fix. It steals our peace, our sleep, and our joy. This is fine—even normal—for short periods of time, but when it goes on for too long, it starts to take its toll. One of the first things to go is emotional stability.

A character in this situation may lose their patience, snap at people, or lash out at others. A different character may constantly be on the verge of tears, overwhelmed to the point of every little thing being the last straw. They may experience wild mood swings, reacting to everyday circumstances in unexpected ways. Again, your character's response will depend on a host of other factors, including their personality and normal emotional range. Figure out which kind of response makes the most sense and you'll be consistent in your portrayal of them, even in the most pressing of situations.

Mistakes. Characters under extreme pressure don't always make the best decisions. Their distractibility, combined with any insecurities they may be feeling, can lead to mistakes that get them into trouble. For a character who is usually level-headed and logical, this can be like a neon sign to others that something isn't quite right.

If your character is a go-get-'em type who systematically eradicates obstacles as they arise, internal conflict will make them uncomfortable. After all, it causes questions to bubble up that don't have easy answers, and this delays the gratification they gain through taking action. Chances are, they'll put a lid on their feelings and charge ahead, and their impulsiveness will come with consequences. Not only will they now have to deal with fallout from not thinking things through, the original problem will still be unresolved.

Shifting Beliefs. A character going to great lengths to hide his inner turmoil may be successful to a degree. But when his struggle concerns fundamental beliefs, such as moral questions and resulting changes to his values, the important people around him will take notice. For example, Adam may have been an outspoken opponent of euthanasia in the past, but recent conversations with close friends show his stance slipping as he examines the dilemma from a new perspective. He's not embracing anything yet, but he's voicing thoughts and toying with ideas that he never would have before.

He isn't trying to tip his hand; the last thing he wants is for anyone to know what he's considering. But it's natural for some of his new thoughts to work their way into his speech, especially in stressful or high-emotion moments when his guard is down. Those honest moments can clarify for readers some of what's happening internally with the character.

LESSONS IN FAILURE: POINTING THE CHARACTER TOWARD GROWTH

Anyone who has raised a toddler has seen firsthand the process of learning to walk. In the beginning there's not a lot of success. Conflict comes in the form of weak muscles, a lack of balance, physical obstacles, gravity, and fear. Mostly, it's a lot of falling down. But letting our children fall is a necessary part of them growing and learning. The same is true for our characters.

FAILURE ACCENTS THE CHARACTER'S FLAWS

A well-rounded and believably built character will have defects—weaknesses, blind spots, and personality flaws he's either unaware of or is unwilling to change. No one is perfect, so these foibles add authenticity, making characters relatable. But a character on a change arc trajectory will have a specific flaw that is directly blocking him from goal achievement. This stumbling block keeps coming up in the story, knocking him flat and cutting him off from fulfillment.

The **fatal flaw** is your character's antiquated and ineffective approach to dealing with life's problems. It consists of mental and behavioral components that work in tandem to protect the character from experiencing emotional hurt. For example, someone who believes people will exploit his vulnerability if he lets them get close may embrace unfriendliness, speaking abrasively to everyone he meets. Technically, this approach works; it certainly keeps people from taking advantage of him. But it does a lot of damage because no one is willing to risk a verbal lashing to have a relationship with him. Over time, he'll feel isolated and lonely and will probably start to doubt his own worth because he can't seem to build connections with anyone.

A fatal flaw is the character's blind spot. He doesn't see the damage it does, only the benefit of it stopping a problem before it can start. In the story, the fatal flaw will stand in the character's way of what he wants most. Until he realizes how his dysfunctional behavior and attitudes are limiting him and adopts a healthier approach, he will continue to fail to achieve his heart's desire. Ironically, failure aids in this process by shining a light on the character's flaw and making it harder and harder to ignore.

Let's view this process in action by looking at *A Few Good Men*.

Lieutenant Daniel Kaffee is a lawyer in the Navy JAG Corps who is quickly gaining a reputation for his plea-bargaining abilities. He seems proud of this unusual skill, but it becomes apparent that he's using it to keep from trying an actual case in the courtroom. The reasons for this are found in his past, where he grew up in the shadow of his highly successful attorney father. He's afraid that if he tries a case for real, he'll never measure up and will always be second best.

Screenwriter Aaron Sorkin does a masterful job of providing the perfect conflict opportunities that allow Kaffee to recognize and confront this flaw.

> Opportunity #1: Kaffee is assigned a murder case involving two marines at Guantanamo Bay. It's a chance for him to be a true lawyer and test his skills in the courtroom, but he falls back on old habits and immediately tries to plea-bargain the case. His failure results in disbelief and open disdain from his co-counsel, who will continue to challenge Kaffee throughout the story.

> Opportunity #2: It becomes obvious that his clients are going to trial, so Kaffee digs into the details and realizes that it's a complicated case—definitely not open and shut. He once again tries to sidestep a trial by encouraging his clients to plead guilty. Men of honor, they refuse, highlighting Kaffee's cowardice.

In each of these situations, Kaffee has a choice: do what he's always done (play it safe and underachieve) or test his mettle as a true attorney. His first two chances result in failure as he continues to avoid the courtroom. But those failures draw attention to his flaw, bringing it into focus and making it difficult for him to ignore.

FAILURE HIGHLIGHTS THE NEED FOR CHANGE

> Opportunity #3: Filled with uncertainty, Kaffee agrees to try the case in court, which is a big step forward. He knows that Colonel Jessep, his clients' commanding officer, ordered them to do what they did, thereby making Jessep culpable. If Kaffee can just get Jessep to admit that he ordered the Code Red, he can convince the jury that his clients were following orders, and they'll be off the hook. But the colonel is a powerful Marine, highly decorated and respected. If Kaffee accuses him of issuing the Code Red and the colonel denies it, Kaffee will be court-martialed and dishonorably discharged from the Navy. This risky path is the only one that will allow him to win his case, and if he succeeds, he'll establish himself as a truly great trial attorney. But he chooses to go another, safer route.

Kaffee's first two failures have made him well aware of his issues. He's afraid to enter the courtroom, and he knows why. He recognizes that he's living below his true potential and that there is dishonor in his constant attempts to avoid being who he was meant to be. He doesn't want to continue living this way. He sees that if he's ever to step out of his father's shadow (and if his clients have a prayer of avoiding jail), he has to make changes.

Taking his case to the courtroom is a huge step in the right direction for him. But he's still hedging his bets, only willing to go partway in the defense of his clients. And when this third opportunity comes along for him to fully disown his former flaws and embrace his true potential, his doubts win out, and he falls back on his old habits.

FAILURE PUSHES THE CHARACTER TO EMBRACE NEW METHODS

Opportunity #4: Kaffee's plan falls apart when his primary witness commits suicide. It's down to the wire now; the trial is wrapping up with his cross-examination of Jessep, and he's faced again with the decision to do the really hard thing that must be done if he wants to win. Finally, he puts everything on the line and takes the big risk—and it pays off. In one of cinema's most memorable scenes, he gets Jessep to admit that he ordered the Code Red. The colonel is hauled off to jail, and Kaffee exits the courtroom with confidence, a man who finally has found honor.

It is through this last opportunity that Kaffee chooses to fully test himself to see if he can live up to his father's reputation. He risks everything, finally rejecting his old, ineffectual habits and replacing them with new ones that will allow him to be a truly exceptional lawyer.

"Finally" will always show up toward the end of a character's arc because growth is a process. As we see from this example, Kaffee needed multiple conflict opportunities to face his demons. In the beginning, he failed spectacularly, which magnified his feelings of self-doubt and reinforced (in his mind) the need to cling to methods that weren't working. Toward the middle, he had more successes—but they were only partial victories. Growth still needed to happen. And then, in the end, once he fully dedicated himself to his clients and the case, he was *finally* able to win.

This is the one-step-forward-two-steps-back formula that works so well in stories because it mirrors real life. It takes time and courage to see flaws for what they are and choose the hard road to discard them and their limitations. Success and failure are intermingled, both parts of a process that eventually result in meaningful growth. Conflict is the vehicle through which we provide these necessary opportunities for our characters.

For a handy visual on the relationship between conflict and failure or growth, see **Appendix A**.

CONFLICT, CHOICES, AND CONSEQUENCES

When we think about the mechanics of a story, our minds immediately go to plot and character, the two titans of fiction. And, hey, that's not wrong—we do need a central character and outer events that will challenge and shape them. But unless we can connect these two so that the character is actively moving toward their goal, these elements simply exist, in stasis … waiting. We don't have a story. It's the equivalent of putting on a wedding dress or tuxedo and then standing at the altar alone. Nothing happens. There is no "next."

So how do we connect the character and plot to get the story ball rolling?

Your first thought might be the inciting incident—an opportunity, conflict, or problem that fish-slaps your character by upsetting their status quo. And, yes, this is an essential event that will help kickstart the story, but it's not what gets your protagonist's feet moving. The power to do that comes directly from the character in the form of a **choice**.

Throughout the story, your protagonist faces options—*Do this or that? Stay or go? Obey or rebel?*—and their decisions dictate what comes next. Their first important choice might be to address the inciting incident, but it is only one of many. Choices will be made again and again, scene after scene. It is an important spoke in the conflict-choice-and-consequence wheel that turns until the final page.

Conflict is the event that demands a response; external or internal, it drives the character to make a decision. And there's no way out of it, because not choosing is also a choice that generates its own consequences.

Consequences are the result of the character's choice and can be positive (the right decision leading to a reward) or negative (fallout that hurts the character and makes the goal harder to achieve). In storytelling, consequences usually have strings attached—meaning, even if a character goes with the best option, there will be new problems, challenges, and unforeseen circumstances to navigate.

Our job as writers is to keep the pressure on and not let up on this 3-C pattern, pushing the character to fight with everything they have to achieve the goal. To hold the reader's attention, we want to escalate the tension and stakes, making this wheel spin faster as the story progresses. The decisions should become harder as we jack up the consequences and cost of failure (stakes). As the character closes in on the objective, the margin for error narrows. With the complications and risks piling up, they can only succeed by making the right choices.

There's no denying it; this is the fun zone for writers. We get to embrace our inner evil, tightening the vice around our character and forcing impossible choices. But even as we cackle maniacally and jab them yet again, we want to make sure we're making good choices too— namely, creating stimulus-response scenarios that will push the story forward. We do that by making sure most of our 3-Cs tie in with character arc. Are characters being challenged to grow or change? Is there room for internal reflection and personal epiphanies? If not, we're missing valuable opportunities to ensnare the reader's emotions. For readers to truly care, they need to see our character struggling to make the right decisions and experiencing the weight of failure. This is how readers become more involved in the story and feel more deeply connected to the plight of the protagonist.

MAKE CHOICES PERSONAL

In every scene, your character is making choices—big ones and small ones. Some will be obvious and require little to no thought, but others will be muddier, with no clear "better" option. These choices, provided the character feels personally invested in the decision, act as a test, revealing who they are. Here are some of the possible conundrums your character can face.

> **Minor:** These choices will be relatively simple, and the consequences won't have much impact. Examples include decisions about what to order off a menu, which outfit to wear to the office, or whether to make an appointment now or later.

> **Win-Win:** This is the one that every character wants but rarely gets, because … writers are evil, and all that. A win-win means both options are good. Either way, the character comes out ahead and anyone impacted by the choice will be happy with the outcome. Win-wins are conflict killers, so if you use one, make sure it comes with some unforeseen price tag attached to it.

> **Win-Lose:** These choices appear obvious; one is a good option, the other is not. It means someone will be happy and someone won't, and this might be okay depending on who is on which end of the stick. For example, if the choice means your protagonist gets what he wants and his rival doesn't, well, that's the perfect happily-ever-after. But this scenario can be a hard one if the character has a close relationship with the person who loses. Consider your character's anguish if he and his friend have both been poisoned, and there's only one dose of the antidote. If he takes it, it means his friend will die. That's a hard choice to make.

> **Dilemmas:** When neither choice is ideal, you have a dilemma. Decision-making can require a lot of weighing and measuring, because no matter what choice is made, there will be blood. These choices often come down to what the character is willing to sacrifice and for how long. Preferences will also factor into the choice. Would the protagonist rather lose time or money? Should they admit the truth and suffer ridicule for a short time, or drag it out with denials that everyone will see through anyway?

> **Hobson's Choice:** Have you ever been offered something you don't really want, but maybe it's slightly better than nothing? That's a Hobson's choice. An example would be applying for a promotion and instead being given the choice of a deep pay cut or being laid off.

Sophie's Choice: This scenario is one where the character must choose between two equally horrible options. Named for the book (and movie) *Sophie's Choice*, in which the character must decide which of her two children will be killed, this is known as the impossible, tragic choice. However, it can also simply be a time-and-place decision, when the character can only be in one place at that time. And the ramifications don't have to be catastrophic. They can be minor—as in the case of the character being able to attend their own college graduation or their grandmother's 100th birthday party. Regardless of the decision, guilt will accompany the character's choice in this kind of scenario.

Morton's Fork: This choice is agonizing because both options lead to the same end. It's Max (*Mad Max*) handcuffing Johnny the Boy to a gas tanker that has a time-delay fuse and handing him a hacksaw. Dying from the explosion or the loss of blood from cutting off his own ankle … it's a deceptive choice because there is only one outcome.

Moral Choices: Moral choices (Sophie's Choice is one kind) are those requiring the character to decide between two competing beliefs or choose whether or not to follow a moral conviction. Do they tell the truth because honesty matters—even when it will deeply hurt someone? Protect a loved one or turn him over to the police? Use an advantage to get ahead, knowing it would be wrong to do so? Moral choices require the character to rationalize the decision so they can feel okay about making it.

Do Something or Nothing: In some cases the character can choose to intervene or not get involved. They may not be personally impacted by the outcome either way, or there might be a cost: a risk to their reputation (if not acting paints them as a coward), the moral repercussions of deciding to do nothing (after, say, letting someone die), or even a safety cost (if they choose to save someone who turns out to be a threat).

Whatever choices you weave into the story, find ways to create inner conflict. One method is to pair options that are equal in some way, such as choices that represent two fears, two needs, or two types of risks or sacrifices. You can also focus on elements that are in direct opposition to each other, such as pitting a fear against a need, duty against freedom, or a want against a moral belief. Conflicting emotions, especially the big ones, can also be used to give readers a front-row seat to a meaningful inner struggle.

Once the decision is made, the psychological turmoil can continue in the form of doubt and second guesses. Were the character's motives pure? Should someone else have made the decision? A choice's fallout, especially when the consequences negatively impact others, will add still more weight to the character's burden of guilt and regret. And the closer they are to those impacted by the choice, the worse the fallout will be.

COMPLICATE THE CHARACTER'S CHOICE

To make things even harder on the character, consider these challenge questions. They may help you brainstorm possible complications that will not only stress your character further and increase the stakes or fallout but also will help you create a fresh twist for your scenario.

- What unforeseen consequences could happen as a result of this choice?

- Is there an unknown factor or missing piece of information that can allow me to create a reversal of the consequences and a fresh twist of fate?

- What sacrifice can I build into this choice that disconnects the character from a safety net that's actually holding them back (especially when this separation is needed for the character to grow and change)?

- How can I tempt the character into making the wrong choice?

- How can I raise the stakes further?

SURPRISE READERS WITH A THIRD OPTION

When it comes to wowing readers, one technique that never fails is to find the third option. We've all seen the scenario: the walls have closed in, and your character has only two foreseeable choices. Readers are tense, wondering which one the character will pick because neither is ideal, but there seems to be no other route forward.

Then you, incredible story wizard that you are, provide a new, ingenious, and completely viable option that allows the character to unexpectedly blaze his own trail. This third path will delight readers because it's a door they should have seen themselves but didn't, and it upends their expectations in the best possible way.

The Firm provides a great example of this. Fresh out of law school, tax lawyer Mitch McDeere lands a too-good-to-be-true job at a law firm in Memphis. This dream job turns into a nightmare when he discovers the firm is engaging in white-collar crime for mobsters in Chicago. When he's approached by the FBI, he's given two choices—either continue with the corrupt law firm and eventually be thrown in jail, or work for the FBI as an informant, be disbarred, and be targeted by the mob.

The pressure is on and it seems there are no other options, but Mitch comes up with a third one: to turn over evidence for a lesser crime (mail fraud) that targets the firm instead of the Morolto crime family. This allows him to continue working as a lawyer, avoid jail, and escape the FBI's noose.

When your character finds a third option that allows him to sidestep nasty consequences, he gets to keep his head above water and fight another day. And his ingenuity will give readers yet another thing to love about the character.

ADVERSARIES IN FICTION: WHO IS STANDING IN YOUR CHARACTER'S WAY?

Conflict often arises when your protagonist's goals, needs, and desires clash with an adversary's. These two characters might have a shared history, be new acquaintances, or be aware of each without having physically met. Whatever the case may be, friction exists, and as the stakes escalate and the characters' goals come within reach, tensions between the two grow. They eventually battle it out in a contest of wills, might, and minds until one is victorious.

Your character's adversary is going to cause a lot of conflict, so it's important for you to know their intentions and motivation. While this isn't an exhaustive list, here are some of the adversaries your protagonist might go up against, along with the subtle (and important) differences between each.

Competition: This adversary is someone who has the same goal as the protagonist and will challenge anyone competing for it. Competition can get ugly, of course, but it can also be completely depersonalized. Whether your character is up against a peer for a scholarship, a job, an award, or something else, a true competition is one in which those involved are evenly matched, with abilities, skills, resources, or other assets that make the outcome uncertain. Whether the competition is between individuals or groups, the clash of wills and strengths generates conflict, and the uncertainty of who will win creates tension.

Rival: Like a competitor, this type of opponent wants the same thing as your protagonist. What's different is that the rival is just as invested in defeating the protagonist as they are in winning. For a rival, the victory is personal because there's history between the two characters. Perhaps they were rivals in a previous competition, and the challenger wants redemption while the victor is fighting to retain their title. Maybe the two come from different places or belong to competing teams or families. Alternatively, differences in beliefs, backgrounds, or advantages may play a part in the relationship. In this case, winning can be synonymous with proving worthiness. Some of the most interesting and memorable rivalries are those involving multiple factors that put the two characters at odds.

Consider the ongoing feud between Johnny Lawrence and Daniel LaRusso (and, later, their competing dojos) in *Cobra Kai*. Johnny and Daniel took very different paths since their initial battle in *The Karate Kid*. Daniel became a wealthy and successful businessman while Johnny worked handyman jobs and flirted with alcoholism as an escape from his personal failings, losses, and abuse trauma. Old wounds are reopened when Daniel's daughter destroys Johnny's car in a hit-and-run, Johnny reopens Cobra Kai to empower youths, and Johnny's son trains with Daniel to get back at his dad. Further complications abound as their teenage kids start dating and Johnny fights to change and become someone better while Daniel holds firm to old biases. The result of all this friction? A boatload of misunderstandings, mistakes, and conflict.

Antagonist: This is often a catchall term that represents the many adversaries in your novel, whether they oppose the protagonist at a pivotal point or many times throughout the story. They can be a group, like Yondu Udonta and his clan of Ravagers in *Guardians of the Galaxy.* Typically, this is the main adversary in the story; they may have a personal vendetta against the protagonist or the protagonist may just be someone who's making it harder for them to reach their goal. If the antagonist is a person, they will have a mission or agenda that counters the protagonist's and likely are prominent enough to have a character arc of their own.

Antagonist Force: The foe standing between your character and their goal doesn't need to be a person to be a powerful adversary. Depending on the story, the antagonistic force might be the weather or an element of nature (the brutal polar vortex in *The Day after Tomorrow*), an animal (the wolf pack hunting plane crash survivors in *The Grey*), or an unjust system or society (the social factions in *Divergent*). As technology further integrates itself into our world, we see more instances of its insidiousness being explored in fiction and film; *I, Robot* and *The Terminator* are well-known examples. Another interesting possibility is when your character is their own worst enemy, and the fight between fear and hope takes place within.

Villain: A villain is different than an antagonist or enemy (see below) in the sense that there is an element of evil or a specific intent to hurt others. Something has skewed their worldview and made them into who they are—a person whose moral code runs on a completely different track. Villains view their own goals and desires as more important than everyone else's and so have no qualms about mowing down anyone who gets in their way.

Villains place a specific target on the protagonist for personal reasons—either the protagonist did something to cause them pain or they represent someone or something that threatens their self-worth. Either way, villains are motivated to annihilate the protagonist, which they see as the only way for them to secure their goals.

With the highest of stakes (death stakes) involved, conflict between the two will be intense and the repercussions of failure brutal. As the story progresses, emotions will escalate between them, especially when they're evenly matched. Inner conflict will also rise as both struggle with what they're willing to sacrifice and how far they'll go to win. A villain may have no issues crossing moral lines but may have to give up other goals or needs to come out on top. The protagonist, on the other hand, will suffer as he tries to discern right and wrong when so much is on the line.

Enemy: This type of foe is a threat to your protagonist and those they're aligned with. An enemy can be a person, collective, family, or even a concept that threatens to do great damage. If the enemy is someone your character once had an amicable relationship with, the moment the two choose opposition, previous attachments are cast aside and no concessions are given.

What's interesting about these players is how those on both sides of a conflict will see the other as "the enemy." Why? Because this label is bestowed by viewpoint rather than facts. In a war, each side has an enemy. In a family feud, every participant sees opposing relatives as the bad guys. Consider two groups fighting for the same life-saving resources in an end-of-the-world scenario. Who's good and who's evil? It depends on which shoes you're wearing.

Invader: Another type of adversary is the one trying to disrupt the status quo: they want what you have—be it land, power, resources, or lives—and are there to take it. They're the aliens showing up on Independence Day, the death-eaters laying siege to Hogwarts, and the highwaymen from *Alas, Babylon.* Invaders believe they are entitled to something, so they grab it. They might believe doing so will liberate people from tyranny or repression (which may or may not be true), and just as with an enemy, labeling someone as an invader instead of a liberator will depend on which side of the fence your character is on.

Frenemy: This interesting type of adversary is someone your character can get along with and may align with at times, but a competition exists that requires an emotional shield to always be in place. Your character knows she can trust this person only so far before self-interest kicks in, and then it's every man or woman for themselves. Frenemy relationships often occur between peers (co-workers, members of the same social clique, warriors in the trenches, etc.), and peace is kept as long as conditions remain as they are. As soon as the character's position is elevated (they're given more attention, an advantage, offered an opportunity), the gloves come off and the competition is on. Frenemy relationships are prone to jealousy that overrides the friendship, as well as a focus on reclaiming power. Sometimes a resolution will restore the status quo, while other times the two become hard-and-fast enemies.

Hater: This adversary is one who sees your character as being underserving of the good that comes to them. In general, haters struggle with the success of others, possibly due to envy, jealousy, and feelings of personal inadequacy. But if they latch onto your character, it's because there's something specific that the hater craves. These adversaries can be deceptive, calculating, and manipulative and make it their mission to strip your character of whatever they feel is undeserved: accolades, respect, a positive reputation, happiness, or something else. Haters are disruptors and saboteurs who look for opportunities to cause problems for your character and "take them down a peg."

Bully: This type of adversary gains power by controlling others. Bullies can exist in any environment, from the mean-spirited boss who enjoys pushing your character around at work, to the older sibling that never lost his adrenaline rush of sliding the brotherly knife in, to the rude, demanding customer who feeds her own inflated sense of self-importance by making everyone else feel small. Bullies can be anyone, and the closer they are to your character, the more they can exploit weaknesses.

Aggressor: Some people who struggle to manage their feelings in social situations have a go-to response to emotional discomfort or fear: aggression. Their misreading of an innocent comment, a facial expression, or even a person's presence may activate their insecurity. When a threat is perceived, the aggressor responds impulsively, using intimidation, verbal and emotional abuse, or physical violence to neutralize the threat and regain control. Aggressors are volatile and dangerous because once they've been triggered, they do not back down, and their need to regain control usually results in harm for their target.

Meddler: Chances are there will be people around your character who have strong opinions and aren't afraid to share them. But if they cross the line by consistently trying to insert themselves or interfere, they become meddlers. This type of adversary is somewhat passive-aggressive, offering unsolicited feedback and intrusive advice—or, worse, actively interfering to achieve a specific end because they believe it is for the best. Meddlers can be a challenge to deal with because they're often family members or people the character has an emotional attachment to. So, rather than directly calling them out and denouncing the behavior, your character may put up with it until they eventually explode. Meddlers can be helpful when you need to add a complication, encourage relationship friction, or force a passive character to take over and steer their own life and decisions.

Nemesis: Once in a very great while, an adversary will come along who is powerful, relentless, and enduring. This is a foe that, to date, has not been bested. Your character's nemesis is the shadow at the end of a dark street, the figure that's always there, just out of sight. They hamper your character's happiness and fulfillment because their very presence is a thorn that can be obsessed over but not removed. Superman has Lex Luther, Professor Xavier has Magneto, and Harry Potter has Voldemort. Both characters long for the destruction or removal of the other but are unable to bring that about. Nemesis-protagonist relationships are great for epic stories and series that, instead of a definitive confrontation and resolution, feature a chess match in which each side wins some and loses some.

Challenger: Sometimes your character is at the top of the food chain—happy, secure, and in control. They might be the director of an important area of the government, have the most prosperous grocery store in town, or they're dating the prom queen. In other words, life is good. But savvy authors realize that happy people in a happy world can't hold the reader's interest for long. Enter the challenger—someone who will disrupt the status quo by challenging what your character has. Whether it's a new guy at football tryouts vying for your character's position or a town councilor who decides to run against your incumbent character for political office, challenge equals conflict. What was once sure is now uncertain, and rather than breeze to victory, your character will have a fight on their hands. Challengers can be a refreshing alternative to the good guy/bad guy dynamic because they don't need to have some dark, demonic motivation for wanting the same thing as your character. In fact, sometimes your protagonist is the challenger in this dynamic.

Supernatural Force: Inhuman adversaries present a specific challenge to your protagonist because they'll have powers and abilities your character does not. This makes the matchup uneven, especially if your protagonist's rules and laws don't apply to the supernatural force. This may be the situation if your character must oppose the wishes or interests of a godlike being who commands vast power and will not be pleased with the challenge. Supernatural forces can also be malevolent by nature—meaning, your character's sanity, life, or soul (or those of a loved one) may be at stake.

Adversarial conflict can be direct or indirect, but it always requires a reason for existing. Choosing an antagonist just because your character needs someone to beat will generate hollow conflict. Instead, dig into this relationship and make it meaningful. Unearth each character's *why* by defining their goals and how the other person stands in the way. Give the two credible reasons for being at odds. Who has something to prove and why? Do they have deeply embedded morals that won't allow them to turn away from their individual and perilous paths? Is one of their identities on the line?

Think about what each might be willing to sacrifice and why, and who is being steered by biases, past pain, or an inability to forgive or forget. Understanding each character's motivation gives credibility to their actions. Even if readers can't condone someone's tactics, they can still respect why that person is in the fight, what's at stake for them, and see how winning will lead to fulfillment.

SOURCING CONFLICT FOR YOUR STORY OR SCENE

At this point, we've established that conflict has many purposes. It provides opportunities for both failure and growth, elevates what's at stake, and escalates emotion for both the character and readers. We also know that our stories will need many instances of conflict, both at the story (macro) and scene (micro) level. But how do we know what kinds of conflict to add to the mix?

First and foremost, the conflict must further the story. There are lots of interesting and compelling scenarios that we authors might like to pursue. But, as with every aspect of storytelling, we must separate ourselves from the process to make sure we're not projecting ourselves—our interests and desires—onto the character and the story. Sure, we might want to write a drunken brawl scene, but would that scenario be likely for our protagonist? Will it reveal something about the character, like a weakness or need, or is it just there to "spice up" a boring scene?

Thinking in terms of the overall story will keep you on track, ensuring you're mixing meaningful conflict into each scene's foundation rather than inventing obstacles to beef up your word count. The latter isn't likely to improve the story and may actually do the opposite. If your story drags because the scenes are more about throwing rocks than triggering epiphanies and change, it's time to grab your editorial scissors and start trimming.

The best way to incorporate convincing conflict scenarios is to pull them organically from the elements you've already added to the story. This can be done in the planning stage or as you're drafting—whatever works for your process. Conflict is lurking all around your characters and the story world, so grab a stick and start poking to see what shakes loose.

START WITH THE STORY'S CAST

Where does most of our conflict come from in real life? That's right: other people. Loved ones, extended family, roommates, co-workers, neighbors, friends, complete strangers—if they're someone who will interact with your character, they're a potential source for trouble.

This is why planning your story's cast ahead of time can be so beneficial. Think about what kinds of people might have crossed swords with your character at some point, will rub him the wrong way, or have goals that are in opposition to his own. Think about which traits might get under your character's skin. What attitudes or morals will be difficult for him to accept?

Then—you guessed it—build characters with those traits, habits, histories, and goals into the story. If each character stays true to form, tensions will inevitably rise. Not a planner? Not a problem. When you need a reasonable conflict scenario that will provide a certain outcome, consider who in the character's life you could use to make that happen. The list of adversaries from the previous section can provide inspiration in this area.

LET YOUR CHARACTERS TALK

Since we're discussing characters, let's pull over for a minute and look at one of the main vehicles that can be used to sow strife among your cast. Dialogue is beautiful for this because it can cause minor, surface-level tension or set the ball rolling for something huge, like the end of a relationship or a global clash. Because you'll already be including it in your story, make it do double duty by using it to initiate problems for your character.

When you need something minor, think about the everyday annoyances or offenses that happen when people talk—all the irritating things another person might do that will elevate your character's emotional state, causing overreactions or a change of opinion about that person.

Unintentional Clashes

So much of conflict is unintentional—meaning, the person causing the problem isn't trying to ruffle feathers. Maybe a personality mismatch is to blame, such as someone who is always interrupting, a tactless party who unknowingly causes offense, or a chronic multitasker who doesn't listen carefully and makes the protagonist feel undervalued. Of course, any of these irritations can be applied to the protagonist instead of the other party, and you get the same result. Enough of these slight aggravations can add up throughout one conversation (or over the course of many) and lead to explosions. When a character loses control of their emotions, they are much more apt to speak their mind, cut the other person down, or reveal information they meant to hold back. And what do all of these lead to? More conflict.

Confrontational Communicators

Purposeful conflict in dialogue can be subtle or overt, depending on the situation and the goal being pursued. The character may be looking to manipulate an exchange to achieve a specific outcome, inflame everyone's emotions, damage a reputation, or completely eviscerate an enemy with words. Consider the following techniques designed to escalate tensions and lead to confrontations.

- Deceiving the other party through lies, omissions, and exaggerations
- Making a threat or saying something to intimidate
- Deploying insults, sarcasm, and belittlement
- Manipulating the conversation toward a topic or away from one
- Shifting the focus to someone else to put them in the hot seat
- Purposely asking about something that will make the other person uncomfortable
- Bringing up a sensitive topic to provoke an emotional reaction
- Revealing a secret, a stance, or a mistake to damage a rival's standing in the group
- Asking questions the character knows the other person can't answer, making them look bad

- Calling the protagonist out (for a mistake, something they said or did, etc.) to steal their self-esteem
- Deliberately provoking an argument
- Making insinuations (about someone's loyalty, capabilities, etc.) to sow doubt
- Making a derogatory statement and passing it off as a joke
- Suggesting disloyalty if the other party doesn't agree, which forces them to do just that

When two or more characters are battling it out in conversation, each is seeking the upper hand. The exchange may appear respectful if others are watching or a certain level of decorum must be observed. In these cases, it may not be what the characters say as much as how they say it, or what sort of doublespeak or innuendo they can safely deploy to score a hit that will go over everyone else's heads. To show that a comment has left a mark, don't be afraid to use body language, facial tics, and vocal shifts that reveal the character's waning level of emotional restraint.

Opposing Motivations
One of the main drivers for conflict in dialogue is that the people involved don't always have the same purposes. One party might be trying to connect with the protagonist while the protagonist is only engaging to gain information. One may be seeking to protect a secret while the other is trying to bring it to light. Another person might be pursuing a conversation because they want to share knowledge and enlighten others while the other participant only wants to prove their own rightness.

Motivation plays a huge part in conflict development at all story levels because conflict typically arises when characters don't get what they want. So when you're planning your protagonist's conversations, consider what they're after. What are they hoping to achieve through that discussion? Then pit them against someone whose goal is in opposition to theirs.

This is just a sampling of the techniques you can incorporate into a conversation to generate authentic conflict. If you're ever at a loss for ideas, think about the conversations you've recently had that irked you, even a little bit. Examine the tactics involved and incorporate them into your character's interactions with others.

MINE THE SETTING FOR CONFLICT GOLD
The character's environment is ripe with opportunities to generate or escalate conflict, and with so many locations to choose from, the options for where to set your story's events are limitless. Sometimes, a blah scene can turn into one that pops simply by picking the right location.

Choose Settings Thoughtfully
Some setting choices are obvious. If you need your character's car to break down in an isolated area, then a country road, campsite, or quarry might do the trick. But conflict very often happens in an ordinary setting, like a retail store or at home. In cases like these, when the story has dictated where events will occur, up the ante by choosing a specific location that holds emotional value for your character. Instead of choosing just any store, pick one with an

emotional association—such as the place the character was caught shoplifting as a teenager. Good or bad, any setting that plays upon their emotional volatility will increase their chances of saying or doing something they'll regret.

And while we're talking about emotional value, don't underestimate the symbolic weight of the objects within the scene. The backyard may be a generic place to have a difficult conversation, but put the characters next to the treehouse their son used to play in before he got sick, and you've already heightened their emotions, potentially adding additional conflict to the scene.

It's also important to think about which settings contain infrastructure that will make the character's goal harder to reach. Maybe it's a ravine the protagonist will need to cross, a locked door to get through, or a security guard to evade. Remember that the character's journey to achieve their goal shouldn't be a walk in the park. Conflict is necessary in every scene, so choose settings that contain obstacles or provide poignant emotional roadblocks.

Add a Complication

Think about how conflict naturally evolves. The character has an objective. They put together a plan and start pursuing that goal. Then complications come along and make things interesting. Luckily, there are lots of ways we can manipulate the setting to create additional conflict scenarios.

Mess with the Weather. Unexpected showers, a heat wave, an icy driveway, the threat of a tornado—how can small and large weather considerations create problems for your character?

Take Away Transportation. No matter what setting you choose, your character will need to move from one place to another. What kind of transportation disruptions will make it harder for them to get where they need to go?

Add an Audience. Falling down in private is totally different than doing it in a crowd of people. Both may be physically painful, but the latter adds an element of emotional hardship. Who could you put in the environment as a witness to the character's missteps or misfortune?

Trigger Sensitive Emotions. Conflict is easier to handle for an even-keeled, emotionally cool character. So use the setting to throw them off balance. If they're struggling to put food on the table, place them in a locale where wealthy characters are eating lavishly and throwing away leftovers. Likewise, a character with daddy issues can be triggered in an environment that highlights healthy and loving father-daughter relationships. So when you're planning the setting for a scene, ask yourself: What could I add specifically for my character in this situation that will elevate their emotions?

Exploit What They Don't Have. If your character doesn't have a light source, place them in a dark place, like a cave or deserted subway tunnel. No weapon? Surround them with physical threats. If they're lacking something vital, capitalize on that.

Make Them Uncomfortable. Vulnerability sets the character on edge and elevates their emotional state. So whenever you can, put the character in a location where they have no experience, don't know the rules, or aren't really suited to navigate it. This can work for small- or large-scale settings, from a character who has to traverse an alien planet to someone who's averse to kids having to host a child's party.

Use Symbolism. Nothing impedes progress like fear and self-doubt. Think about which symbols can be added to the environment to remind the character of an area of weakness, a past failure, a debilitating fear, or an unresolved wound.

Add a Ticking Clock. One surefire way to up the ante is to give the character a deadline. Instead of them having unlimited time to complete the goal, make them dependent upon elements within their environment, such as having to avoid rush-hour traffic, reach the bank by four p.m., or get home before sunset.

DON'T FORGET THE WORKPLACE
If your character's anything like the rest of us, they'll be spending a lot of time at work. And most people admit to not being 100 percent happy with their jobs, so a lot of conflict can happen in the workplace. Again, think about the people your character will encounter there and how might they create tension. Or, how could the character's work cause problems? What changes (in hierarchy, duties, hours, or location) may create friction with the important people at home? How might their insecurities or flaws contribute to a work-related situation, creating drama that will have to be dealt with?

USE INTERNAL CONFLICT
Remember that the most compelling conflict is often the internal kind. Monitor your characters and their situations to see what kind of inner turmoil you can add to an already difficult situation. Where might they be conflicted, confused, or uncertain? What moral questions would keep them up at night? Which decisions are they struggling to make and why?

Internal conflict is the trickiest to write because it has to make sense for the character. Their personality, moral code, sense of identity, missing basic needs, motivations, and desires will all determine how they think and feel about what they're going through. So get to know your character intimately to get this important piece of the conflict puzzle right.

USE THE ENTRIES
It's not always easy to find the right conflict scenario for an important scene or come up with the perfect combination of situations that will lead your character where they need to go. But that's the whole purpose of this book—to give you ample ideas to pull from. Flip through the Table of Contents to see all the possibilities, then brainstorm options for your project. If you know the kind of conflict you need but you're not sure exactly what it should look like, use the category breakdown to jumpstart that process. For instance, if you want tension in an important relationship or need your character to make a crucial error, look at the Relationship Friction and Failures and Mistakes sections to see which scenarios might fit the bill.

On the flip side, *The Conflict Thesaurus* can also help when you know which conflict scenario you want to use, but you're not sure about the specifics. Need a low-level response to what's happening? Check out the Minor Complications field for that entry. Do the same when you're looking for Potentially Disastrous Results. And Possible Internal Struggles can offer you a variety of inner turmoil scenarios that can be used to add gravitas to the situation.

JUST LOOK AROUND

If all else fails and you can't figure out what kind of conflict to use, look around. Conflict options surround us all hours of the day or night—at home, at work, driving down the street, with enemies, with family members, and with our closest friends. Inventory your recent conflicts. Think about what's happened to the people you know to raise tension and stakes for them personally. Train your brain to watch others so you can catch conflict scenarios as they unfold in real time.

You can also find options by turning on the TV. What kinds of conflict do you see? What levels are there? How do those scenarios play out? Movies, shows, and books can be a great source of inspiration for finding the right kinds of clashes and contentions. What's awesome is that these conflicts can happen in pretty much any location; just tweak the setting to make them work for your memoir, contemporary fiction story, historical fiction epic, dystopian novel, or space opera.

FINAL WORDS FROM THE AUTHORS

Conflict really is such an important part of a successful story. And not just any conflict; you want the kinds that are going to create tension in all areas of the character's life, stand in the way of them achieving their goals, and generate psychological turmoil. It needs to escalate over the course of the story, with stakes that become more personal and devastating. And it needs to be part of every story and scene. We hope this book can guide you toward the right conflict options for your story so you can incorporate them in the most beneficial way.

The categories can help you narrow down your options to a short list of possibilities, making it easier to find what you're looking for. If what you need isn't here, you might find what you need in the second volume of *The Conflict Thesaurus*. A full list of the entries to be included in that publication can be found at the back of this book.

With so many options for story complications, we couldn't include them all. Instead, we aimed for a mixture of conflict types and levels. It should also be noted that while conflict can be generated by a specific event, it often begins with the simple act of having to choose. The temptation to cheat or lie can cause different fallout than the acts themselves, often resulting in that all-important internal tension that is so important to include in our stories.

It's our sincere hope that this book, like all our others, will provide you with the tools and knowledge you may have been lacking, enabling you to elevate your storytelling. Best of luck to you, and enjoy the journey!

THE
CONFLICT
THESAURUS

Relationship
Friction

A DIVORCE OR BREAKUP

MINOR COMPLICATIONS
Awkwardness arising from running into one's ex in social situations
Being lonely
Having to attend social events and functions alone
Wanting to get back together when the other person has no desire to do so
Decreased productivity at work or school
Having to change habits and routines to avoid running into the ex
Becoming single and drifting away from friends who are in relationships
Having to split up assets, household items, and pets
Dealing with loved ones who share unhelpful advice: *You'll find someone even better*, or *How long are you going to mourn that loser?*
Being saddened by hobbies or interests that were shared with the other person and being at loose ends

POTENTIALLY DISASTROUS RESULTS
A difficult and drawn-out divorce settlement
A bitter custody battle
The character's children suffering
Losing friends or family members who choose sides
Being financially ruined by a prenup, shared debts, or legal fees
Having to move to a new house, neighborhood, or city
Sinking to new lows in an effort to win the person back (stalking, manipulation, nagging their friends for information, etc.)
Being pursued by the other person (if the character initiated the breakup)
The breakup triggering or aggravating a mental condition (depression, panic attacks, OCD, etc.)
The ex seeking power by spreading rumors, deliberately poaching the character's friends, poisoning their child against him or her, etc.
Having to continue to work with an ex who is a co-worker or business partner
Getting into a toxic rebound relationship
Refusing to take any ownership for one's part in the breakup; being destined to repeat the same mistakes in future relationships

RESULTING EMOTIONS: Anger, Anguish, Bitterness, Conflicted, Denial, Depressed, Despair, Desperation, Devastation, Emasculation, Grief, Guilt, Homesickness, Hurt, Insecurity, Jealousy, Loneliness, Panic, Powerlessness, Remorse, Resentment, Resignation, Sadness, Self-Pity

POSSIBLE INTERNAL STRUGGLES
Second-guessing the breakup
Knowing the decision is best for everyone but feeling guilty about the effect on the kids

Taking the high road and not disclosing the ex's infidelity to one's kids, yet resenting the fact that he or she is responsible for the marriage ending

Being relieved the relationship is over but worrying that nothing better may lie ahead

Wanting to move on but feeling insecure about one's attributes and whether or not one will find a good match

Wanting to love again but struggling with trust and vulnerability

Feeling relief about the relationship ending but mourning the loss of dreams that were destroyed or put on hold, such as getting married or having children

Not wanting to end up in another bad relationship but knowing one won't be happy single

Worrying that bitterness and resentment might taint new relationships

NEGATIVE TRAITS THAT MAY WORSEN THE SITUATION: Addictive, Controlling, Cynical, Gullible, Insecure, Manipulative, Martyr, Needy, Obsessive, Pessimistic, Self-Destructive

IMPACT ON BASIC NEEDS

Self-Actualization: A character whose identity is tied to being married, starting a family, or wanting children by a certain age might find their dreams upended in the aftermath of a divorce or breakup.

Esteem and Recognition: Characters who are dumped may worry others will view them as defective and not relationship-worthy.

Love and Belonging: Too many breakups (or one really bad one) can cause the character to avoid relationships in the future. Over time, this self-protection strategy can backfire, compromising their need for of love and belonging.

Safety and Security: Codependent, obsessive, or mentally unstable characters might lose their grip on reality after a divorce or breakup and vent their pain on others.

POSITIVE TRAITS TO HELP THE CHARACTER COPE: Appreciative, Centered, Creative, Friendly, Funny, Happy, Independent, Objective, Optimistic, Playful, Uninhibited

POSITIVE OUTCOMES

Recognizing the part the character played in the breakup and taking steps to make changes and grow

Making the most of the time without a partner; the character learning to be comfortable and happy on their own

Taking the opportunity to do some internal work; seeking to understand their sensitivities or triggers and processing any trauma that's keeping them from fulfillment

Distance revealing truths about the other person that the character had been reluctant to see

Being free to find someone who is a better fit

Having more time to engage in meaningful activities and pursuits

Building deep, lifelong relationships with other singles

A CHILD WANTING TO LIVE WITH ONE'S EX

EXAMPLES
A teenage child choosing to live with the character's ex after a divorce
A child taking every opportunity to tell the character how much better life would be if they lived with their other parent
A child admitting in a custody hearing that they'd prefer to live with the character's ex
Siblings choosing to live with different parents and being split up into two households

MINOR COMPLICATIONS
Struggling with the "empty nest" situation on days when the child is with the other parent
Having to pack up a child's things and relocate everything to their new home
Not being with the child for holidays or important events
Siblings growing apart or experiencing unequal treatment because they live in different households
Complications arising from blended and extended families
Being manipulated by a child playing their parents against each other to get what they want
The character feeling like an outsider while spending time with the ex and their child at Christmas concerts, graduations, or other important events
Having to accommodate the ex's schedule
Dealing with a reluctant child every time the character picks them up from the ex's
Having to explain the custody situation to other people

POTENTIALLY DISASTROUS RESULTS
A long, drawn-out custody battle
Co-parenting with an ex who has vastly different rules, beliefs, or ideas about discipline
Suspecting the ex's environment may be unhealthy or unsafe for the child
The character seeking full custody (against the child's wishes), resulting in resentment and anger
Guilt driving the character to make poor parenting choices
The child being influenced by the ex's lies or negativity toward the character
Awkwardness and distance growing between the character and child
Not being there to offer guidance, support, and advice when it's needed

RESULTING EMOTIONS: Anger, Anxiety, Apprehension, Betrayed, Bitterness, Concern, Defensiveness, Depressed, Despair, Devastation, Grief, Hurt, Insecurity, Jealousy, Neglected, Powerlessness, Reluctance, Resentment, Resignation, Self-Pity, Shame, Unappreciated

POSSIBLE INTERNAL STRUGGLES
Wanting the child to stay but also wanting to grant their wishes
Having to disappoint the child when something doesn't go as planned
Fighting the urge to speak negatively about the ex, even when they're to blame
The character feeling guilty for being closer with the children they live with than the child who lives with the ex

Fighting the temptation to ask their child about the other parent
Struggling with shame for enjoying one's child-free time
Being tempted to compete for the child's affections by trying to be the "fun" parent
Feeling like a failure as a parent for not being their child's top choice

NEGATIVE TRAITS THAT MAY WORSEN THE SITUATION: Abrasive, Catty, Controlling, Defensive, Insecure, Irrational, Jealous, Manipulative, Needy, Oversensitive, Possessive, Pushy, Resentful, Stubborn, Uncooperative, Vindictive

IMPACT ON BASIC NEEDS

Self-Actualization: If the character's dreams included being a highly involved parent, they may struggle to find satisfaction and happiness with the changes.

Esteem and Recognition: Any person whose child chooses someone else over them is going to question their own self-worth, believing they have failed as a parent. Other people may also assume negative things about the character because the child chose to live with someone else.

Love and Belonging: A character whose child is their whole world can become so focused on being available as a parent that they don't make room for other relationships. At some point, the character's loneliness may cause discontent, but they may not recognize it or know how to fix it.

POSITIVE TRAITS TO HELP THE CHARACTER COPE: Appreciative, Confident, Easygoing, Empathetic, Generous, Objective, Optimistic, Supportive, Tolerant, Unselfish, Wise

POSITIVE OUTCOMES

The parent and child relationship strengthening as a result of time spent apart
The child finding new appreciation for the character after living with the ex for a while
The character using the time alone for internal reflection, gaining insight that makes them a better parent
The character finding balance by taking advantage of the time alone to travel, pursue a new hobby, or advance their education
The child thriving in a new living arrangement and the character realizing it was the right choice
The character being able to empathize with and offer support for parents in their circle who are going through the same situation
Connecting with another single parent and going through life together

A LOVE INTEREST TAKING UP WITH SOMEONE ELSE

EXAMPLES
A girlfriend or boyfriend breaking up with the character to try again with an ex
A promising match from an online app canceling a date because they've met someone else
The character discovering they've been used by a love interest to get close to a friend, roommate, or sibling
Attending a party or other social event with a date only to have them leave with someone else
The character developing feelings for a co-worker who begins dating someone else
A long-time crush embarking on a romantic relationship
A long-distance lover breaking things off to pursue a local relationship
Being too slow to act on a mutual attraction and the other party moving on to someone else

MINOR COMPLICATIONS
Awkward moments when the character and love interest run into each other
Having to retrieve belongings left at the other's apartment
Canceling reservations, theater tickets, or plans for a shared trip
Embarrassment at having to explain to people what happened
Changing their social media status to "single" and feeling pitied
Flying solo at events
Having to start over in the dating department
Becoming the "third wheel" at social functions
Carefully selecting activities and group hangouts to minimize chance run-ins

POTENTIALLY DISASTROUS RESULTS
The character confronting the love interest or their new flame in a fit of jealous rage
The betrayal of discovering that a friend is the one who took the character's place with the love interest
An unexpected pregnancy
The character becoming obsessed and stalking the love interest and their new partner
Discovering that the love interest gave the character a sexually transmitted disease
Being unable to move on; missing out on meaningful new relationship opportunities
The character building up the lost relationship in their mind and holding every potential suitor to an impossible standard
Swearing off of dating altogether

RESULTING EMOTIONS: Anger, Anguish, Annoyance, Betrayed, Bitterness, Confusion, Despair, Devastation, Disappointment, Disillusionment, Emasculation, Embarrassment, Envy, Hurt, Inadequacy, Insecurity, Jealousy, Loneliness, Longing, Obsession, Resentment, Resignation, Stunned, Unappreciated

POSSIBLE INTERNAL STRUGGLES

Wanting to remain friends so the relationship isn't completely lost but harboring resentment at being discarded

The character feeling at fault that things didn't work out and worrying their personal deficits (real or imagined) make them an unsuitable romantic partner

Wanting to be happy for the love interest but feeling jealous and hurt instead

The character trying to date someone new but not being able to shake the feelings for their former partner

The character measuring themselves against the new guy or girl and coming up short

Beating oneself up for missing certain signs, not doing enough, or acting too late

NEGATIVE TRAITS THAT MAY WORSEN THE SITUATION: Catty, Childish, Cocky, Controlling, Insecure, Martyr, Possessive, Self-Destructive, Vindictive, Volatile

IMPACT ON BASIC NEEDS

Self-Actualization: If the character assumed their life path would include the person they lost, they may have a hard time adjusting and feel uncertain about the future.

Esteem and Recognition: When a relationship ends in a way the character doesn't expect, it causes them to question where they went wrong and why they weren't good enough for the other person, damaging their self-esteem.

Love and Belonging: A newly single character without the prospect of an immediate relationship may feel alone in the world, craving love and belonging. If the breakup was an ugly one, they could develop a fear of intimacy that affects future relationships.

POSITIVE TRAITS TO HELP THE CHARACTER COPE: Adaptable, Adventurous, Ambitious, Analytical, Centered, Confident, Easygoing, Independent, Mature, Optimistic, Sensible, Supportive, Unselfish

POSITIVE OUTCOMES

The character enjoying their newly single life and learning to appreciate their own company

Being emotionally available when a new, better-suited love interest comes into the picture

The character realizing they've escaped from a toxic or dead-end relationship

Gaining a new perspective on how much it hurts to be let go and resolving to take greater care when parting ways with friends or lovers in the future

The character developing a friendship with the love interest's new flame—someone they wouldn't have met otherwise

Being able to focus on important things, such as work, education, or developing other relationships

The character being able to envision more clearly what they do or do not want from a romantic partner

A PARTNER BEING UNWILLING TO COMMIT

EXAMPLES
The character's significant other not wanting to get married
Having a partner who doesn't want to move in with the character
The partner refusing to call the relationship exclusive even though there is no one else
Being engaged for a long time to someone who is reluctant to set a date or plan the wedding
Being in an on-again-off-again relationship with a person who is constantly breaking up with the character when things get serious

MINOR COMPLICATIONS
Arguments and friction in the relationship
Having two of everything—two homes, beds, closets and sets of clothes, etc.
Fielding awkward questions from family and friends
Being judged or talked about by those outside the relationship
"Bleeding" money because finances and assets are not consolidated
Feeling like an outsider around the partner's family
Experiencing envy when friends get married or announce pregnancies
Wanting to talk to someone about the situation but not wanting to be the subject of pity
One's family showing animosity toward the partner for keeping the relationship in limbo
Having to make excuses for the significant other's reluctance to commit

POTENTIALLY DISASTROUS RESULTS
The character delivering an ultimatum
The partner leaving the relationship
The character looking elsewhere for the commitment they desire (engaging in emotional cheating or an affair)
A rival seeking to move in due to a belief that the existing relationship isn't serious
A pregnancy forcing the issue or upping the ante
A catalyst event that makes things worse, such as the partner being promoted but her work requiring frequent travel, further restricting time spent with the character
The partner being required to move to another city (to care for an elderly family member, for work, etc.) and a long-distance relationship being proposed
Other dreams being denied (e.g., turning down a promotion that would require a relocation) because the character is pinning their hopes on the other person eventually committing
Learning a devastating reason for the other person's reluctance—because they're married or their family wouldn't approve of the character, for instance

RESULTING EMOTIONS: Conflicted, Disappointment, Frustration, Hurt, Insecurity, Longing, Neglected, Powerlessness, Resignation, Self-Pity, Unappreciated, Vulnerability, Wistfulness

POSSIBLE INTERNAL STRUGGLES
Loving someone yet hating the part of them that can't commit
Feeling defective, yet knowing the commitment issues lie in the partner's painful past

Wanting to respect the partner's fears and love them unconditionally but also resenting them for not being able or willing to meet the character's needs

Wondering if they're making a mistake by staying in the relationship

Wanting marriage and a family but being unsure if their partner will ever "get there"

Fearing lifelong regret either way—from leaving and losing the love of a lifetime or staying and giving up the dream of being a parent, for example

Wanting to be happy about attending weddings and baby showers but being jealous instead

Doubting the partner's motives; wondering if their reluctance to commit is really due to past pain or is just related to a character flaw

Pushing for a commitment and feeling selfish for doing so

Knowing there are some problems in the relationship but believing commitment will fix them

NEGATIVE TRAITS THAT MAY WORSEN THE SITUATION: Confrontational, Insecure, Jealous, Martyr, Needy, Possessive, Selfish, Uncommunicative, Withdrawn, Worrywart

IMPACT ON BASIC NEEDS

Self-Actualization: A character whose dreams involve being part of a forever relationship may feel they're being kept from living their true purpose.

Esteem and Recognition: Having a partner who is unable to commit might cause the character to look within for reasons why and begin to believe they have an internal deficiency.

Love and Belonging: The distance created by a lack of commitment could leave the character feeling they're not fully loved or appreciated, creating friction in the relationship.

POSITIVE TRAITS TO HELP THE CHARACTER COPE: Appreciative, Centered, Easygoing, Honest, Independent, Kind, Loyal, Mature, Persistent, Tolerant, Unselfish

POSITIVE OUTCOMES

Realizing in the waiting that the other party is a mismatch and being able to break ties before the relationship becomes more complicated

The situation causing friction that encourages the character to search within for reasons why, leading to personal growth and positive life changes

The character prioritizing their own happiness by choosing to walk away and seek something better rather than settling for "good enough"

The character letting go of certain visions of the future and focusing their energy toward other things that will lead to happiness and fulfillment

A ROMANCE BEING STYMIED

NOTES: Many romances have obstacles and stumbling blocks that keep them from thriving. For clarity, this entry will only explore relationships being affected by forces outside of the couple's control.

EXAMPLES
An interfaith couple being blocked by loved ones or members of their religious communities
Teens being forbidden by parents to pursue a relationship
The character's wealthy family disapproving of a love interest from a humble background
Children of feuding families struggling to make a romantic relationship work
A royal being discouraged from pursuing a love interest who is beneath their station
Loved ones discouraging a character from pursuing an unhealthy or toxic relationship
Parents with deeply ingrained bias (involving race, sexual identity, etc.) forbidding the relationship

MINOR COMPLICATIONS
The couple having to sneak around to be together
Joining a romantic partner's family, culture, or religion and causing strife with their own family
Tension with family members
Having to lie and keep secrets
Not knowing which family members to trust with the truth
The couple having to come up with creative ways to communicate, such as sending letters in code or using burner phones
Family tension bleeding into the romantic relationship, causing friction and conflict
Being asked by the partner to change in order to be accepted into their family
Being guilted by loved ones to respect the family's wishes or adhere to duty

POTENTIALLY DISASTROUS RESULTS
The character choosing to cut family members out of their life to pursue the relationship
A head of state's untraditional marriage triggering instability, violence, or a war between nations
The couple's children not being accepted by the family or religion because the relationship wasn't sanctioned
Refusing to end things and being financially cut off or ousted from the family
The character denouncing their own beliefs to be with their romantic interest
Eloping to avoid drama and conflict (creating new family tensions when the news goes public)
The relationship ending badly, leaving both parties with deep emotional wounds
One or both parties being punished or jailed as a result of their union
Being forced to hide a marriage or pregnancy from families or authorities
Disagreements between feuding families escalating to violence or death
Being forced to marry someone chosen by the character's family when the character is in love with someone else

Being expelled from a culture or religion due to the character's choice of life partner
The character's partner caving to family pressure and ending the relationship

RESULTING EMOTIONS: Anger, Anguish, Anxiety, Betrayed, Bitterness, Defensiveness, Determination, Devastation, Fear, Intimidation, Loneliness, Regret, Scorn

POSSIBLE INTERNAL STRUGGLES

The character struggling with their love life being on display for others to scrutinize
Moments of doubt about whether the romantic partner and the relationship are worth the cost
Letting negative feeling toward a partner's family affect the way they view their partner
The character longing to be accepted by the partner's family, even if their misgivings are beyond the character's ability to change (such as race, religion, or station in life)
Losing hope for a happy future with the love of their life
Resentment at being asked to change to "make things easier" but wanting to be accepted
The character's love of their family dimming as prejudice, bias, and control issues come to light

NEGATIVE TRAITS THAT MAY WORSEN THE SITUATION: Addictive, Impulsive, Inhibited, Melodramatic, Possessive, Rebellious, Self-Destructive, Uncommunicative, Vindictive

IMPACT ON BASIC NEEDS

Self-Actualization: At the heart of a stymied romance is repression. An otherwise happy life can fail to satisfy if the character isn't free to choose who to spend it with.

Esteem and Recognition: A character who is constantly criticized for their choice of romantic partner may begin to doubt their judgment and instincts.

Love and Belonging: Being forcibly separated from a love interest or one's family can easily affect the character's feelings of belonging.

Safety and Security: Financial support being withdrawn when the character chooses love over their family's wishes could cause financial hardship in some cases.

Physiological Needs: In a society where choosing the wrong partner is punishable by jail or execution, the character may face dire consequences for pursuing the relationship.

POSITIVE TRAITS TO HELP THE CHARACTER COPE: Affectionate, Courageous, Discreet, Focused, Optimistic, Passionate, Patient, Persistent, Persuasive, Protective

POSITIVE OUTCOMES

A couple becoming stronger after overcoming resistance to their union
The character finding immense fulfillment after adopting a partner's religion
Friends being inspired by the character's courage to pursue their own true desires
The character realizing after the romance fell apart that their loved ones were right and the other person was all wrong for them
Those in opposition realizing they had been wrong and choosing to let go of biases
A character who is abandoned by their partner being free to find someone who places love and romantic loyalty above all else

A ROMANTIC COMPETITOR
ENTERING THE SCENE

EXAMPLES
A love interest's old flame showing up and wanting to resume a relationship
Someone new expressing a desire for the character's love interest
Being "just friends" with someone, yet wanting more when competition shows up
A rival seeking ways to hurt the character, including stealing their love interest
The character dating someone who won't agree to be exclusive

MINOR COMPLICATIONS
Having to find ways to one-up the competition
Having to go to a special event solo because the character lost to the competitor
Distraction causing trouble at work, at school, and in other areas of responsibility
Having to work twice as hard to be noticed by the love interest
Being teased or pitied by friends
Time lost to worry and anxiety
Jealousy creeping into the relationship, triggering arguments
Discomfort at putting oneself out there (if the character hasn't made their feelings known to the love interest)

POTENTIALLY DISASTROUS RESULTS
Jealousy that gets out of hand and causes a breakup
Getting caught spying on the love interest while they're out with the competition
Becoming obsessed and driving the love interest toward the competition
Losing the love interest because the character demanded they make a choice
Turning the love interest off by trying to buy their affection
Pretending to be interested in someone else and it backfiring
Getting into an altercation with a rival, spurring the love interest to walk away from both parties
Desperation pushing the character to do something that ends in humiliation, like publicly popping the question and being rejected
Losing oneself in the race to win the love interest's affection (becoming obsessed with one's looks, losing weight, bulking up in an unhealthy way, striving for a certain social status, etc.)
Giving up, then living with regret
Breaking up and developing a new emotional wound: unrequited love

RESULTING EMOTIONS: Anticipation, Anxiety, Defeat, Depressed, Desire, Despair, Desperation, Determination, Disappointment, Doubt, Envy, Hopefulness, Humiliation, Hurt, Inadequacy, Insecurity, Intimidation, Jealousy, Loneliness, Longing, Love, Obsession, Self-Pity

POSSIBLE INTERNAL STRUGGLES
Insecurity causing neediness that leads to self-loathing

Anguish over the partner's indecision

Feeling "not good enough" but also angry for being made to feel that way

Being ashamed of one's anger toward the rival, since he or she is really a good person

Wrestling with trust issues regarding the love interest

Wanting to share negative information about the rival but not wanting to be viewed as jealous or catty

Being tempted to cross a moral line to come out ahead

Wanting to be free of the situation but loving the other person too much to let go

The character becoming confused about which is more important: winning the love interest or beating the other person

NEGATIVE TRAITS THAT MAY WORSEN THE SITUATION: Catty, Childish, Confrontational, Controlling, Dishonest, Foolish, Impulsive, Insecure, Melodramatic, Needy, Nosy, Obsessive, Paranoid, Possessive, Pretentious, Pushy, Reckless, Suspicious, Whiny

IMPACT ON BASIC NEEDS

Esteem and Recognition: Learning about a competitor can create all sorts of problems with the character's self-esteem. Having someone to measure herself against can shake her confidence, bring out insecurities, and play havoc with her emotions. This might cause her to behave erratically, doing things she might not normally do that will cause embarrassment, humiliation, shame, or regret.

Love and Belonging: A competitor showing up can shake the foundation of your character's existing relationship—depending on the love interest's reaction. If they are entertaining the idea of trading her in for someone else, this could push them to do so. If your character loses the love interest because she never let her feelings be known, this can lead her to believe unhealthy or untrue things about herself, making it more difficult for her to pursue a romance in the future.

Safety and Security: Depending on how obsessive the character is and how far she may go to win the heart of the one she loves, she may burn through her savings. This can lead to financial strain if the character overextends herself and has bills to pay.

POSITIVE TRAITS TO HELP THE CHARACTER COPE: Affectionate, Charming, Creative, Flirtatious, Funny, Easygoing, Kind, Loyal, Passionate, Patient, Perceptive, Persistent, Persuasive, Playful, Sensual, Sentimental, Whimsical

POSITIVE OUTCOMES

The appearance of a new competitor nudging the love interest toward appreciating and valuing the character more

The character reflecting on whether the relationship is worth fighting for or not

A character finally finding the strength to push through the mental blocks that are holding them back and voice their true feelings to the love interest

A character who has a hard time seeing her own strengths finding clarity when she compares herself to the other person and finds them lacking

AN EX INTERFERING IN ONE'S LIFE

EXAMPLES
An ex causing friction with the character's new love interest
A past partner stalking the character (appearing at a favorite coffee shop, place of work, etc.)
The ex misrepresenting the breakup to shared friends, manipulating them into picking sides
The character being blackmailed by an ex with intimate details about their life
The ex making unreasonable demands surrounding alimony, shared property, or custody arrangements
An old flame spreading untrue rumors in the character's social circle or workplace
An ex buying the character's place of employment or becoming a client
An ex-spouse going after something important to the character (the kids, his or her job, etc.) as a way of getting back at or controlling the character

MINOR COMPLICATIONS
Friction with the character's current love interest because of the ex
The character being forced to change routines to avoid running into their past partner
Having to consult with the ex before making decisions (if finances or property are involved)
Frequent arguments with the ex
Hesitating to pursue new romantic relationships because of the past partner's volatility
Trust issues with family, friends, or co-workers who may be sympathetic to the ex
Losing friends who picked sides after the breakup
Work or friendships suffering because the character is always dealing with the ex's demands, jealousy, or unreasonable behavior
Avoiding communication from the ex and missing other important correspondences
The situation putting a character on edge, always wondering what else is coming

POTENTIALLY DISASTROUS RESULTS
Giving in to rage and lashing out (defacing the ex's property, slashing their car's tires, or stealing something of theirs) and being arrested and charged
The character's deepest secret being shared publicly
The character getting fired because of the ex's influence with their employer
A confrontation with the ex that leads to violence
A new relationship ending because the ex's meddling becomes too much
Emotional scars causing the character to sabotage new relationships or avoid them all together
A past spouse using intimate knowledge of the character to get revenge (releasing nude photos, publishing a drunken video of them, sharing personal or financial information online, etc.)

RESULTING EMOTIONS: Anger, Anxiety, Apprehension, Defiance, Desperation, Dread, Emasculation, Embarrassment, Fear, Frustration, Intimidation, Tormented, Unease, Worry

POSSIBLE INTERNAL STRUGGLES
Being responsible for a bad breakup (by not handling it well or being the reason the relationship ended) and believing on some level they deserve the mistreatment

The character forming an opinion that love always ends badly, affecting future relationships
Anger making them lose sight of what's really important
Struggling to take the high road and resist the urge to sink as low as the ex
The character regretting choosing the ex in the first place, feeling responsible for the predicament
Being tempted to just give in and do what the ex wants because it's easier than resisting
Feeling judged by family or friends who tried to warn the character away from the relationship

NEGATIVE TRAITS THAT MAY WORSEN THE SITUATION: Confrontational, Controlling, Gullible, Inhibited, Insecure, Martyr, Needy, Nervous, Obsessive, Reckless, Subservient, Violent, Volatile, Worrywart

IMPACT ON BASIC NEEDS
   Self-Actualization: If battling the interference takes all of the character's energy, they may lack the reserves needed to pursue the important things in life.
   Esteem and Recognition: Rumors and lies spread by the ex could embarrass the character and hurt their reputation, changing the way people view them.
   Love and Belonging: Emotional scars from an ex's behavior can lead the character to doubt love is possible, causing them to reject other romantic opportunities that become available.
   Safety and Security: A spiteful ex stalking a character (online or off) can threaten their sense of safety and security.

POSITIVE TRAITS TO HELP THE CHARACTER COPE: Bold, Calm, Confident, Diplomatic, Disciplined, Independent, Just, Patient, Persuasive, Proactive, Protective, Resourceful, Wise

POSITIVE OUTCOMES
The character recalling what they wanted in life before they met the ex and going for it
Learning from a failed relationship and building a stronger one the next time around
A character getting sick of the ex's drama and taking steps to remove him or her from their life for good
Getting an ex out of their system and finally being ready to move ahead with someone new
The character learning to be happy on their own

AN UNWANTED ROMANTIC ADVANCE

EXAMPLES
Having a friend who doesn't want to stay in the friend zone
Being pursued by someone in a position of power or authority (the boss, a university professor, one's landlord, the security guard in one's building, etc.)
Romantic advances from someone crossing a moral line (the best friend's significant other, a sister's ex, the fiancé's mother, etc.)
An acquaintance who makes the character uncomfortable—because of their beliefs, off-putting personality traits, or an undefined *something* that triggers the character's instincts

MINOR COMPLICATIONS
Awkwardness around the pursuer
Feeling embarrassed and flustered in the moment
Coming up with strategies to de-escalate the situation (having excuses ready, making sure another person is nearby, not saying or doing anything that could be misconstrued as interest, etc.)
Having to keep the situation secret from an important person (one's spouse, best friend, sibling, etc.) to avoid drama or repercussions
Inconveniences arising from trying to avoid the pursuer

POTENTIALLY DISASTROUS RESULTS
Other people finding out and important relationships being damaged as a result (even if the character never encouraged the pursuer)
Trying not to hurt the pursuer's feelings and inadvertently giving them false hope
A potential love interest giving up because they think the character is already involved with someone
The relationship dynamic worsening—e.g., losing a friend because that person wants more and the character can't comply
The pursuer refusing to take *no* for an answer (becoming obsessed, stalking the character, trying to manipulate them, etc.)
The pursuer becoming depressed or suicidal at the character's rejection
Being pressured by others to accept the unwanted advances
Giving in, even though the character doesn't fully return the pursuer's feelings
The character having to leave their job, school, or neighborhood to get away from the pursuer
The rejected pursuer using their position of power to punish the character

RESULTING EMOTIONS: Apprehension, Conflicted, Disbelief, Dread, Embarrassment, Empathy, Flustered, Frustration, Guilt, Pity, Powerlessness, Reluctance, Stunned, Unease

POSSIBLE INTERNAL STRUGGLES
Feeling conflicted about pursuing something more with the other person, especially if the two are good friends
Struggling with guilt from having to reject them

Wanting to respond respectfully but being angry or embarrassed about being put in the situation

Not wanting that type of relationship but knowing the person is emotionally fragile and being afraid of causing more damage to their ego

The character analyzing their own behavior, banter, and actions, trying to see if something they said or did was misconstrued

Knowing the other person isn't a good fit but fearing what could happen if they are refused

Feeling trapped because the pursuer has some sort of leverage over the character

NEGATIVE TRAITS THAT MAY WORSEN THE SITUATION: Abrasive, Apathetic, Callous, Cruel, Disrespectful, Gossipy, Nervous, Tactless, Worrywart

IMPACT ON BASIC NEEDS

   Self-Actualization: If the character takes drastic steps to avoid the pursuer (such as changing jobs or turning down promising work projects), they may become limited in their opportunities.

   Esteem and Recognition: Too many unwanted advances from different people could cause the character to wonder what vibe they're giving off that draws undesirable people to them. They also may worry they're being too picky and will never be satisfied with anyone.

   Love and Belonging: If the pursuer is connected to the character through a close relationship (perhaps they are married to a relative, engaged to the character's best friend, or used to date a sibling), others may assume the character did something to encourage the advance. And, if the pursuer takes rejection badly, they could reframe events to say the character was the one doing the pursuing, creating rifts in those important relationships.

   Safety and Security: A rejected pursuer in a position of authority could cause the character to lose their job or be evicted from their home, resulting in danger to their well-being.

   Physiological Needs: If the situation turns dark and the pursuer becomes obsessed, the character's life may be endangered.

POSITIVE TRAITS TO HELP THE CHARACTER COPE: Courteous, Diplomatic, Gentle, Kind, Loyal, Merciful, Persuasive, Proactive, Professional

POSITIVE OUTCOMES

A boost in confidence that comes from being found desirable

Learning to give bad news graciously and respectfully

The situation clarifying the character's true feelings in some way—realizing they love someone else or recognizing the importance of a vital relationship in their life

Having an opportunity to reflect on what they do or do not want in a romantic relationship

Becoming more self-aware of behavior and actions that can easily be misunderstood

Recognizing flirtatiousness isn't always fun and games and people can be hurt by it

BEING BETRAYED OR ABANDONED BY A TRUSTED ALLY OR FRIEND

EXAMPLES
The character being framed by a trusted co-worker to cover for their own mistake
Being set up by a friend or loved one to take the fall for their crime
Being abandoned by an ally in a life-threatening situation, such as a battle, violent confrontation, or extreme weather event
Being forced out of a shared business by a long-term partner
A best friend not standing up for the character who is being publicly embarrassed or bullied
A friend revealing a closely held secret (the character's sexual orientation, an embarrassing mistake from the past, their involvement in a crime, etc.)
Being dumped by a friend when it suits their purposes (because a better "friend" opportunity came along, because sticking with the character through a troubling time is too much work, etc.)
The character learning an ally was never really on his or her side

MINOR COMPLICATIONS
A framed character having to prove they did nothing wrong
Loss of credibility with employers due to the co-worker's lies
Running into the former friend at social events or a shared favorite gym or coffee shop
Financial complications and loss of time from having to unwind a long-term business partnership
Embarrassment when a video capturing the betrayal or confrontation goes viral
Legal complications (if allegations of a crime are involved)
Losing the friend but still having to work with him or her
The inconvenience of having to replace the ally or partner
Temporarily putting other goals on hold to stabilize a business after the partner's departure

POTENTIALLY DISASTROUS RESULTS
Losing other friends who take the betrayer's side because they don't know the whole story
The character being fired and losing their financial livelihood
The character becoming obsessed with avenging him or herself
Responding in the moment of betrayal with violence
Financial ruin for the character's extended family or friends who invested in the business
The character being seriously injured or dying when left behind in a life-threatening situation

RESULTING EMOTIONS: Anger, Appalled, Betrayed, Bitterness, Confusion, Defensiveness, Defiance, Denial, Devastation, Disappointment, Disbelief, Disillusionment, Emasculation, Hatred, Hurt, Powerlessness, Rage, Stunned, Unappreciated

POSSIBLE INTERNAL STRUGGLES
Holding a grudge that clouds the character's judgment in other situations going forward

Wanting to hold onto the friendship but being unable to get past the betrayal

Finding it hard to trust or commit to others

Struggling to do the right thing when a future situation arises where the character could help the ex-ally or leave them to their own devices

The character internalizing the betrayal or abandonment and taking the blame for it

Being able to see the other's reasons for their choice but still being hurt by it

The character running themselves down for not seeing the other's true nature

Starting to believe the worst about people and expecting future allies to be faithless

Over-analyzing the motives of others, unable to shake the belief that more betrayals will come

NEGATIVE TRAITS THAT MAY WORSEN THE SITUATION: Gullible, Insecure, Macho, Needy, Oversensitive, Paranoid, Resentful, Timid, Uncommunicative, Vindictive

IMPACT ON BASIC NEEDS

Self-Actualization: Most meaningful goals cannot be achieved without trust and open-mindedness. So holding onto the betrayal and refusing to forgive may limit the character's ability to fully pursue their dreams.

Esteem and Recognition: If a friend doesn't stand up for the character when others are being critical or are making fun of them, the character may start to believe the criticism is true.

Love and Belonging: Being abandoned or betrayed by someone they care about can lead to trust issues, hampering the character's ability to connect meaningfully with others in the future.

Safety and Security: An abandonment or betrayal that results in loss of freedom or causes financial challenges can undermine the character's sense of security.

POSITIVE TRAITS TO HELP THE CHARACTER COPE: Cautious, Confident, Decisive, Easygoing, Independent, Inspirational, Optimistic, Perceptive, Persuasive

POSITIVE OUTCOMES

Being able to recognize the signs of a false friend or ally in the future

The character succeeding on their own and growing in confidence

Winning a legal suit against a former business partner and receiving a cash windfall

The character finding a new, more fulfilling career path after losing their job or business

The character vowing to be loyal and keep their word, never putting anyone through their own horrible experience

Building alliances with people who demonstrate they have the same values, ethics, and goals

Learning firsthand the personal benefit of forgiving others and letting go of a wrong

The character valuing the trustworthy people in their life all the more

BEING CHEATED ON

EXAMPLES

Finding out a spouse has been fooling around with someone else

Discovering sexy text messages on a partner's phone

Starting a fledgling but promising relationship only to find out the other person is still sleeping with their ex

The character coming home to find their partner in bed with their best friend

Being dumped by a partner and realizing they've been involved with someone else for a while

The character discovering their significant other, who travels frequently for work, has another family in a different city

MINOR COMPLICATIONS

Fielding questions from the kids, who can see something's wrong

Friction around the home (if the couple is still living together)

Having to attend couple's counseling to try to work things out

Ending the relationship with the cheater

Contracting an inconvenient but treatable sexually transmitted disease due to a partner's infidelity

Seeking to gain the upper hand in a divorce and having to take actions to catch the cheater in the act (by hiring a detective, setting up hidden cameras, monitoring their phone, etc.)

Having to confront the cheating partner about their actions

Becoming the "bad cop" in the relationship (forcing the partner to find new work away from their lover, requiring transparency of financial statements, etc.) to move forward

The character hiding what they know (and the pain that comes with it), hoping the partner will come to their senses and the situation will resolve on its own

Broken relationships with people who knew about the affair and said nothing

POTENTIALLY DISASTROUS RESULTS

Contracting a serious disease such as AIDS or Hepatitis C due to a partner's infidelity

A child witnessing the cheating behavior and not knowing what to do

Rage giving way to violence and the character severely injuring or killing the cheater

The character finding out they're pregnant

The cheater's infidelity leading to a pregnancy in their other relationship

The character engaging in extra-marital relations to get even

Discovering that the cheating has been going on for a very long time

Finding out a partner's ongoing affairs have been covered up by family for years

Staying for personal reasons (because a disability keeps the character financially trapped, they want the kids to have stability, etc.) and being trapped in a relationship characterized by bitterness, mistrust, anger, and dysfunction

Being gaslit by the partner into believing the character must prove they deserve the partner's love

RESULTING EMOTIONS: Anger, Anguish, Betrayed, Denial, Desperation, Emasculation, Grief, Humiliation, Hurt, Hysteria, Panic, Self-Pity, Shame, Shock, Skepticism, Stunned, Vulnerability, Worthlessness

POSSIBLE INTERNAL STRUGGLES

The character's self-confidence being shaken until they falsely think they are to blame
Needing support and advice but being too humiliated to share the infidelity with family and friends
Being torn between kicking the cheater to the curb and wanting to hang onto the relationship
Feeling guilty for wishing ill toward the partner who cheated
Choosing to stay in the relationship for the kids' sake and being unsure how to move past one's anger and resentment
Being unsure of what to do
Feeling overwhelmed by the sudden changes (being a single parent, having in-laws turn cold and uncommunicative, starting over, etc.)

NEGATIVE TRAITS THAT MAY WORSEN THE SITUATION: Addictive, Controlling, Cynical, Hypocritical, Impulsive, Indecisive, Insecure, Needy, Obsessive, Possessive, Self-Destructive, Subservient, Weak-Willed

IMPACT ON BASIC NEEDS

Self-Actualization: Whatever meaningful goals and higher fulfillment the character was working toward will be put on hold as they divert energy and focus to either fixing this relationship or dissolving it.

Esteem and Recognition: Discovering a partner has turned to someone else for intimacy can shake the character's self-worth. Underlying insecurities may deepen, further eroding their esteem.

Love and Belonging: Being cheated on may make it difficult for the character to pursue other relationships; they may even decide being alone is better than risking their heart again.

Safety and Security: Fallout from the cheating in the form of STDs (sexually transmitted diseases), financial difficulties, or emotional trauma can cause safety or security issues for the character.

POSITIVE TRAITS TO HELP THE CHARACTER COPE: Analytical, Centered, Confident, Mature, Optimistic, Proactive, Sensible

POSITIVE OUTCOMES

The character acknowledging they deserve better and leaving the relationship
The couple working through counseling and building a stronger relationship
Growing in independence and confidence by leaving and starting over
Finding love with someone who is devoted and loyal
Being able to counsel others who have experienced the same pain
Gaining perspective over time that ending the dysfunctional relationship saved the character from a lifetime of unhappiness and unfulfillment

BEING FORCED TO MARRY

EXAMPLES

An arranged marriage where one or both parties do not consent
A strategic match based on pedigree, wealth, power, or politics
Because of an unplanned pregnancy
For protection
Under threat of violence (often in a conflict zone, being captured, kidnapped, trafficked, etc.)
At the direction of a ruler or community leader

MINOR COMPLICATIONS

In a situation like this, there really are no minor complications. But there are immediate complications and then ongoing or escalated complications. Immediate ones for a character in this situation might include:

Having to move
Having to give up favorite interests, pastimes, and recreational activities
Having to leave home or one's comfort zone
Being forced to sever relationships (either through distance, pressure to no longer be in touch with certain people, or under threat of violence)
Losing the freedom to make independent choices
Having to hide their true feelings
Being forced to embrace new responsibilities the character may not be prepared for
Having to let go of other people they were romantically interested in

POTENTIALLY DISASTROUS RESULTS

Being forced to embrace a new way of life, beliefs, or religious practices
Living in fear of what is to come (due to a lack of control, a violent spouse, civil unrest, sexual expectations, new obligations, being in the public eye, etc.)
Depression at the direction the character's life has taken, especially over what was lost
Being placed in harm's way (due to new associations, family vendettas, assassins, etc.)
Being forced to bear children
Witnessing violence
Experiencing domestic violence, torture, slavery, or other forms of abuse
Being trapped in a loveless marriage
Being trapped in a relationship with an unfaithful partner

RESULTING EMOTIONS: Anger, Anguish, Appalled, Betrayed, Defiance, Depressed, Despair, Desperation, Intimidation, Panic, Powerlessness, Resignation, Sadness, Vulnerability

POSSIBLE INTERNAL STRUGGLES

Being torn between what the character wants (personal desires) and what family members want or need (duty)
Struggling with the decision to choose the good of the many or the good of the few

Having no good options

The character feeling like they're losing the battle between hope and despair

Marrying to protect another but being cut off from that person and feeling anguish over not knowing if the sacrifice paid off

Viewing important events, such as the birth of a child, with mixed emotions

Having to cross moral lines against one's will

Wanting to run away but being responsible for people in this new life

Needing to safeguard loved ones (children, friends, others who have been taken) but having no power to do so

Grieving over what was lost but being relieved over what was gained (safety, security, financial certainty, etc.)

Resentment toward the people who pressured the character into this fate

Wrestling with jealousy and bitterness toward people who have the freedom to make their own choices

NEGATIVE TRAITS THAT MAY WORSEN THE SITUATION: Controlling, Impulsive, Pessimistic, Rebellious, Resentful, Self-Destructive, Uncooperative, Vindictive, Worrywart

IMPACT ON BASIC NEEDS:

Self-Actualization: A character who is forced to marry may never be truly happy or fulfilled because they lack something vital: the freedom to choose their own path.

Esteem and Recognition: When the character's worth is tied up in what they offer as a marriage asset, this can lead to feelings of powerlessness and low self-esteem.

Love and Belonging: If family members do nothing to stop a forced marriage—or worse, are pushing for it to take place—those relationships may become strained, cutting the character adrift from the important people in his or her life.

Safety and Security: If the character is entering a marriage where their safety or personal rights are negotiable, these needs may become compromised.

POSITIVE TRAITS TO HELP THE CHARACTER COPE: Adaptable, Ambitious, Appreciative, Cooperative, Happy, Loyal, Obedient, Optimistic, Persuasive, Traditional

POSITIVE OUTCOMES

Discovering a new purpose in a tough situation

Developing personal resilience

Building valued friendships and community in the new situation

Embracing the situation and, over time, finding love

Being able to safeguard loved ones (rescuing them from harm, giving them immunity, etc.) because of the marriage

Escaping danger, poverty, or violence

Having access to better education, new opportunities, and a stronger financial standing

Gaining power and prestige from the family name and using it to make life better for others

BEING IGNORED OR BLOWN OFF

EXAMPLES
The character's mails or texts going unanswered (ghosting)
People talking over the character at a family dinner
Talking to someone who doesn't bother to respond
The character reaching out to someone who always lets the character's call go to voicemail
Being stood up for a date
Decisions being made for the character without their input
The character's ideas being dismissed without fair consideration
Being ditched for someone else by a friend at a social event
A friend using a lame excuse to cancel plans at the last minute
Being relegated to the outskirts of a group; being denied access to the inner circle
Being assigned menial work tasks; not being considered for a promotion or important project
Discovering the friend who canceled their plans is out with other people

MINOR COMPLICATIONS
The character's time being wasted
An assignment falling through the cracks when the character forgets the other person didn't get back to them
Venting to someone who tells the offending party what the character said
Not doing anything and being viewed as weak by others
Having to self-invite to be included

POTENTIALLY DISASTROUS RESULTS
Losing one's temper and saying things that damage a relationship or make one look bad
Accusing the other person of deliberate disrespect when it was really a misunderstanding
The character prematurely deciding to cut the person out of their life
Becoming more withdrawn and engaging less with others
The character not sharing their ideas or opinions at work, thereby lowering their value in the eyes of co-workers or the boss
Using unhealthy coping measures (bingeing, seeking love from anyone who will provide it, the character changing to please others, etc.)
Not addressing the problem and letting it escalate into a bullying or toxic situation

RESULTING EMOTIONS: Anger, Annoyance, Apprehension, Bitterness, Confusion, Denial, Determination, Disappointment, Emasculation, Embarrassment, Flustered, Frustration, Humiliation, Insecurity, Intimidation, Powerlessness, Resentment, Unappreciated, Worthlessness

POSSIBLE INTERNAL STRUGGLES
Wanting to bring up how one is feeling but worrying it will sound pathetic
Heightened insecurity as the character wonders what they've done wrong and how to fix it
Wondering if they really are as unimportant and irrelevant as others make them feel

The character's mind going in circles as they try to decide if the other person's actions are deliberate or coincidental

Constant analysis of other people and how they command respect that the character lacks

Assuming other people are ignoring the character because this one person has done it

NEGATIVE TRAITS THAT MAY WORSEN THE SITUATION: Abrasive, Addictive, Insecure, Jealous, Martyr, Melodramatic, Needy, Oversensitive, Paranoid, Vindictive, Worrywart

IMPACT ON BASIC NEEDS

Self-Actualization: Someone who is consistently sidelined by others at work will be limited in their influence and ability to contribute. Even if they don't take the slights personally, they could become frustrated due to their inability to live up to their full potential.

Esteem and Recognition: Most people who are repeatedly ignored or blown off by others will begin to take it personally, believing the behavior is due to a flaw in their own character. This will inevitably lead to feelings of insecurity and self-doubt. On the flip side, people who don't stand up for themselves are often looked down upon, which can lead to a lowered perception by others.

Love and Belonging: This kind of treatment and the self-esteem issues that occur can make it difficult for the character to be vulnerable with others and create meaningful connections.

Safety and Security: A character who doesn't respond properly to this behavior may begin coping in unhealthy ways that could threaten their physical and mental well-being.

Physiological Needs: In extreme cases, people who are consistently ignored may become isolated, depressed, and even suicidal. A subset may even devolve and seek retribution for being overlooked by society. If their actions are violent, they could be shot and killed by police.

POSITIVE TRAITS TO HELP THE CHARACTER COPE: Centered, Charming, Diplomatic, Extroverted, Funny, Patient, Persistent, Persuasive, Responsible, Talented, Witty

POSITIVE OUTCOMES

Learning to be more assertive and stand up for oneself

Being able to read superficial or insincere people more accurately

Confronting the individual and finding out it was a misunderstanding, thereby learning the importance of communicating before jumping to conclusions

Learning the truth about the offending party and limiting one's contact with them

Striving to surround oneself with positive and uplifting people

Becoming more self-aware and determining not to treat other people in such a hurtful way

Using the situation to seek out others who may be quiet, shy, or reserved and build connections with them

BEING INSULTED

EXAMPLES
The character being told their outfit or hairstyle is out of fashion
A physical disfigurement being made fun of
A rude gesture, profanity, or hateful words being hurled at the character
A younger person assuming an elderly character can't make decisions for him or herself
Being dismissed by someone because of assumptions about the character's intelligence, integrity, or abilities
Being treated as less than (being denied the same level of service that others are given, being disrespected, others assuming the character shouldn't be allowed where they are, etc.)
The character being subjected to insults relating to their race or religion
Being belittled through ongoing verbal abuse
Experiencing insults via brainwashing, gaslighting, or other deliberate attempts to alter the way the character sees him or herself

MINOR COMPLICATIONS
The character returning the insult and escalating the situation
A child or impressionable character witnessing the insulting behavior
Being uncomfortable around the insulter in future interactions
Having to report the insulting behavior to a parent, boss, or authority
The character avoiding places where they might run into the person who insulted them
Friends or family being dragged into the confrontation
Seeking out an apology and it not being granted
Reacting in a way that lowers the character in the eyes of others
Telling a trusted friend, who then downplays the incident or tries to rationalize what happened

POTENTIALLY DISASTROUS RESULTS
Responding with violence
The character becoming desensitized and adopting rude or hateful attitudes toward others
The character doing nothing and the disrespect escalating
Wanting to fight the disrespect but being coerced by a boss, spouse, etc. into doing nothing
The character changing who they are to avoid reproach
Not responding when one should and discouraging others from opposing harmful behavior
The character's children witnessing the disrespect and developing anxiety that the same thing will happen to them
A character standing up for him or herself and being seen as a troublemaker, resulting in unfair consequences

RESULTING EMOTIONS: Anger, Annoyance, Anxiety, Appalled, Bitterness, Confusion, Defensiveness, Disbelief, Fear, Humiliation, Hurt, Insecurity, Intimidation, Shame, Shock

POSSIBLE INTERNAL STRUGGLES
Becoming obsessed with fitting in or pleasing others to avoid criticism

The character making changes to fit in and then feeling repressed or trapped
Wanting to ignore the insult but letting it get under their skin
The character internalizing the insult until they begin to believe it
Analyzing the offense to see if they read too much into it; doubting what they experienced
Struggling with shame because they believe, on some level, the insult is true
Wanting to report the incident but not wanting anyone to know what was said
Silent rage building inside the character because they know they'll be punished if they complain
The character feeling shame about something they can't change and anger at being made to feel that way

NEGATIVE TRAITS THAT MAY WORSEN THE SITUATION: Abrasive, Catty, Childish, Cocky, Confrontational, Insecure, Melodramatic, Needy, Obsessive, Oversensitive

IMPACT ON BASIC NEEDS
   Esteem and Recognition: A character subjected to continuous insults may start to believe them, which could negatively affect their self-esteem.
   Love and Belonging: If the insult occurs within the character's inner circle and it's brushed off rather than called out, the character will realize their position in the group is not equal to that of everyone else. This disillusionment will erase any feelings of belonging.
   Safety and Security: If the insults go unchecked, eventually they could escalate, creating a situation where the character is at risk of physical harm.

POSITIVE TRAITS TO HELP THE CHARACTER COPE: Bold, Calm, Confident, Cooperative, Courteous, Diplomatic, Disciplined, Easygoing, Innocent, Just, Mature, Persuasive, Playful, Professional, Uninhibited

POSITIVE OUTCOMES
The character developing bonds with others who have suffered the same treatment
The character recognizing a grain of truth in the insult and seeking to better him or herself (by overcoming a fault or embracing a good quality)
The character's confidence growing after confronting the insulter
Getting involved in a movement to counteract discrimination and hurtful stereotypes
The character exposing a bully and being free of their damaging insults
Confronting the accuser and stopping them from hurting others
Learning not to care so much what other people think
Recognizing that not every insult or offense needs to be confronted
The character realizing unfounded insults say more about the insulter than they do about them

BEING MANIPULATED

EXAMPLES
Being gaslighted by someone who makes the character question what they know to be true
An undercover cop infiltrating the character's circle of friends to gain information
A love interest feigning romantic feelings for the character to gain access to their friend
A character being kidnapped and falling victim to Stockholm Syndrome, developing sympathetic feelings toward their captor
The character being blackmailed with proof they engaged in unethical behavior
A cult or governmental regime using propaganda to brainwash the character
The character's children using guilt to convince him or her to do what they want
An organized crime boss threatening to harm the character's loved ones if they fail to follow certain orders
Being scammed or phished by a con artist
A rival preying on the character's weakness to sow self-doubt
A parent using guilt or coercion to get a child to behave
Being deceived by a love interest who only allows the character to see what he or she wants them to see
Being catfished by a suitor who wishes to gain access to the character's wealth
A manipulator telling the character half-truths or innuendo so they form incorrect conclusions

MINOR COMPLICATIONS
The character being coerced into doing something minor they normally wouldn't have done (telling a lie, covering for a co-worker, etc.)
Awkwardness and anxiety from having to confront the manipulator
A manipulated victim developing romantic feelings for their abuser and entering into a relationship
The character being blackmailed and having to lie so loved ones won't find out
The character being embarrassed that they were taken in
Friction arising when a character in denial is confronted by loved ones about the manipulator
Resulting inconveniences from cutting ties with the manipulator (having to find a new accountant, losing a carpool associate and having to drive the kids to school every day, etc.)

POTENTIALLY DISASTROUS RESULTS
Unknowingly giving sensitive information to the manipulator that is used against the character or loved ones
The character losing their livelihood or freedom
A confrontation with the manipulator that turns violent
The character fundamentally changing to please the manipulator
The character committing unethical or unsavory acts they never would have done on their own
Harm befalling loved ones when the character disobeys a blackmailer or crime boss
A kidnap victim helping a captor commit further crimes or take more victims
The character questioning their own memories and sanity
Experiencing mental or emotional trauma from the manipulation

The character cutting out the important and healthy people in their life, leaving them with no support system
The character overcompensating and becoming a controlling person

RESULTING EMOTIONS: Anxiety, Appalled, Apprehension, Betrayed, Confusion, Denial, Devastation, Horror, Inadequacy, Intimidation, Panic, Powerlessness, Shame, Skepticism

POSSIBLE INTERNAL STRUGGLES
Recognizing manipulation but not confronting it out of a desire to avoid conflict
Struggling with guilt over the acts they were forced to commit
Being plagued with self-doubt; worrying that they will be manipulated again
Knowing right from wrong but still wrestling with making the right choices
Reluctance to take responsibility for their actions; blaming the manipulator
Developing deep-seated resentment toward the organizations or groups that did the manipulating

NEGATIVE TRAITS THAT MAY WORSEN THE SITUATION: Apathetic, Gullible, Indecisive, Insecure, Macho, Needy, Paranoid, Resentful, Timid, Weak-Willed

IMPACT ON BASIC NEEDS
   Self-Actualization: A manipulated character is usually not meeting their own needs and desires. This can stymie the pursuit of their passions and restrict their ability to live life to the fullest.
   Esteem and Recognition: Depending on the level of manipulation, the character may feel deep shame or self-loathing for allowing it to happen.
   Love and Belonging: If the character was manipulated by a loved one, they may become uncomfortable with vulnerability, keeping them from opening up to others in the future.
   Safety and Security: A codependent character may continue in a dysfunctional relationship even after they realize they're being manipulated. This can lead to emotional, mental, or physical trauma.

POSITIVE TRAITS TO HELP THE CHARACTER COPE: Adaptable, Ambitious, Bold, Confident, Just, Perceptive, Sensible, Spunky, Uninhibited

POSITIVE OUTCOMES
The character confronting the manipulator and ending the relationship
Recognizing manipulation more easily in the future
Being able to help friends who are being manipulated because the character recognizes the signs
The character realizing it's important and healthy to stand up for themselves
Recognizing the manipulation tactics and setting clear boundaries among family members, employers, and friends

BEING REJECTED BY A POTENTIAL LOVE INTEREST

EXAMPLES
Asking out a stranger or acquaintance and being turned down
The character asking someone out and being "friend-zoned"
Asking out a promising love interest for a second date and being rejected
Planning to ask someone out, then learning they aren't interested (via an intercepted text or email message, overhearing a conversation, etc.)
The character asking someone out that they know they shouldn't be with (a co-worker, a best friend's ex, etc.) and being scorned

MINOR COMPLICATIONS
Responding awkwardly, compounding embarrassment
Having to see the person regularly (at work, school, church, in the neighborhood, etc.)
Being reluctant to ask anyone else out
Having to answer questions from well-meaning friends about how it went
Being embarrassed publicly (if the rejection happened in a public place or online)
Lying about the encounter (saying it didn't happen, for instance) and getting caught
Disparaging the other party to others and the character's words being reported to him or her
Retreating to lick one's wounds and missing out on fun, time with friends, and other romantic opportunities
The rejection being witnessed by a rival or enemy

POTENTIALLY DISASTROUS RESULTS
The character's entire future falling apart (because they're in love with the other party)
Rebounding by jumping into an unhealthy relationship with anyone who is willing or available
A recovering addict being triggered into a relapse by the rejection
Doing something stupid in the aftermath as a way of making oneself feel better (picking a fight with someone, having a one-night stand, etc.)
Swearing off romantic relationships forever (if this was the latest in a series of rejections) and being alone
Not taking no for an answer by continuing to pursue the other party, stalking them, or intimidating them
Coming onto the person's friends to try and make them jealous
Becoming a source of gossip (if the rejection went badly)
Becoming too cautious when asking people out in the future and missing out on opportunities
Being unwilling to look too closely at one's rejections, thereby missing problems in one's approach that could be avoided in the future

RESULTING EMOTIONS: Depressed, Determination, Disappointment, Emasculation, Embarrassment, Flustered, Hurt, Inadequacy, Insecurity, Longing, Sadness, Self-Pity

POSSIBLE INTERNAL STRUGGLES

Struggling with feelings of insecurity and self-doubt

Placing too much importance on the rejection and becoming depressed by it

Developing a fear of rejection (if it has happened repeatedly)

Struggling with one's ego because getting a *yes* is usually a sure thing

Comparing oneself to others and coming up short

Negative self-talk that contributes to low esteem (*You're so stupid, She was way out of your league, No one wants to be with you,* etc.)

Trying to decide if one should stay friends (and win over the love interest eventually) or move on

The character questioning their instincts because they thought they had read the signs correctly

Being unable to move on because the character is in love (unrequited love)

NEGATIVE TRAITS THAT MAY WORSEN THE SITUATION: Addictive, Controlling, Hostile, Insecure, Macho, Martyr, Possessive, Self-Destructive, Volatile

IMPACT ON BASIC NEEDS

Esteem and Recognition: Rejection is almost always followed by a self-inventory to determine what might be wrong with the character: *What did I do?* or *What's wrong with me?* Their sense of self-esteem can easily be undercut by multiple rejections (or an important one), leaving them feeling insecure.

Love and Belonging: Rejection is painful; too many instances can convince the character they're better off alone, which will eventually cause them to feel disconnected and unhappy. This is especially true if the character has experienced emotional wounds involving rejection or abandonment.

POSITIVE TRAITS TO HELP THE CHARACTER COPE: Bold, Charming, Confident, Easygoing, Funny, Mature, Optimistic, Persistent, Playful, Uninhibited

POSITIVE OUTCOMES

Being able to move on after learning the other person isn't interested

Recognizing mistakes in one's technique and improving the process for next time

Recognizing the other person wasn't a fit and being ok with that

Appreciating singleness and the benefits it brings

Becoming aware of a pattern in the rejections that helps the character realize they're targeting people for the wrong reasons—focusing on their looks instead of compatibility, for instance

The character realizing the first rejection wasn't as terrible as they thought, making it easier for them to risk it again

Determining to be careful when rejecting others to avoid hurting them unnecessarily

BEING TAKEN FOR GRANTED

EXAMPLES

A character looking after their household and children while an overcommitted or ungrateful spouse pursues their career goals

Being expected to work long hours without extra pay or recognition

The character supporting an unappreciative, selfish, or manipulative friend through difficult times and them not returning the favor

The character constantly sharing their possessions—a car, internet bandwidth, clothing, etc.—with an entitled friend or roommate

A parent financially supporting an adult child who, in turn, expects them to do so

The character taking on the lion's share of work (at school, on the job, when volunteering or child-rearing, etc.) while their peers do little or nothing

The character always being asked to do favors or take on unpleasant jobs

Not ever being acknowledged for the way the character contributes (to a business, marriage, friendship, as a caregiver to an elderly parent, etc.)

MINOR COMPLICATIONS

Missing time with family and friends due to extended work hours

Having to miss an anticipated event to help with someone else's "emergency"

The character becoming so dissatisfied at work that they quit or decide to look for another job

Having houseguests who overstay their welcome, hindering the character's personal life

Having to make personal sacrifices because they're giving their money to others

Giving up things the character wants—turning a craft room back into a bedroom, missing out on social activities, etc.—to meet the needs or desires of others

Work quality being affected because of exhaustion or distraction

Domestic disputes arising from an imbalance of responsibilities

The character being inconvenienced in their own home (because a house guest is messy or ignores established quiet times)

Awkwardness arising when the character sets boundaries with others

The character losing interest in things they used to enjoy

The character gravitating toward relationships with people who don't take them for granted but are bad for them in other ways (having an affair, getting involved with an abuser, etc.)

POTENTIALLY DISASTROUS RESULTS

Arguments and fights arising from growing bitterness

Being fired from a job after complaining about the unfairness

Exhaustion causing the character to make a serious or dangerous mistake, such as misplacing a large sum of money or falling asleep at the wheel of their car

The character adopting destructive behaviors to gain attention, such as heavy drinking, excessive spending, or drag racing

The character accepting the ingratitude as normal or fair

The character saying something that can't be taken back, damaging an important relationship or closing the door to an opportunity

RESULTING EMOTIONS: Anger, Annoyance, Bitterness, Conflicted, Contempt, Desperation, Disillusionment, Dissatisfaction, Frustration, Hurt, Irritation, Neglected

POSSIBLE INTERNAL STRUGGLES

Struggling to stay positive while feeling underappreciated and overworked
Becoming obsessed with perfection in an attempt to gain recognition
Developing a martyr complex and continuing to help out while complaining bitterly about being underappreciated
The character wanting to say no but not wanting to upset a spouse or boss
Wanting to help a friend or family member who is struggling but not knowing how to set boundaries
The character losing touch with their own feelings and desires while focusing on serving others
Wanting to be accepted but resenting when teammates take credit for the character's work

NEGATIVE TRAITS THAT MAY WORSEN THE SITUATION: Cynical, Insecure, Martyr, Needy, Obsessive, Perfectionist, Resentful, Subservient, Timid

IMPACT ON BASIC NEEDS

Self-Actualization: Putting the needs of others before their own may make the character lose sight of what's important to them and impede their ability to live their best life.

Esteem and Recognition: Someone who is constantly taken for granted may begin to wonder why they're treated that way and whether they deserve a healthy and positive relationship.

Love and Belonging: When resentment over ingratitude creeps into family relationships, the character may question whether they are connected to others by love or by duty.

POSITIVE TRAITS TO HELP THE CHARACTER COPE: Adaptable, Bold, Confident, Decisive, Independent, Persuasive, Uninhibited

POSITIVE OUTCOMES

The character leaving an unsatisfactory work environment and finding a more fulfilling job
Requiring an adult child to support themselves monetarily and seeing them take responsibility for their own finances
The character ending a toxic relationship and experiencing freedom
Breaking off an unhealthy romance and experiencing true, unconditional love with someone new
Learning to set reasonable boundaries
The character demanding recognition and finally receiving appreciation for the work they do
Recognizing signs of entitlement or selfishness in others and addressing those behaviors head on
The character realizing they have value and deserve to be treated better

BEING UNABLE TO FORGIVE SOMEONE

EXAMPLES

The character being unwilling to reconnect with a parent who abandoned them as a child

Reconciling with an unfaithful spouse but not being able to stop thinking about them with someone else

Sibling rivalry as adolescents causing trust issues that the character carries into adulthood

Holding a grudge against a high school friend who betrayed the character long ago

A parent who once played favorites with her children trying to act like it didn't happen and the character being unable to forgive her

Not being able to forgive a stranger whose irresponsibility or selfishness changed the character's life significantly

Suffering an assault or abuse by a known person and being expected to let it go so everyone can move on

MINOR COMPLICATIONS

Tensions rising from the character making snide comments about the offender at social gatherings, family events, or work functions

Arguments between the character and the offender

The character passing up beneficial opportunities (such as a great job or an all-expense paid trip) because it comes from the person they can't forgive

Having to endure token apologies

The person trying to buy the character's forgiveness through gifts or grand gestures

Awkward interactions with estranged family members at holiday gatherings

Family members taking sides in the dispute

Friends growing tired of the character complaining about the person they can't forgive

Having to socialize with a high school bully at a reunion, wedding, or funeral

Needing to attend emotionally challenging counseling sessions to address one's bitterness

POTENTIALLY DISASTROUS RESULTS

A marriage or friendship ending because the character is unable to move forward

The character interfering with the offending person's relationships, job, or family in an attempt to even the score

Plotting revenge that escalates to acts of violence or death

Unresolved feelings for an estranged parent affecting the character's ability to bond with their own children

The character losing their faith (because forgiveness is an important part of their religion and they're unable or unwilling to comply)

The character holding onto their anger and forbidding their child to pursue a relationship with a member of the hated family

The character spitefully cutting a family member or former loved one out of their will

RESULTING EMOTIONS: Anger, Betrayed, Bitterness, Conflicted, Contempt, Doubt, Guilt, Hatred, Obsession, Regret, Resentment, Schadenfreude, Scorn, Shame, Unappreciated

POSSIBLE INTERNAL STRUGGLES

Wanting to move past the betrayal but being unable to turn off the constant replaying of the event in their mind

Becoming obsessed with making the offending party miserable

Putting up walls in future relationships so they won't be hurt the same way again

Becoming paranoid and seeing ill intent in situations where there is none

Carrying insecurities stemming from a childhood abuser into adulthood

Missing the closeness they once shared with the wrongdoer; feeling alone

Struggling with prejudice against people who share the wrongdoer's race, nationality, gender, religion, etc.

Wanting closure through forgiveness but knowing that it also requires justice

NEGATIVE TRAITS THAT MAY WORSEN THE SITUATION: Callous, Cruel, Cynical, Defensive, Inflexible, Manipulative, Pessimistic, Rebellious, Resentful, Uncooperative, Vindictive

IMPACT ON BASIC NEEDS

Self-Actualization: Holding a grudge can take tremendous energy and cause the character to become lost in their own bitterness rather than moving toward healthy, fulfilling goals.

Esteem and Recognition: Someone who wants to forgive but finds it hard to do so may begin to question their own morality—especially if pressure is coming from others to do the "right" thing.

Love and Belonging: A character who suffered at the hands of another may become oversensitive to slights and hurts. If they find themselves unable to forgive even normal transgressions, they will only be able to offer conditional love. This dysfunction will likely lead to more relationships ending, which will deepen the character's bitterness and emotional wounds.

Safety and Security: The inability to forgive others can deeply impair a character's mental health, leading to anxiety, depression, denial, and unhealthy coping mechanisms. All of this can affect their mental and physical well-being.

POSITIVE TRAITS TO HELP THE CHARACTER COPE: Cooperative, Courageous, Easygoing, Empathetic, Generous, Humble, Idealistic, Kind, Merciful, Nurturing, Spiritual

POSITIVE OUTCOMES

Being able to let go of toxic feelings that held the character hostage to unhappiness

The character experiencing growth as they seek to learn to forgive—even if they aren't ready or able to actually do so yet

Recognizing forgiveness can be granted without the character removing healthy boundaries and embracing the person who hurt them

The character moving on from a bad person or situation without looking back

DISAPPOINTING SOMEONE

NOTES: This entry explores the character disappointing someone they look up to, such as a parent, a mentor, or a coach. It also refers to situations where the character lets down someone who looks up to them—a younger sibling or a clergy member's parishioner, for instance. For information on conflict produced by the reverse scenario, see the entry on BEING BETRAYED OR ABANDONED BY A TRUSTED ALLY OR FRIEND.

EXAMPLES
The character choosing a different career than the one their parents want them to pursue
The character bombing an interview or business meeting set up by a mentor
A younger cousin witnessing the character abusing alcohol, drugs, or another person
Being suspended as a coach for behaving unethically or making insensitive comments
Immoral behavior being exposed (such as a congregation discovering the character—their pastor, priest, etc.—has embezzled church funds or engaged in an extra-marital affair)
Sports fans discovering the character is taking steroids to enhance their performance
The character using his position of power to get items that are in short supply, such as life-saving medicines earmarked for others or extra food rations
Rallying others to join a team, fight for a cause, or take a risk when the character isn't willing to do the same

MINOR COMPLICATIONS
Enduring embarrassment and shame as word gets around
Becoming the focus of ugly gossip
Having to grovel to get back into a mentor's good graces
The character overcompensating to make up for their behavior
The character's reputation being sullied when their behavior goes public on social media
Having to release a statement and apologize, promising to do better
Not being invited to events or family gatherings
Losing the trust of an impressionable younger cousin or sibling
Having to attend counseling or sensitivity training to save face

POTENTIALLY DISASTROUS RESULTS
Being excommunicated from a church the character has dedicated their life to
Being fired
The character losing a scholarship or being cut off financially by their parents
An impressionable youth mimicking the character's mistakes and getting into serious trouble
The character being arrested for their actions
A mentor revoking their endorsement, resulting in the loss of special privileges or opportunities
Getting sued (if the disappointing behavior was against the law)
The damage to one's reputation being so severe that a life goal must be given up
Being cast out of the family
The character removing themselves from their family or community so they won't be responsible for disappointing anyone again

RESULTING EMOTIONS: Agitation, Anguish, Anxiety, Appalled, Apprehension, Concern, Devastation, Disappointment, Guilt, Remorse, Self-Loathing, Self-Pity, Shame, Worthlessness

POSSIBLE INTERNAL STRUGGLES

Being overwhelmed by shame, guilt, and self-doubt

Replaying the event, thinking of all the different choices that could have been made

Feeling less enthusiastic about certain choices after learning a parent or mentor disapproves of them

Wondering if it's best to give certain things up to get back on someone's good side

Experiencing anxiety when making decisions out of the fear of screwing up again

The character being angry that they're held to a higher standard than others but being unable to show it

Regret over hurting people but knowing it was the right decision

The character feeling remorse about cutting corners but also resenting the unfair level of pressure and expectation that led them to do so

NEGATIVE TRAITS THAT MAY WORSEN THE SITUATION: Foolish, Insecure, Irrational, Needy, Nervous, Oversensitive, Perfectionist, Self-Destructive, Withdrawn

IMPACT ON BASIC NEEDS

Self-Actualization: A character who is afraid of disappointing others may make choices based on what others want instead of pursuing goals that will make them happy.

Esteem and Recognition: Whoever the character disappoints will likely lose respect for them. And if the character admits to letting someone else down, their self-respect may lessen, as well.

Love and Belonging: Disappointing beloved friends or family members can leave the character feeling unworthy of love, causing them to hold back and isolate themselves.

Safety and Security: Someone who doesn't want to disappoint others again may become subservient to the point of being mistreated or abused.

POSITIVE TRAITS TO HELP THE CHARACTER COPE: Honorable, Humble, Just, Mature, Persuasive, Proactive, Professional, Responsible

POSITIVE OUTCOMES

Reconciliation, brought about by the character taking ownership and making amends

The character deciding to follow their own dreams instead of trying to impress others

The character becoming motivated to change disappointing behaviors and make personal improvements

Making a deliberate effort to not make the same mistakes again

The character recognizing their actions have consequences for others and vowing to be a better influence

DISCOVERING A SPOUSE'S SECRET

NOTES: Trust is paramount in a marriage, so discovering a spouse has been harboring secrets can be devastating. Considering the array of events and information human beings have been known to hide from one another, the options for information your character's spouse might withhold from them are vast. Below are a few possibilities.

EXAMPLES
An affair
An unhealthy addiction
Being fired or laid off
The existence of a separate family
Aspects of who they really are
An escalating mental health condition
Their identity as a serial criminal (killer, rapist, child abuser, drug or human trafficker, etc.)
Events from their past (significant traumas, their biological parents, their medical history, etc.)
A terminal or communicable disease
An unusual paranormal power
Their manipulation or gaslighting of a potential threat
Illegal activity at work (embezzling, passing off other people's ideas as their own, blackmailing, etc.)

MINOR COMPLICATIONS
Lost sleep due to worry and uncertainty
Relationship friction with the spouse
Awkward conversations with others as the character tries to gain information
Embarrassment over being the last to know
Having to explain the situation to other loved ones
The character missing work so they can meet with people (doctors, lawyers, a private investigator, etc.) to unearth the truth
The character standing up for the spouse against allegations, then realizing they've been played
Becoming the subject of neighborhood gossip once the secret is out

POTENTIALLY DISASTROUS RESULTS
The character's reputation being ruined by association
The marriage ending in divorce
Fallout for the character's children
The character being implicated as an accomplice despite their ignorance
Going bankrupt (due to the spouse's financial irresponsibility, unpaid bills, etc.)
One's home and assets being seized by police
Developing a panic disorder or falling into depression
Serious physical ailments, such as heart disease or an STD
The character having to start over on their own (with little education or experience in the workplace, as a single parent, under a load of debt, etc.)

Confiding in the wrong person and the character's words being used against them and their spouse

The spouse disappearing, leaving the character to pick up the pieces alone

RESULTING EMOTIONS: Anger, Appalled, Betrayed, Confusion, Denial, Despair, Devastation, Disappointment, Disbelief, Disillusionment, Embarrassment, Empathy, Fear, Guilt, Horror, Humiliation, Hurt, Overwhelmed, Powerlessness, Shock, Vulnerability, Worry

POSSIBLE INTERNAL STRUGGLES
Loving the spouse but struggling to trust them again
Being torn between working things out or giving up on the relationship
Torment over what to tell one's children, family members, and friends
Self-doubt over how one didn't see what was happening
The character wondering why the spouse didn't open up about their struggles and if maybe the character wasn't providing them with what was needed
Guilt over the part the character's ignorance or naïveté played

NEGATIVE TRAITS THAT MAY WORSEN THE SITUATION: Addictive, Callous, Confrontational, Cruel, Hypocritical, Irrational, Insecure, Judgmental, Gullible, Volatile

IMPACT ON BASIC NEEDS
    Esteem and Recognition: Most characters will blame themselves (however unnecessarily), believing they should have seen the signs or known what was going on, leading to feelings of self-doubt and insecurity about their instincts.
    Love and Belonging: If the character believes they somehow contributed to the spouse's situation or mental state (by being too demanding or not showing enough support), they may doubt themselves to the point of being reluctant to get involved with others.
    Safety and Security: Changes that come about in the aftermath of this secret coming to light may impact the character's safety and security (having to move, being less financially secure, being physically beaten by the spouse, their children being bullied, etc.).
    Physiological Needs: The character's life may be threatened depending on the spouse's response to the secret being discovered—say, if they have violent tendencies or want to keep their information hidden at all costs.

POSITIVE TRAITS TO HELP THE CHARACTER COPE: Adaptable, Calm, Cautious, Empathetic, Gentle, Perceptive, Protective, Resourceful, Supportive

POSITIVE OUTCOMES
Being determined not to be blindsided in this way again
The character taking control of their life instead of letting others be in charge
Becoming an advocate for the people the spouse mistreated
Deciding to support the spouse and work through the challenges ahead

DOMESTIC ABUSE

NOTES: The most common association with domestic abuse involves physical assault by one's spouse or partner. This entry will address this along with other kinds that can have devastating consequences, including a character's sexual, emotional, and verbal abuse by any family member.

EXAMPLES
Verbal abuse in the form of continuous insults or criticism from someone in the home
The character being forced to cut ties with friends and family to prove their loyalty to a spouse
A partner controlling every aspect of the character's life, including monitoring their movements, phone calls, emails, and access to money
A child being sexually abused by a guardian
A spouse or child sustaining injuries from a family member's violent outbursts
A child being isolated and controlled by denying them access to education, communication, or interaction with the outside world

MINOR COMPLICATIONS
Answering questions from concerned friends, family, employers, or teachers
Having to use makeup, sunglasses, long sleeves, or scarves to hide cuts and bruises
Having to cater to the abuser to avoid repercussions
Having to cancel plans repeatedly to appease a controlling family member
Frequently visiting the emergency room to treat minor injuries caused by violence
Lying to the abuser about day-to-day activities
Lying to family and friends to cover for the abuse
Being unable to access help or an advocate as a minor
Not having the financial freedom to enjoy everyday things, such as a new book or a coffee with a friend
Suffering (from pain, hunger, loneliness, etc.) at the abuser's whim

POTENTIALLY DISASTROUS RESULTS
Becoming a prisoner in one's own home
The character being forced to give up their support system of family and friends, leaving them isolated, alone, and more susceptible to abuse
A child taking up with a gang to avoid their difficult home life
A child running away from home and being trafficked
A parent taking the brunt of an abuser's wrath to protect a child
Having to go into hiding and adopt a new identity
Being raped by one's partner
Violence that brings about serious injury or death
The character injuring or killing their abuser in self-defense
The character committing suicide to escape their abuser
A codependent spouse staying with an abuser even when children are witnessing the abuse or being harmed by it

The character giving up their own desires to appease the abuser and missing out on things they once loved

RESULTING EMOTIONS: Acceptance, Anger, Anxiety, Betrayed, Bitterness, Defeat, Defiance, Desperation, Dread, Fear, Hatred, Intimidation, Loneliness, Nervousness, Powerlessness, Terror

POSSIBLE INTERNAL STRUGGLES
The character believing their abuser's lies about their lack of worth
Resentment toward those who turn a blind eye to the abuse
Wanting to leave but not feeling strong or capable enough
The character wanting to leave to save their children but not knowing how to support them
The character struggling to move on with their life even after they've escaped the abuse
Difficulty trusting others, especially when they show kindness

NEGATIVE TRAITS THAT MAY WORSEN THE SITUATION: Addictive, Confrontational, Controlling, Hostile, Impulsive, Inhibited, Macho, Needy, Nervous, Subservient

IMPACT ON BASIC NEEDS
Self-Actualization: A character in an abusive relationship will likely not have the freedom or resources to focus on their own growth until they are removed from the situation.
Esteem and Recognition: If the character is submitted to continuous criticism, they may internalize it and start to believe the abuse. Feelings of unworthiness may cause the character to crave the abuser's respect, motivating them to accept unreasonable behavior and demands.
Love and Belonging: When an abuser also professes to love the victim, that person may adopt a dysfunctional view of love, associating it with verbal or physical mistreatment.
Safety and Security: When there is a threat or pattern of physical abuse in the home, the character's safety will be jeopardized.
Physiological Needs: Abuse often escalates—meaning, it could realistically lead to the accidental or intentional death of the character.

POSITIVE TRAITS TO HELP THE CHARACTER COPE: Adaptable, Ambitious, Calm, Cautious, Confident, Diplomatic, Observant, Persuasive, Proactive, Protective

POSITIVE OUTCOMES
Finding the courage to leave and start over fresh
The character learning they deserve to be treated well and standing up to their abuser
Escaping the abusive situation and founding a nonprofit organization to help other survivors
Recognizing the signs of abuse in someone else and being able to help them
Finding a hobby, passion, or area of expertise that builds the character's confidence and enables them to escape their situation
Experiencing unconditional love from someone else and recognizing the abuser's love as false and undesirable

FAMILY SECRETS BEING REVEALED

EXAMPLES
A parent's extra-marital affair coming to light
Discovering the existence of half siblings—say, at the reading of a parent's will
Finding out a crime was covered up (someone was paid off, a family member was "sent away to school" to avoid consequences, victims were threatened, etc.)
A family member being outed for drug abuse, alcoholism, or a gambling habit
Discovering a family member's fetish or unconventional sexual preferences
Learning about a hidden pregnancy or adoption
Discovering one's ancestors were war criminals, racists, or slavers (or supported such things)
Discovering ties to the occult
Learning the family's wealth or power was obtained illegally or through immoral means
Finding out one family member is blackmailing another
Uncovering the source of a feud
Family abuse (physical, emotional, or sexual) being exposed
Finding out a mental health condition or physical disease runs in the family
Uncovering an ability that runs in the family (psychic sensitivities, a gift that has always been suppressed or hidden for safety, etc.)

MINOR COMPLICATIONS
Strained relationships
Awkwardness arising from the family member's secret being out in the open
Family members taking sides
Being pressured by family members to let it go or keep it quiet
The secret getting out, resulting in unwanted scrutiny for the character
Having to lie or feign ignorance about it (to avoid danger, to protect someone, etc.)
The burden of knowledge erasing one's innocence and changing how family members are viewed

POTENTIALLY DISASTROUS RESULTS
Investigations, litigation, or other actions being taken against the family or one of its members
Having to course correct (pull the family out of debt, cover something up, make reparations for a family misdeed, etc.)
Having one's reputation destroyed by a family member's transgression
Losing one's power, a position, or an opportunity because of "guilt by association"
The character being ostracized or maligned because they refuse to keep the family's secret
The information benefiting an enemy, giving them power over the character or the family

RESULTING EMOTIONS: Betrayed, Conflicted, Devastation, Disbelief, Disgust, Disillusionment, Embarrassment, Empathy, Guilt, Horror, Hurt, Nostalgia, Panic, Relief, Resentment, Scorn, Shame, Shock, Tormented, Uncertainty, Vengefulness, Vindication, Worry

POSSIBLE INTERNAL STRUGGLES

Struggling with disillusionment; feeling like one's life has been a lie

Love, anger, and disappointment facing off when a role model's unsavory secret is revealed

Relief at having answers yet being angry at being kept in the dark

Feeling adrift from one's family after trust was broken

Regret over things the character said and did when they didn't have the whole story

Feeling betrayed yet still loving the one who caused the emotional harm

Being torn between keeping quiet and speaking out

Needing someone to talk to but not being able to trust anyone

Wanting to run away but knowing that doing so will make things worse

Wishing one could go back to not knowing; feeling cowardly because of it

NEGATIVE TRAITS THAT MAY WORSEN THE SITUATION: Addictive, Confrontational, Cowardly, Gossipy, Gullible, Insecure, Irresponsible, Jealous, Judgmental

IMPACT ON BASIC NEEDS

Self-Actualization: If a character learns something that causes them to question their sense of identity, they may doubt who they are and suffer a fracture of self.

Esteem and Recognition: Learning a difficult truth (like the character being adopted) may introduce new questions about their worth, especially if they were given up freely because they weren't wanted.

Love and Belonging: A secret could blow a family apart, fracturing relationships and leaving the character to feel adrift and unloved.

Physiological Needs: Some secrets come with high levels of danger. If family members are willing to go to great lengths to keep the secret hidden, they may try to end the character's life rather than risk exposure.

POSITIVE TRAITS TO HELP THE CHARACTER COPE: Cautious, Disciplined, Honorable, Loyal, Patient, Persistent, Persuasive, Proactive, Resourceful, Supportive, Unselfish

POSITIVE OUTCOMES

Relief at finally knowing the truth about something the character has always suspected

Certain things that have always bothered the character finally making sense

The need to uncover the truth (or keep it secret) turning feuding family members into allies

The character experiencing healing once a wounding event has become fully known

Access to the whole story allowing the character to make better informed decisions

The character regaining a sense of control once everything is out in the open

The revealing of the secret destroying the power of those who have had knowledge of it or kept it hidden

HAVING TO BETRAY A FRIEND OR LOVED ONE

NOTES: A betrayal occurs when loyalty is discarded, often for selfish reasons: possibly to satisfy a desire, get ahead, or put personal needs first. But your character may also choose to set aside loyalty for legitimate reasons—say, when a friend is a danger to themselves, a loved one needs help but won't take it, or the cost to others will be too high.

EXAMPLES
The character turning in a loved who has committed a crime
Staging an intervention to confront a family member about their substance abuse problem
Telling a friend's spouse that the friend is cheating on them
Being blackmailed into revealing family secrets that will hurt a loved one's reputation
Revealing damaging information about a friend to avoid threats to one's own family
Reporting a friend's suicidal thoughts or plans to a counselor, teacher, or family member
Having a loved one in need of mental health intervention committed for evaluation
Suspecting a friend of child abuse and reporting them to the authorities
Telling a parent about a sibling's dangerous behavior
Refusing to lie, provide a false alibi, or break the law so a family member can avoid jail time

MINOR COMPLICATIONS
Awkwardness around the other person
Spending valuable time providing proof of wrongdoing
Being dragged into a couple's marital dispute or custody hearing
Friends and family members choosing sides when the betrayal causes a rift
Having to take personal time from work to make statements or file paperwork
Having to defend oneself to others when the betrayed person lies about the situation
People in the character's support system rejecting them for speaking out
Being constantly pumped for information by gossipy friends and family

POTENTIALLY DISASTROUS RESULTS
Losing an important relationship because of the betrayal
The friend or loved one enacting vengeance by betraying in kind: sharing the character's secrets, helping their enemies, or sowing discord and turning people against the character
The character's reputation being ruined when the accused refutes the claims and there is no proof
The accused friend or loved one committing suicide
Being pushed by police and having to violate the loved one's privacy by accessing their phone, computer, or safe to gain proof of wrongdoing
One's finances being strained from supporting a loved one through counseling or hospitalization
The friend losing their job or marriage because of their behavior and loved ones blaming the character

RESULTING EMOTIONS: Anguish, Anxiety, Conflicted, Devastation, Disappointment, Dread, Fear, Guilt, Pity, Reluctance, Resignation, Scorn, Uncertainty, Vulnerability, Worry

POSSIBLE INTERNAL STRUGGLES
Being torn between loyalty to the loved one and doing the right thing
Deep feelings of guilt affecting the character's ability to enjoy daily life
The character struggling with feelings of hypocrisy because they have their own secrets to hide
Being tempted to believe the other person's lies even while being certain of the truth
The character second-guessing their actions, questioning whether they made the right decision
Being tempted to give in to the accused's request to lie or turn a blind eye to their actions

NEGATIVE TRAITS THAT MAY WORSEN THE SITUATION: Confrontational, Controlling, Gossipy, Hypocritical, Impulsive, Judgmental, Martyr, Melodramatic, Unethical, Weak-Willed, Worrywart

IMPACT ON BASIC NEEDS
Self-Actualization: A character who is overcome with guilt over betraying a loved one or who has to spend considerable time dealing with the fallout may end up in survival mode, unable to pursue the things that give them joy and fulfillment.

Esteem and Recognition: There will always be those who believe family trumps all else. Their judgment and scorn over disloyalty could shake the character's self-belief that they did the right thing.

Love and Belonging: Losing the friend or loved one is a difficult thing to deal with, even if the betrayal was the right thing to do.

Safety and Security: If the accused's actions involve other criminals or there are people involved who would go to great lengths to keep things quiet, the character's safety may be at risk.

POSITIVE TRAITS TO HELP THE CHARACTER COPE: Analytical, Confident, Courageous, Decisive, Diplomatic, Discreet, Honorable, Just, Objective, Responsible, Socially Aware, Traditional

POSITIVE OUTCOMES
The betrayed friend expressing gratitude (after a time) for the character's intervention
The accused turning their life around because of the character's actions
The character taking solace in the fact that they have saved a friend's life by reporting their thoughts of self-harm—even if the friend doesn't appreciate their intervention
The character's children watching events unfold and recognizing the importance of doing what's right even when it's difficult
People affected by the friend's behavior or actions experiencing happier and safer lives now that the harmful activity has stopped

HAVING TO BREAK SOMEONE'S HEART

NOTES: This entry deals with the complications arising from having to break the heart of a love interest. For similar entries having to do with non-romantic relationships, see the entries for DISAPPOINTING SOMEONE and HAVING TO BETRAY A FRIEND OR LOVED ONE.

EXAMPLES
A college-aged character growing apart from their high school sweetheart and seeking to end the relationship
A character realizing they're engaged to someone for the wrong reasons and canceling their upcoming wedding
Having to be blunt with a persistent admirer to convey that the character is never going to be interested in a romantic relationship
The character breaking up with someone to save them from harm, possibly because an abusive ex is making threats against the love interest or the character is terminally ill and doesn't want to put the loved one through that
The character ending the relationship because they believe they're not capable of love (due to a wounding event, perhaps) and the other person deserves better
The character relocating to a place where the other person can't follow, such as an off-the-grid compound, prison, or a witness protection program and deciding it's kinder to break things off
Having to push someone away to keep them from discovering an important secret

MINOR COMPLICATIONS
Dealing with the uncomfortable and painful conversation when the news is delivered
Losing the support of friends or family who disapprove of the character's actions
Inconveniencing friends or family members who have invested financially in the wedding
A breakup dragging on for an extended period of time
The logistics and frustrations arising from having to move out of a shared home
Having to cancel scheduled plans with the other person
Complications arising from the character procrastinating giving the bad news
Losing valued friendships with ancillary people who take the other person's side

POTENTIALLY DISASTROUS RESULTS
The other person reacting with violence or retaliation
The character waffling, contributing to an on-again-off-again relationship that does more harm than good
The rejected person slipping into depression because of the breakup
The character regretting their decision and wishing they could turn back the clock
The partner refusing to be rejected, causing the character more emotional agony—especially if they love the person and really don't want to break up but feel they have to
Fallout from having to continue working or raising children with the other person

RESULTING EMOTIONS: Anguish, Anxiety, Apprehension, Bitterness, Conflicted, Depressed, Desire, Determination, Devastation, Dread, Grief, Guilt, Hurt, Loneliness, Longing, Panic, Relief, Reluctance, Sympathy, Uncertainty, Unease, Wistfulness

POSSIBLE INTERNAL STRUGGLES

Wanting to support the other person through the difficult time but knowing the character's continued presence will prevent the other party from moving on

The character knowing they made the right choice but struggling with the guilt they carry

Experiencing guilt over the sense of relief at having broken things off

The character second-guessing their decision and wondering if they did the right thing

The character's guilt affecting their ability to function in their day-to-day life

Feeling responsible for the other party's poor response upon receiving the news

Replaying the conversation mentally and realizing the character could have handled things better

Feeling brokenhearted because the breakup wasn't what the character wanted

NEGATIVE TRAITS THAT MAY WORSEN THE SITUATION: Addictive, Callous, Cowardly, Cruel, Haughty, Tactless, Uncommunicative

IMPACT ON BASIC NEEDS

   Self-Actualization: Guilt over breaking someone's heart may devastate the character, making it hard for them to pursue or enjoy their own dreams. If the breakup leads to unrequited love, they may actively avoid fulfillment to punish themselves for the hurt they put the other person through.

   Love and Belonging: A gun-shy character who is afraid to enter into new romantic relationships because they don't want them to end the same way may become isolated and unhappy over time.

POSITIVE TRAITS TO HELP THE CHARACTER COPE: Ambitious, Analytical, Centered, Decisive, Diplomatic, Discreet, Efficient, Gentle, Honest, Humble, Just, Kind, Proactive, Simple

POSITIVE OUTCOMES

The character finding they enjoy their own company and embracing a fulfilling single life

Feeling lighter and more empowered after being honest with the other person

Enjoying the freedom to pursue activities the partner wouldn't have approved of

Being free from the constant dread brought on by an admirer's unwanted attention

Being free to find a new love interest who is a better match

The partner being thankful for the character's honesty and ending things amicably

The character knowing they did the right thing in a difficult situation

LOSING ONE'S TEMPER

EXAMPLES

The character telling off their boss, a kid's coach, or a nosy neighbor for a perceived injustice

Exploding and making a scene (at work, at a family barbeque, etc.) because of unreasonable expectations, a lack of respect, or rudeness

Pushing, hitting, or slapping someone when rage takes over

Saying something in frustration or anger that can't be unsaid—perhaps revealing a secret, outing someone's addiction, or insulting them

Becoming enraged and walking out (of an interview, in the middle of a game, etc.)

Speaking in a way that makes someone cry (a child, someone in a sensitive condition, etc.)

Going off on a rant

Damaging or breaking something

Giving in to road rage

Intimidating or bullying others (to get something done, put someone in their place, etc.)

Setting an ultimatum that is completely unreasonable

Reacting with anger to a child's infraction instead of responding with understanding or patience

MINOR COMPLICATIONS

Being thrown out of an establishment

Being reprimanded at school or work

Losing the respect of others

Minor property destruction that must be fixed (breaking a knickknack, punching a hole in the wall, kicking a car door, etc.)

The outburst causing a rift in a relationship that the character must then address

The outburst being recorded and posted publicly

POTENTIALLY DISASTROUS RESULTS

Losing a friend or damaging a relationship beyond repair

Being arrested and charged for assault, destruction of property, slander, or breaking and entering

Getting fired

The situation devolving into a physical fight

Seriously injuring someone

Losing someone's trust or respect

The character's insults damaging the target's self-esteem and confidence

Destroying an important piece of property (an antique, something that holds emotional significance for the other party, etc.)

Getting in a car wreck

Loved ones (a child, niece or nephew, protégé, etc.) following in the character's footsteps and repeating the abusive behavior

Slipping into a dysfunctional behavior pattern of losing one's temper when angry

Viewing the tendency as normal rather than something that is disrespectful and needs correction

The behavior reinforcing harmful stereotypes about the character's occupation, race, gender, birthplace, etc.

RESULTING EMOTIONS: Anger, Defensiveness, Defiance, Disillusionment, Embarrassment, Frustration, Guilt, Horror, Humiliation, Rage, Regret, Schadenfreude, Self-Loathing, Shame

POSSIBLE INTERNAL STRUGGLES
Feeling intensely guilty following the outburst
Knowing it's wrong but enjoying the sense of power the outburst brings
Wanting to respond differently but feeling powerless to do so in the moment
Struggling with shame or self-loathing
The character feeling they have let others down

NEGATIVE TRAITS THAT MAY WORSEN THE SITUATION: Abrasive, Callous, Confrontational, Controlling, Cruel, Defensive, Disrespectful, Hostile, Impatient, Impulsive, Macho, Perfectionist, Stubborn, Violent, Volatile

IMPACT ON BASIC NEEDS
Self-Actualization: Loose cannons are seldom placed in charge or appointed to lead others. Their lack of self-control will create limitations, stymieing their aspirations.

Esteem and Recognition: When a character is unable to control their negative emotions and it results in a messy outburst, damage to their reputation is almost certain.

Love and Belonging: Loved ones are often the target of outbursts because the character feels safe letting off steam around them. The damage from repeatedly losing control in this way will become harder to forgive or excuse, and the distance this creates usually cannot be erased.

Safety and Security: Anger can easily spiral into a situation that is physically and emotionally unsafe.

Physiological Needs: History is, sadly, full of court cases involving murders that were not premeditated. While this is an extreme example, it's definitely possible that unchecked anger can lead to extreme, unintended circumstances, even death.

POSITIVE TRAITS TO HELP THE CHARACTER COPE: Calm, Centered, Empathetic, Gentle, Honest, Kind, Loyal, Merciful, Objective, Patient, Pensive, Protective, Spiritual, Tolerant

POSITIVE OUTCOMES
Seeing the damaging results and vowing to be more controlled
Recognizing a dangerous pattern of behavior and determining to make a change
Regaining control and being able to talk things through satisfactorily
Being in conflict with someone who remains calm and seeing how managing anger in this way gains the respect of others

ONE'S INFIDELITY BEING DISCOVERED

EXAMPLES
The character being spotted by their spouse or child while out with a lover
Former love interests contacting the character's spouse to make claims of infidelity
A significant other discovering a paper trail of hotel receipts, lavish gifts, or text messages
A celebrity character's affair being exposed by the media
A character confessing to cheating after giving their long-term partner a sexually transmitted disease, being caught in one too many lies, or being overcome with guilt
A character's spouse catching the character and a mutual friend in the act
A former lover leaving the character a large inheritance, leading to difficult conversations and a confession
The appearance of an illegitimate child who couldn't have been conceived with one's partner

MINOR COMPLICATIONS
The character softening the details of the affair to make it less damning
Telling so many lies the character has trouble keeping track of them
Having to convince the person who discovered the infidelity to keep it a secret
Trying to continue the extra-marital relationship while enduring much more scrutiny
Trying to do damage control (saying it didn't mean anything, apologizing, etc.) and failing
Discomfort and awkwardness arising from having to admit wrongdoing
Having to temporarily relocate to a hotel or friend's house to give the partner space
The couple deciding to keep the infidelity quiet while they figure out what to do and having to act as if everything is fine
The infidelity being made public, exposing the character's spouse and children to humiliation
The character having to explain their actions to loved ones and face judgment
Being shunned by certain family members or friends
Awkwardness around friends and family members who have learned about the cheating
The character ending the relationship with the other party but still having to see them socially or work with them

POTENTIALLY DISASTROUS RESULTS
The character responding to accusations irrationally and the kids bearing witness to the meltdown or someone being hurt
Having to deal with a public relations nightmare
The character being kicked out of their house
The character or their significant other becoming dangerously ill from a sexually transmitted disease acquired outside the relationship
Placing a burden on one's children to keep their knowledge of the affair a secret
Being blackmailed by the person who discovered the infidelity
The character's spouse forgiving them but never trusting them again
The character choosing to continue the affair
The character losing their spouse or long-time partner because of the infidelity

The character's spouse seeking violent vengeance against the lover
The character's children rebelling or pulling away from the character because of his actions

RESULTING EMOTIONS: Anxiety, Apprehension, Defensiveness, Denial, Desperation, Determination, Disbelief, Dread, Fear, Flustered, Guilt, Horror, Humiliation, Panic, Regret, Relief, Remorse, Resentment, Self-Loathing, Self-Pity, Shame, Shock, Stunned

POSSIBLE INTERNAL STRUGGLES
Loving two people and struggling to choose between them
Feeling a duty to stay but a yearning to go
Feeling terrible for causing pain yet desperately wanting to be with the lover
Anguish and guilt at unintentionally following in a parent's footsteps (if infidelity was the cause of an unhappy childhood home)
The character wondering what's wrong with them and worrying they'll never be happy in a monogamous relationship
Being crippled by guilt, shame, and regret for putting their spouse and family through this
Anger at being caught but feeling relief because the secret had to come out sometime

NEGATIVE TRAITS THAT MAY WORSEN THE SITUATION: Apathetic, Confrontational, Controlling, Defensive, Devious, Dishonest, Evasive, Hostile, Irrational, Irresponsible, Manipulative, Resentful, Self-Destructive, Uncooperative, Violent, Volatile

IMPACT ON BASIC NEEDS
Esteem and Recognition: A character who engages in affairs but believes they're wrong may feel weak and suffer from self-loathing and shame. Once the infidelity becomes known, they will also be ostracized by many who will lose all respect for the character.
Love and Belonging: In the wake of infidelity, the character will be abandoned by many of the important people in their life, resulting in them being left without a community or support system.
Safety and Security: A character may deal poorly with the fallout of this situation, turning to drugs and alcohol or becoming a workaholic as a way of avoiding the truth. Unhealthy coping mechanisms like these will only cause problems for the character over time, impairing their mental and physical health.

POSITIVE TRAITS TO HELP THE CHARACTER COPE: Adaptable, Calm, Charming, Cooperative, Honest, Honorable, Imaginative, Passionate, Persistent, Persuasive, Responsible

POSITIVE OUTCOMES
No longer having to live a lie or a double life
The character seeing the situation as a wake-up call and deciding to be more responsible and unselfish in the future
Attending couple's counseling and the marriage growing stronger as a result
The character being forced to face their commitment issues and deal with them

PEER PRESSURE

EXAMPLES

The character doing something irresponsible or dangerous because others are doing it (using drugs, diving into unknown waters, etc.)

Giving in to a dare (picking a fight with a stranger, vandalizing property, etc.)

Going too far physically because they've been pressured to do so

Laughing at an off-color joke because others do, even though it doesn't feel right

Seeing wrongdoing and not pointing it out due to fear of losing friends

Covering for someone who's doing something they're not supposed to do

Taking part in a prank

Allowing oneself to be subjugated to someone else (laughing off insults, agreeing to ideas the character doesn't believe in, etc.)

Participating in activities one isn't really passionate about because important people in the character's life are involved (joining a country club, trying out for a sports team, etc.)

Living beyond one's financial means (buying a luxury car, taking expensive trips, only wearing designer clothes, etc.) to keep up appearances

Expressing support for political, religious, or social ideals one doesn't actually believe in

Going to great lengths to maintain a certain appearance simply to look like everyone else

Making important life decisions based on what others are doing (where to send one's kids to school, what career to pursue, where to live, etc.)

MINOR COMPLICATIONS

Embarrassment over the foolish decisions one has made

Getting into minor trouble at school or work

One's reputation being damaged

Having to adopt the group's disagreeable viewpoint on a topic

Having to change plans quickly to accommodate one's peers

Having to run errands, be inconvenienced, or make unimportant things a priority to appease the group

Reputation by association (being lumped in with the group rather than being seen as an individual)

POTENTIALLY DISASTROUS RESULTS

The character losing their sense of personal identity and values

Experiencing physical, mental, or emotional trauma from the consequences of one's choices (getting pregnant, developing an eating disorder, being abused, getting into a car accident, etc.)

Being guilty by association

Choosing dysfunctional relationships over healthy ones; losing the friends and loved ones who would speak wisdom into the character's life

Seeking other unhealthy ways of gaining control (self-harming, controlling people outside of the peer group, etc.)

Going into debt

The character being arrested

Being pressured to take the fall for a guilty peer
Getting suspended or expelled from school
Getting fired
Becoming codependent and losing the ability to think for oneself
Living an unhappy or unfulfilled life
Hurting someone else (if the peer pressure involves oppressing or bullying others)
Developing severe self-esteem issues stemming from the unkind critiques of important peers

RESULTING EMOTIONS: Appalled, Apprehension, Conflicted, Confusion, Discouragement, Dread, Emasculation, Embarrassment, Flustered, Guilt, Humiliation, Hurt, Inadequacy, Insecurity, Intimidation, Nervousness, Regret, Reluctance, Resignation, Self-Loathing, Shame, Worry

POSSIBLE INTERNAL STRUGGLES
Feeling powerless and trapped, like the character isn't in charge of their own life
Struggling with feelings of insecurity and self-doubt
Constantly feeling conflicted over what one is doing and what one really wants to do
Struggling with the idea that maybe the group's treatment is an indication of the character's worth
Experiencing anxiety when peers go silent or shift positive attention to another member of the group

NEGATIVE TRAITS THAT MAY WORSEN THE SITUATION: Callous, Cruel, Cynical, Defensive, Gullible, Hypocritical, Indecisive, Insecure, Subservient, Timid, Weak-Willed

IMPACT ON BASIC NEEDS
Self-Actualization: If the character's need to fit in becomes strong enough, they may lose sight of who they are and what they need. Eventually, they'll become dissatisfied because they're living someone else's truth and not their own.
Esteem and Recognition: In the aftermath of giving in to peer pressure, the character's self-esteem may plummet as they question their strength of will and worry about being a pushover or an easy mark. Others may also view the character as weak and easily led.
Safety and Security: A character who is easily pressured by others can end up doing things that aren't safe or healthy. They may even be prone to dysfunctional or unhealthy relationships that can threaten their physical or emotional well-being.

POSITIVE TRAITS TO HELP THE CHARACTER COPE: Alert, Cautious, Diplomatic, Funny, Honorable, Independent, Intelligent, Perceptive, Persuasive, Responsible, Socially Aware

POSITIVE OUTCOMES
Recognizing manipulation in others so it can be avoided in the future
The character becoming aware of someone's toxicity and cutting them out of their life
Learning to take personal responsibility, even for things that happened because one stood passively by
Deciding to be a leader instead of a follower

SEEING AN EX WITH SOMEONE NEW

NOTES: Learning an ex is seeing someone else can be a painful experience, especially if the character is still emotionally attached. The amount of conflict this generates for your character will depend on many factors, the most impactful being who the ex is with and where they are seen.

EXAMPLES:

The character running into the ex and their new beau at a favorite restaurant

The character realizing their "replacement" is a friend or family member

Running into one's therapist, pastor, or trusted mentor and their date … who happens to be the character's ex

Showing up for a team sport and seeing the ex with one's rival

Running into the ex and seeing them entwined with someone they always denied liking, which may become a double blow if the character suspected the partner of cheating in the past

Attending a corporate social event and discovering the boss' significant other is the ex

Seeing the ex at a funeral, being comforted by someone else

The character returning to the old place to retrieve their stuff and being greeted at the door by their replacement

Attending class or a school dance and seeing the ex with a hated rival or enemy

MINOR COMPLICATIONS

The character saying something they'll regret later

Awkwardness or unease that causes the character to do something embarrassing (spilling a drink, putting on an obvious act as if everything is fine, etc.)

An onset of tears that can't be hidden, leading to public embarrassment

Skipping school or calling in sick to avoid the new couple and getting in trouble for it

Avoiding the ex by canceling plans with a mutual friend and creating tension in that relationship

Old feelings cropping up, causing temporary uncertainty about a current romantic partner

Becoming possessive or needy with one's romantic partner

POTENTIALLY DISASTROUS RESULTS

Getting into a physical altercation with the new person

Struggling and failing to be calm and collected in the aftermath (screwing up a job interview, yelling at a child, fighting with a friend over something stupid, etc.)

Obsessing about the breakup and ruining one's current romantic relationship

Seeking revenge against the ex

Engaging in unhealthy coping mechanisms (getting drunk, spending large amounts of money, etc.)

Pushing the current romantic relationship to the next level before either party is ready to go there

Seeking to get the ex back (even if the ex was a bad fit, the relationship was toxic, etc.)

Seeking the ex out for a confrontation

RESULTING EMOTIONS: Agitation, Anger, Betrayed, Conflicted, Contempt, Depressed, Desire, Flustered, Hurt, Inadequacy, Jealousy, Loneliness, Longing, Nostalgia, Obsession, Powerlessness, Resentment, Sadness, Self-Pity, Shock, Stunned, Vengefulness, Vulnerability

POSSIBLE INTERNAL STRUGGLES

Comparing oneself to the new person and being disappointed

Romanticizing the old relationship—only recalling the good memories, remembering things more positively than they actually were, etc.

Needing to process the new information but having to hide one's emotions

Difficulty finding closure (if the new person is someone the character will see often)

Still having feelings for the ex and not knowing what to do with those

Second-guessing the decision to split up in the first place

The character struggling with dark thoughts (that they will always be single, they're unworthy of being loved, they're broken and inadequate, etc.)

Slipping deeper into an existing mental condition (depression, anxiety, having thoughts of suicide, etc.)

Revived feelings of remorse or guilt over the part one played in the breakup

Being happy the ex moved on but resenting that they did so first

NEGATIVE TRAITS THAT MAY WORSEN THE SITUATION: Abrasive, Addictive, Catty, Confrontational, Controlling, Impulsive, Insecure, Jealous, Macho, Melodramatic, Needy, Obsessive, Oversensitive, Possessive, Self-Destructive, Self-Indulgent, Vindictive, Weak-Willed

IMPACT ON BASIC NEEDS

Esteem and Recognition: If the character was responsible for the breakup (for example, if they cheated or were toxic in some way), seeing the ex again can reawaken feelings of worthlessness.

Love and Belonging: The character may be unable to achieve love with someone else until they're able to let go of residual feelings for the ex.

Safety and Security: A character who is struggling with the breakup may be triggered by the sight of their ex dating someone else, sending them back into a pattern of unhealthy or self-destructive coping practices.

POSITIVE TRAITS TO HELP THE CHARACTER COPE: Centered, Confident, Easygoing, Friendly, Mature, Patient, Proper, Sensible, Supportive, Tolerant, Whimsical, Witty

POSITIVE OUTCOMES

Eventually gaining closure from seeing that the ex has moved on

The character realizing their new love interest is a much better match than their ex

Seeing one's faults more clearly and being motivated to change them

Being freed emotionally to let go and pursue a new relationship

SEXUAL DYSFUNCTION

EXAMPLES
The character not being able to perform during sex due to erectile dysfunction
Having to abstain from sex because of a medical risk or an injury that makes the act impossible
Being unable to have sex for emotional or mental reasons (due to being sexually abused or assaulted, a phobia, etc.)
Being unable to have or enjoy sex because of side effects from a necessary medication
Avoiding sex due to discomfort or pain after a birth, illness, or surgery

MINOR COMPLICATIONS
The character having awkward conversations with their partner about emotions, sexual desire, or intimate body parts
Having to lie or make up excuses to avoid sexual intimacy with a partner
The character faking arousal or orgasm to avoid admitting or discussing their dysfunction
Dealing with side effects from medication prescribed for the problem
Trying to find solutions to the issue—eating foods or taking supplements that claim to increase libido, trying acupuncture, seeing a specialist, etc.
The embarrassment of having to see a doctor or attend therapy—alone or with a partner—to address the issue
A well-meaning but ignorant partner trying to solve the problem with ineffective methods, such as suggesting they role play to "spice things up"
Intimacy waning in the relationship because of the issue
Minor arguments and friction about other things because of the underlying problem
Experiencing embarrassment when friends talk openly about sex

POTENTIALLY DISASTROUS RESULTS
The character's partner satisfying their sexual needs outside the relationship—through an affair or porn, for instance
A marriage ending in divorce due to lack of physical or emotional connection
A couple being unable to conceive a child because of their limited sexual activity
Ignoring a doctor's advice to abstain from sex and suffering an injury, aggravating an existing condition, or having a heart attack from the physical exertion
The character being overwhelmed with guilt for not being able to fix the problem
A character with past trauma trying to push through it and suffering a panic attack during sex
Resentment, anger, or frustration building to a boiling point in the relationship
The character ending the relationship out of embarrassment or to free their partner to be with someone who can fulfill them

RESULTING EMOTIONS: Anger, Anguish, Annoyance, Anxiety, Apprehension, Bitterness, Confusion, Depressed, Desire, Despair, Devastation, Dissatisfaction, Doubt, Dread, Emasculation, Embarrassment, Fear, Frustration, Guilt, Inadequacy, Nervousness, Worthlessness

POSSIBLE INTERNAL STRUGGLES
The character wanting to be honest about the problem with their partner but being too embarrassed or afraid of rejection to do so
The character knowing the dysfunction isn't their fault but still feeling broken and defective
Feeling unworthy of a partner's love
Struggling to stay mentally present and relaxed during sex or intimate moments
Difficulty with dating, because the character knows sex will eventually be introduced and become a problem
Constantly being frustrated sexually because the character is unable to have sex
Feeling guilt for being unable to meet a spouse's needs

NEGATIVE TRAITS THAT MAY WORSEN THE SITUATION: Cynical, Evasive, Impatient, Insecure, Nervous, Nosy, Obsessive, Oversensitive, Perfectionist, Pessimistic, Resentful, Self-Destructive, Uncommunicative, Worrywart

IMPACT ON BASIC NEEDS
Esteem and Recognition: Because sex is such a universal occurrence, a character who is unable to participate in it will often internalize this as a weakness or failure, which will deplete their confidence and self-esteem.
Love and Belonging: Without a deep bond of understanding, a prolonged lack of physical intimacy can take its toll on a romantic relationship, generating feelings of frustration or resentment and a general sense of being disconnected. A breakup may follow, leaving both characters alone and dissatisfied.
Physiological Needs: If the result of sexual intercourse is desperately important to the character (to secure a lineage, pass on an important magical ability that's dying out, etc.) but they're unable to participate in it, then this need will be impacted.

POSITIVE TRAITS TO HELP THE CHARACTER COPE: Affectionate, Analytical, Appreciative, Confident, Cooperative, Easygoing, Honest, Kind, Nurturing, Patient, Resourceful, Uninhibited, Unselfish

POSITIVE OUTCOMES
The character finding alternatives or modifications to sex that fulfill them and their partner
Increased intimacy through honesty and open communication with a spouse
Seeking medical help and discovering an unrelated health issue in time to treat it
Counseling leading to a deeper connection for the couple
The character, through therapy, becoming aware of and facing an unresolved past wound which allows them to overcome their dysfunction
The couple making an effort to grow in emotional intimacy to make up for the lack of physical intimacy
Seeking help for the condition and discovering a treatment that can make sex possible again

THE REAPPEARANCE OF AN ESTRANGED RELATIVE

EXAMPLES
An estranged parent appearing at the character's door unannounced
A cousin one broke ties with years ago resurfacing to ask for help
An estranged parent showing up at the hospital to meet their grandchild
A sibling who has made no effort to contact the character for years calling to ask for money
A relative who was banned from the character's wedding showing up anyway
Feuding relatives appearing at a loved one's funeral, wake, or reading of the will
A child with an out-of-control addiction appearing when they run into trouble
A terminally ill relative appearing in their final days, looking for the character's forgiveness

MINOR COMPLICATIONS
Anger prompting rashness and words that can't be taken back
Embarrassment, especially if the person shows up drunk or behaves inappropriately in front of others
Having to answer uncomfortable questions and explain the relative isn't, in fact, dead like the character has claimed
Losing the esteem of others because of the person's bad behavior
Loved ones being exposed to a toxic person
The estranged relative pandering to the character's partner or child to get what they want

POTENTIALLY DISASTROUS RESULTS
Being suckered into believing the person has changed only to find they have not
A child building a relationship with their grandparent only to be abandoned when he or she leaves again
The character's hard-won esteem crashing due to gaslighting
The character falling back into dysfunctional habits they've worked hard to shake
Anger escalating to violence and the police being called
Family drama ruining an important event, such as a wedding reception or graduation
Discovering money or valuable items are missing after the person's arrival
The person's presence touching off a feud, with relatives taking sides
The estranged member causing friction in the character's marriage
People discovering the character's past as they know it is a lie

RESULTING EMOTIONS: Anger, Appalled, Betrayed, Bitterness, Certainty, Conflicted, Confusion, Contempt, Defensiveness, Disillusionment, Dread, Embarrassment, Flustered, Frustration, Guilt, Hatred, Hopefulness, Hurt, Longing, Remorse, Shock, Skepticism, Suspicion

POSSIBLE INTERNAL STRUGGLES
Wanting approval and hating that this is the case

Struggling to not let one's own "ugly side" take over when dealing with the other person
Wanting to repair things but knowing it is impossible
Wanting to tell loved ones the truth about the rift but being unwilling to revisit the source of hurt
Anxiety over traits the character has in common with the estranged individual
The character questioning their memory (especially if gaslighting was a factor)
Feeling raw and exposed at the person's return and embarrassed that others have seen it
Feeling hope and berating oneself for it because it's setting one up to be hurt again

NEGATIVE TRAITS THAT MAY WORSEN THE SITUATION: Addictive, Callous, Confrontational, Forgetful, Hypocritical, Needy, Subservient, Timid, Violent, Weak-Willed

IMPACT ON BASIC NEEDS
Self-Actualization: If the relative who shows up dredges up a past the character has tried to leave behind, they could be triggered and devolve, losing their identity and becoming lost to a resurgence of past trauma.
Esteem and Recognition: Having an abusive person show up (especially a caregiver or parent) that the character tried hard to forget could reawaken feelings of inadequacy and low self-worth.
Love and Belonging: Some relationships are closer than others, but any sort of estrangement means the person was at one point close enough to hold the character's trust. The return of a once-important person to your character's life could have them feeling the loss of what they had all over again, reexperiencing this void. Another scenario to consider is if the person is insidious and manages to turn loved ones against the character, either trying to win their forgiveness enough to reenter their life or for more nefarious reasons. Either way, this person's meddling could create friction in the character's existing relationships.
Safety and Security: If the returning relative brings trouble with them, your character and their loved ones might be in danger by association. Or if the person is there as a financial drain, your character's finances may dwindle away, leaving them vulnerable.

POSITIVE TRAITS TO HELP THE CHARACTER COPE: Alert, Calm, Centered, Observant, Proactive, Protective, Sensible, Wise

POSITIVE OUTCOMES
Being able to forgive and reconcile with the long-lost relative
The character achieving closure through the encounter and being able to move on
The character gaining access to much-needed information, such as medical history, that only the estranged person can provide
The character pursuing a relationship so they can gain proof about the relative's deeds and motives and seek prosecution
The other person showing their true colors, allowing loved ones who have taken sides against the character to see the light

Failures and Mistakes

A LIE IMPACTING SOMEONE ELSE

EXAMPLES
The character concealing (or falsely claiming to have) a medical condition
Misleading others about the status of a romantic relationship
Falsely accusing someone of a crime
Being selective about which details to share about a crime they witnessed
The character concealing their true identity
Falsifying credentials, such as legal documents, licenses, or certificates
Concealing an addiction
Faking a pregnancy or the loss of a pregnancy
Lying to corroborate someone else's alibi
Spreading a rumor about someone else
The character not being honest with their details on a dating website
The character faking their own death
The character concealing parentage from their child
A student lying about grades or their academic standing
Hiding a second family
Concealing involvement in an illegal activity
The character hiding their political or religious beliefs
A character concealing their true feelings toward someone else
Lying on a résumé
Stretching the truth about one's skills or abilities

MINOR COMPLICATIONS
Uncomfortable conversations when the character is confronted about their lies
Stress and exhaustion from keeping up a façade
Having to keep lies straight with different people
Being asked for proof about the claims
Having to take measures to prevent others from digging up the truth
Other people being inconvenienced when the truth becomes known—e.g., them having to take over a project because the character lacks the experience they claimed to have

POTENTIALLY DISASTROUS RESULTS
Broken relationships that can't be mended
A criminal or wrongdoer going unpunished because of the character's lies
A health issue worsening because the character won't be honest about it
The character's children learning that lying is acceptable behavior
The character being fired
Loved ones experiencing trauma and an inability to trust others because of the character's actions
The character losing their marriage or custody of their children
Those victimized seeking retribution
Being faced with criminal charges (for lying under oath, for participating in a crime, etc.)

Other people being pulled into the character's dishonesty or crime because they didn't know the truth

Becoming so desensitized to lying that the character no longer sees it as a problem

RESULTING EMOTIONS: Anguish, Anxiety, Apprehension, Conflicted, Defensiveness, Denial, Determination, Doubt, Dread, Fear, Flustered, Guilt, Nervousness, Shame, Stunned, Uncertainty, Unease, Worry, Worthlessness

POSSIBLE INTERNAL STRUGGLES
Guilt and anxiety at knowingly betraying others
Difficulty determining right from wrong
The character questioning their worth as a spouse, parent, friend, employee, etc.
Being paranoid that others will discover the truth
Wanting to reveal the truth but being too afraid of the consequences
Having to choose between self-preservation and the safety and security of loved ones
Not being truly known by anyone and feeling disconnected

NEGATIVE TRAITS THAT MAY WORSEN THE SITUATION: Antisocial, Apathetic, Callous, Cowardly, Cruel, Devious, Disloyal, Forgetful, Hypocritical, Impulsive, Irresponsible, Manipulative, Paranoid, Reckless, Selfish

IMPACT ON BASIC NEEDS
   Esteem and Recognition: Being caught in a lie that has repercussions to others will force the character to face the consequences of their actions. If the affected person is a loved one, or an innocent, it may be difficult for the character to justify their actions and the weight of shame will be immense, eroding their self-respect.
   Love and Belonging: Lies cause people to put up barriers, so if your character is unable to convince those around them that they've changed, their relationships will lack the closeness they need and crave.
   Physiological Needs: The world can be a dangerous place. Telling a lie that casts suspicion on someone dangerous could have big blowback, putting the character's life at risk.

POSITIVE TRAITS TO HELP THE CHARACTER COPE: Ambitious, Analytical, Cautious, Confident, Creative, Decisive, Diplomatic, Industrious, Intelligent, Meticulous, Persistent, Persuasive, Spontaneous

POSITIVE OUTCOMES
Being given an opportunity to undo the harm of the lie
Realizing the repercussions of lying and resolving to not do it again
The character embracing honesty and discovering people like them for who they are, erasing the misbelief that lying about themselves is necessary
Remaining free (if the lie is one that would send the character to jail)

A PRANK GOING WRONG

EXAMPLES
The character doing something silly that results in their arrest
Changing a family member's clocks on April Fools' Day, causing them to miss an important job interview
Throwing a flaming bag of poop on someone's doorstep and the porch being burned down
Replacing the office treats with marijuana brownies the day before a random drug testing
Setting up a prank for a friend and it backfiring on someone else
Moving or decorating someone's car as a prank and damaging the paint job
Organizing a hazing ritual that ends in someone's injury or death
Participating in an insensitive prank that is shared online, resulting in backlash and a permanent record of the character's ignorance or racism
Telling a lie that is taken as the truth, causing widespread hysteria or panic
Messing with a friend's car so it won't start and them being mugged while walking home

MINOR COMPLICATIONS
Having to apologize for a prank
Being suspended from school or reprimanded at work
A relationship with a friend being damaged because of the prank
The prank causing property damage the character must pay for
The character developing a reputation as a prankster and no longer being taken seriously
Innocent bystanders being harmed by the prank
Having to be hyper-alert to avoid retaliation
Being publicly humiliated as people share what happened on social media
The character being pressured by their peer group to orchestrate more pranks
Being monitored more closely at work or school because trust has been lost

POTENTIALLY DISASTROUS RESULTS
A prank that causes an injury or death
Legal consequences, including fines, probation, or jail time
The character's involvement costing them an opportunity at school or work
The character being expelled or fired
Someone other than the character being blamed for the prank
The generation of a war between the character and their victim, with pranks that escalate in magnitude and destruction
Losing the respect of a loved one
Losing a friendship
The character continuing to initiate pranks because it brings them attention or acceptance

RESULTING EMOTIONS: Anxiety, Appalled, Apprehension, Desperation, Determination, Devastation, Disbelief, Dread, Embarrassment, Empathy, Fear, Guilt, Horror, Indifference, Nervousness, Paranoia, Regret, Sadness, Self-Pity, Shock, Unease, Worry

POSSIBLE INTERNAL STRUGGLES

The character struggling with coming clean or letting someone else take the blame

Wanting to end a prank war but not wanting to give the other party the satisfaction of winning

Feeling conflicted about joining a group but being uncomfortable with the pranks one has to complete to become a member

Feeling pride for the prank's creativeness but regretting it didn't quite go as planned

Regretting the prank but also feeling like the repercussions are overly punitive

NEGATIVE TRAITS THAT MAY WORSEN THE SITUATION: Apathetic, Compulsive, Cruel, Defensive, Dishonest, Foolish, Gullible, Inattentive, Irresponsible, Mischievous

IMPACT ON BASIC NEEDS

Self-Actualization: If a character's reputation is affected because of their involvement in the prank or the criminal record that results, the ability to pursue certain dream vocations or careers might be limited.

Esteem and Recognition: A character feeling shame or regret for their involvement in a prank gone wrong will mentally beat themselves up and think less of themselves for it.

Love and Belonging: If the character's prank hurts a loved one's feelings, causes them injury, or damages their property, that person may hold a grudge or sever the relationship.

Safety and Security: Pranks can be dangerous. What seems like a hilarious idea or harmless bit of fun could turn into a nightmare that injures the character.

Physiological Needs: If the prank puts the character or someone else in a dangerous situation, there is the possibility of serious injury or death when the prank goes wrong.

POSITIVE TRAITS TO HELP THE CHARACTER COPE: Charming, Cooperative, Generous, Honest, Honorable, Innocent, Just, Kind, Nurturing, Obedient, Responsible

POSITIVE OUTCOMES

Turning over a new, more serious leaf when the character sees the error of their ways

The character getting peer recognition for pulling an epic prank and enjoying popularity at school

The character channeling their proclivity for arranging elaborate pranks into more productive avenues, such as organizing parties or school activities

The character making restitution and finding a new skill or passion, such as car detailing or landscape design

A close call helping the character see that their recklessness is going to get them killed if they don't make a change

BEING UNPREPARED

NOTES: Being unprepared for an important event not only has potentially devastating consequences but it can also cause the character to blame themselves for not doing what should have been done—even if that blame is unwarranted. Reasons vary for why a character may not be prepared for a work meeting, interview, presentation, speech, personal conversation, or court case. The examples that follow explore a few of these possibilities.

EXAMPLES
An emergency situation that steals the character's preparation time
Being assigned the duty last minute and having to "wing it"
Poor time management
Taking on too much, so nothing gets done adequately
Procrastination due to an underlying fear or worry
Subconscious self-sabotage—e.g., because the character doesn't really want the promotion
Wanting to sabotage someone else who is involved
Being morally opposed to the project
A travel or weather delay that keeps the character from important last-minute preparations
A rival tampering with the character's materials (ruining a prototype, stealing their laptop, destroying documents, etc.)
Going into the presentation drunk, hungover, very ill, or otherwise impaired
An unexpected inspection or check-in the character wasn't prepared for

MINOR COMPLICATIONS
Looking unprofessional
Losing credibility
Being embarrassed in front of peers or influential people
Letting other people down
Hurting the reputation of co-workers, the character's firm, etc.
Not getting paid for the gig because the character failed to hold up their end of the bargain
Missing out on an opportunity to step up and stand out
Losing the chance to repair a relationship or reconnect with someone

POTENTIALLY DISASTROUS RESULTS
Not getting the desired job, promotion, account, etc.
Being removed from the project and losing out on future opportunities
Failing to bring about change (if the character was speaking at a rally, providing a witness testimony, pleading a case in front of a committee, etc.)
Experiencing health problems (hypertension, ulcers, insomnia, etc.) from the stress or being overworked
Getting fired
Not being able to salvage a relationship (if the character was unprepared for a conciliatory conversation)

Blaming the circumstances or other people instead of taking responsibility; not learning from the mistake

Shying away from similar projects in the future

A rival saving the day—possibly because they sabotaged the character in the first place

RESULTING EMOTIONS: Apprehension, Confusion, Defensiveness, Embarrassment, Flustered, Humiliation, Inadequacy, Nervousness, Powerlessness, Shame, Uncertainty, Worry

POSSIBLE INTERNAL STRUGGLES

Feeling guilty because other parties were impacted by the character's poor planning

Struggling with feelings of inadequacy and insecurity—especially if this isn't the character's first mistake

The character being stuck in a comparison loop, wondering why they fall short when others don't

Being afraid to work as part of a team and let people down again

Reliving the situation and beating oneself up over what should have been said or done

Trying to come up with a way to salvage the situation or get a do-over

Feeling set up or unfairly targeted, especially when others are given an unfair advantage or aren't subject to the same expectations as the character

NEGATIVE TRAITS THAT MAY WORSEN THE SITUATION: Apathetic, Cocky, Defensive, Disorganized, Flaky, Irresponsible, Lazy, Nervous, Perfectionist, Timid, Worrywart

IMPACT ON BASIC NEEDS

Self-Actualization: A character who desperately wants to help or serve others but has weaknesses that make it difficult for them to prepare may become frustrated enough to give up on a meaningful goal.

Esteem and Recognition: It's obvious when someone hasn't done their best work, particularly on a group project or a presentation involving others. In this situation, their reputation and credibility will take a hit, lowering their esteem in other people's eyes.

Love and Belonging: Unpreparedness can cause problems in personal relationships just as it can in the workplace. A loved one or romantic partner who believes the character isn't putting in the necessary effort may pull away or eventually cut their losses.

Safety and Security: Unprepared individuals typically end up rushing and cutting corners, which can lead to accidents and injuries.

POSITIVE TRAITS TO HELP THE CHARACTER COPE: Cooperative, Disciplined, Efficient, Friendly, Honest, Industrious, Intelligent, Meticulous, Proactive, Professional

POSITIVE OUTCOMES

Learning to plan ahead, schedule more carefully, or communicate more clearly so the situation won't be repeated

Taking ownership of their mistakes

The character recognizing they may not be suited for that career field or particular goal

Being open and honest about one's lack of preparation and being rewarded with a second chance Asking for more time to prepare and the request being granted

BREAKING OR DESTROYING AN IMPORTANT ITEM

EXAMPLES
The character's mode of transport breaking (a car no longer working because of poor maintenance, crashing a bike so it no longer rides, knocking a hole in a boat, etc.)
A family heirloom being ruined
A treasured gift (from a mentor, a deceased parent, a child, etc.) being mistakenly thrown out
A phone or laptop getting dropped in the water
Ruining a stuffed animal or security blanket the character's child must have to sleep and feel safe
Prize-winning begonias belonging to the character's grandmother being dug up by the dog
A school assignment or work project being ruined at the last minute
Knocking over the urn containing a relative's ashes
A map or letter containing vital instructions sustaining extensive water damage
The will or deed that entitles the character to something valuable going up in a house fire
A vial containing the only known cure for a devastating disease being broken
A centuries-old weapon or magical item needed to protect a nation or group of people being destroyed
The machine that's supposed to bring back a time traveler being blown up
A lamp or box constraining an evil spirit busting open

MINOR COMPLICATIONS
The character having to confess to people who will be upset by the loss
The character being chastised for their carelessness
Having to clean up the broken item and dispose of it
Hiding evidence of the broken item to avoid discovery
Having to scavenge or buy essential items to fix the item
The character sustaining minor injuries when the item is broken
Looking bad in front of people whose opinions matter
The financial burden of having to replace the item
Time spent unsuccessfully trying to fix the item or find a replacement
The character having to lie about their involvement
Inconveniences arising from the loss (being forced to take the bus to work, going without a phone, having to redo an assignment from scratch, etc.)
Getting a poor grade on an assignment or being reprimanded at work

POTENTIALLY DISASTROUS RESULTS
Destroying something that can never be replaced
Family members not forgiving the character for destroying an irreplaceable item
Being stranded in a dangerous place
Facing prison time for the infraction
Losing a large sum of money because the character doesn't have proof they're entitled to it

A nation of people being made vulnerable
Magic no longer working the way it should
An evil force being unleashed

RESULTING EMOTIONS: Anger, Anguish, Annoyance, Anxiety, Appalled, Apprehension, Defeat, Defensiveness, Despair, Desperation, Determination, Dread, Fear, Frustration, Guilt, Horror, Hysteria, Irritation, Nervousness, Remorse, Resignation, Worry

POSSIBLE INTERNAL STRUGGLES

The character wanting to come clean but fearing people's reactions
Being tempted to blame others instead of taking ownership
Being tormented by the mental replay of the item breaking; wishing for a do-over
Being secretly relieved about the item's destruction but having to pretend the opposite
Being filled with guilt
Resenting that the item seems to be more important to some people than the character is

NEGATIVE TRAITS THAT MAY WORSEN THE SITUATION: Apathetic, Defensive, Devious, Dishonest, Frivolous, Fussy, Impulsive, Irresponsible, Lazy, Perfectionist, Reckless, Resentful, Rowdy, Spoiled, Worrywart

IMPACT ON BASIC NEEDS

Self-Actualization: If the destroyed item is one that will keep the character from pursuing their dreams, they will have to lower their expectations and settle for something else that may not make them truly happy.

Esteem and Recognition: A character who breaks an item that is important to people may become anathema in their eyes. And a character who internalizes this mistake may begin to think poorly of himself.

Love and Belonging: When a person makes a big mistake, they learn quickly who their friends are. If people distance themselves rather than rally with forgiveness and support, the character may feel adrift and alone.

Physiological Needs: If the item is important on a larger scale—say, affecting the security of a region or nation—large numbers of people may be endangered or killed.

POSITIVE TRAITS TO HELP THE CHARACTER COPE: Adaptable, Analytical, Bold, Calm, Creative, Decisive, Diplomatic, Disciplined, Focused, Honorable, Industrious, Persistent, Proactive, Protective, Resourceful, Responsible, Studious

POSITIVE OUTCOMES

Being forgiven and realizing people are more important than material items
The character learning to take responsibility for their actions
The character becoming more careful with the items in their care
The character learning their actions can cause problems for others
Going on a quest to replace the item or solve a problem caused by its breakage and discovering skills and abilities the character didn't know they had

CAUSING A CAR ACCIDENT

EXAMPLES
The character getting into a fender bender because they were texting while driving
Driving under the influence and causing a major accident with another vehicle
Accidentally hitting an animal or pedestrian because the character wasn't paying attention
Falling asleep at the wheel, running off the road, and hitting a tree or structure

MINOR COMPLICATIONS
Being late due to having to wait for a police officer or tow truck
Having to deal with rambunctious children during the wait
A totaled car that leaves the character without transportation
Getting a ticket
Conflict with the other driver
A new or young driver not knowing the protocol
Temporary health problems caused by the accident (a headache, sore muscles, bruises or scratches, etc.)
Damaging someone's property and being financially responsible for repairs
Having to call someone for a ride if the car is not drivable or has been impounded

POTENTIALLY DISASTROUS RESULTS
Sustaining life-threatening injuries, such as internal bleeding, a collapsed lung, or damage to vital organs
Injuries that result in chronic pain or disability (paralysis, traumatic head injury, back pain, etc.)
Death
Being negligent in an accident that results in someone's death
Suffering severe injuries and having no insurance
The accident occurring in a remote location where help won't come for some time
Getting sued
Being trapped in a vehicle
The character losing their license (because this wasn't a first offense, they were drunk, etc.)
A long recovery
The character being unable to work because of the injuries or hours missed during recovery
Accruing debt as medical and legal bills pile up

RESULTING EMOTIONS: Anguish, Anxiety, Apprehension, Defensiveness, Devastation, Disbelief, Dread, Embarrassment, Empathy, Fear, Flustered, Gratitude, Guilt, Horror, Nervousness, Panic, Regret, Remorse, Self-Loathing, Shock

POSSIBLE INTERNAL STRUGGLES
Being tempted to evade responsibility (by leaving the scene, lying to shift blame to the other driver, etc.)
The character constantly wondering what they could have done to avoid the accident

Being overcome with guilt

Depression

Seeing the accident replay over and over in their mind

Developing phobias associated with the accident (a fear of driving, of hospitals, etc.)

Obsessing over what could have been: *What if I had killed someone? If I'd left the house thirty seconds later, I would've missed the whole thing. Why did I drink so much at the party?*

Worrying over what the character's spouse or parents will say

NEGATIVE TRAITS THAT MAY WORSEN THE SITUATION: Addictive, Defensive, Devious, Flaky, Foolish, Impulsive, Inattentive, Irresponsible, Melodramatic, Morbid, Nervous, Obsessive, Spoiled, Volatile

IMPACT ON BASIC NEEDS:

   Self-Actualization: If resulting fears or anxieties limit the character significantly or physical disabilities put certain personal goals out of reach, they may not be able to live the life they saw for themselves.

   Esteem and Recognition: Blame for the accident (from within or from other people) could result in plummeting self-esteem or decreased respect for the character.

   Love and Belonging: In the aftermath of a serious accident for which the character was to blame, loved ones may find it difficult to forgive the character or he may find it difficult to forgive himself, leading him to believe he is unworthy of love and acceptance.

   Safety and Security: By its very nature, a car accident will put the character's safety at risk. If others were involved and decide to seek revenge, safety could continue to be an issue—especially if the character escaped justice because of their connections, being a minor at the time, or a botched police procedure that led to charges being dismissed.

   Physiological Needs: This kind of conflict could realistically result in the loss of life for the character or a loved one.

POSITIVE TRAITS TO HELP THE CHARACTER COPE: Appreciative, Centered, Cooperative, Empathetic, Generous, Honorable, Mature, Objective, Optimistic

POSITIVE OUTCOMES

Gratitude that things didn't turn out as badly as they could have

Being reminded of what's important in life

Becoming a more cautious and patient driver

Being forgiven instead of condemned and determining to be more gracious and forgiving in the future

The character recognizing they have a problem (an alcohol addiction, texting while driving, etc.) and taking steps to address the issue

Partnering with an organization to speak to others about the repercussions of driving while impaired and what it's like to live with what was done

CAUSING A WORKPLACE HAZARD

EXAMPLES
The character using tools, machinery, or technology improperly
Accidentally causing a fire
Handling chemicals or hazardous materials incorrectly
Not following safety and security protocols
Exposing co-workers to a contagious disease
Failing to carry out safety drills
Neglecting routine maintenance, updates, or inspections
Contributing to a toxic environment with bullying, discrimination, or harassment
Bringing an unsafe animal to work
Allowing an unauthorized person onto a work site
Carrying out a violent act at the worksite
Failing to dispose of toxic or hazardous waste appropriately
Falling asleep or becoming distracted during working hours
Careless sharing of sensitive information
Exposing co-workers to allergens
The character saving money by hiring less people, leading to reduced safety for those on site

MINOR COMPLICATIONS
Feeling embarrassment
Teasing or ridicule by one's co-workers
Having to admit fault and notify those impacted
Dealing with the distrust of co-workers
Experiencing increased stress levels
Being required to take a safety course or follow a disciplinary protocol
Having to apologize
Being reprimanded by superiors
Having to pay fines or for repair of damaged tools, machinery, or technology
Being given fewer hours, lower wages, or a different job within the company

POTENTIALLY DISASTROUS RESULTS
Injuring or killing a co-worker
Destroying property
Negatively impacting company and employee earnings
Being held liable for damages and/or loss of life
Being fired
The public becoming aware of the infraction
Difficulty finding new employment
Being sued or charged with a crime
Co-workers' personal and/or financial information being exposed to untrustworthy sources

RESULTING EMOTIONS: Anguish, Anxiety, Appalled, Apprehension, Despair, Devastation, Dread, Fear, Guilt, Horror, Humiliation, Overwhelmed, Panic, Remorse, Self-Pity, Shame, Shock, Tormented, Worry

POSSIBLE INTERNAL STRUGGLES

Feeling guilt and shame at one's lapse in judgment and its impact on others

The character knowing it was an honest mistake but struggling to forgive him or herself

The character reliving their choices over and over

Worry over possible legal or financial repercussions

Trying to remember anything that could have contributed to the mistake that might improve the character's position

Wanting to reach out to co-workers but being afraid to hear what they might say

Dealing with the temptation to deny responsibility (if there's no evidence)

Struggling with post-traumatic stress

Worry over causing another accident rendering decision making difficult

NEGATIVE TRAITS THAT MAY WORSEN THE SITUATION: Antisocial, Apathetic, Foolish, Hypocritical, Inattentive, Perfectionist, Pretentious, Resentful, Uncooperative, Unethical

IMPACT ON BASIC NEEDS

Self-Actualization: Consequences that limit the character's upward mobility at work may result in them being stuck in a job that doesn't fulfill or satisfy them.

Esteem and Recognition: The character may experience intense guilt and shame over being to blame for an accident. They may feel like a failure for not preventing the outcome.

Love and Belonging: Trust from co-workers or team members may be lost, even if the hazard was accidental, leaving the character feeling like they are on unsteady ground at work.

Safety and Security: If the character was suspended without pay for a period of time or an injury occurred and the character was unable to work, their finances may dwindle.

Physiological Needs: Depending on the dangers involved, a severe hazard can lead to death.

POSITIVE TRAITS TO HELP THE CHARACTER COPE: Adaptable, Appreciative, Calm, Confident, Cooperative, Diplomatic, Disciplined, Empathetic, Honest, Objective, Optimistic, Persistent, Proactive, Responsible

POSITIVE OUTCOMES

Exposing a hazard that could have yielded a worse outcome

Reinforcing existing safety and security protocols to prevent future hazards

Being fired but finding a better and more fulfilling job elsewhere

The character pivoting to a less dangerous career that provides an opportunity to gain new skills, leading to greater fulfillment

Extending forgiveness to others more readily as a result of having received it

CONFIDING IN THE WRONG PERSON

EXAMPLES
The character sharing information with someone who can't keep a secret
One's private or personal information being sold to tabloids
Information being used against the character in some way
Being honest about a system flaw or security risk at work and being fired
Revealing corruption and being turned into a scapegoat so those involved can avoid jail time
Being blackmailed with information that was shared in good faith
Sharing sensitive information with a friend, who uses it to turn a profit
Confiding about a lapse of judgment (such as infidelity) and the person turning around and telling the character's partner about it
Revealing information to a co-worker, who uses it to get ahead
Agreeing to an interview where one's responses are sensationalized or quoted out of context
Confessing to feelings that are shared without one's consent
Confiding in someone who makes a moral decision to reveal the information
Making oneself vulnerable by sharing personal information, then being taken advantage of
An anonymous whistleblower's identity being leaked

MINOR COMPLICATIONS
Having to tell a spouse that a family secret is out
Having to do damage control with people upset by confidential information being leaked
Being put on the spot to answer questions or reveal more information (by reporters, investigators, family members, or people involved who were caught unaware)
Being called out by a boss or co-worker
Being put in a compromising situation
Being unfairly blamed for fallout
Being forced to do something one doesn't want to do to fix the situation
Having to call in an expensive favor to undo the damage
Lying to save face or prevent further fallout
Losing access to something (or someone) the character cherished
Being judged publicly for the information that was shared
Damaged relationships and mistrust
Time lost to worry over what other secrets the person might have passed on

POTENTIALLY DISASTROUS RESULTS
A relationship ending because it has been broken beyond repair
Losing a position of prestige
Losing a hard-won advantage
The character's reputation being destroyed
Being betrayed by someone close, leading to an emotional wound
Being blackmailed
Being excommunicated or shunned
Being prosecuted for wrongdoing

Being forced to break the law or sacrifice ethics or morals to reverse the fallout
Destroying one's chances to win something important
Losing out on a once-in-a-lifetime opportunity
Financial hardship from being sued, blackmailed, or dragged through the courts
Losing a chance to be forgiven or make things right
Loved ones believing something that is not true

RESULTING EMOTIONS: Anger, Anguish, Betrayed, Bitterness, Devastation, Disappointment, Disbelief, Disillusionment, Guilt, Humiliation, Hurt, Panic, Powerlessness, Rage, Regret, Remorse, Resentment, Self-Loathing, Self-Pity, Shock, Vengefulness, Vulnerability

POSSIBLE INTERNAL STRUGGLES
Being unable to stop caring about someone even though they betrayed the character's trust
Anger that cherished memories have now been tainted or spoiled by backstabbing
Guilt or self-blame for one's naïveté vying with anger at the one who took advantage
Being upset by what happened yet experiencing relief that the secret is out in the open

NEGATIVE TRAITS THAT MAY WORSEN THE SITUATION: Confrontational, Controlling, Disloyal, Gossipy, Hypocritical, Nervous, Suspicious, Vindictive

IMPACT ON BASIC NEEDS
Esteem and Recognition: Trust is hugely important in both personal and professional relationships—meaning, a character who has been deemed untrustworthy will often be looked down upon by others.
Love and Belonging: When betrayal comes from someone the character trusts most, the knife cuts the deepest.
Physiological Needs: If the character confides in someone about a dangerous individual and that sensitive information comes to light, the character could be made vulnerable or silenced altogether.

POSITIVE TRAITS TO HELP THE CHARACTER COPE: Calm, Honest, Intelligent, Private, Proactive, Protective, Responsible, Tolerant, Wise

POSITIVE OUTCOMES
Taking responsibility for the part one played, even if it was unintentional
The character gaining perspective about where their loyalties should lie and who might be a toxic influence in their life
Being free to address an issue once it's out in the open
Recognizing the need for better friends who have the character's best interests at heart
Being more careful about sharing private or personal information in the future

DOING SOMETHING STUPID WHILE IMPAIRED

EXAMPLES
The character calling or texting an ex to tell them off
Telling the boss or co-workers what the character *really* thinks (about them, the company, etc.)
Contacting an ex via a drunk dial, social media post, or text in hopes of getting back together
Picking a fight with someone
Taking stupid risks (jumping over a campfire, climbing on a roof to stargaze, standing on a high ledge to prove fearlessness, wandering through a dangerous neighborhood, etc.)
Driving under the influence
Getting naked and indecently exposing oneself
Sleeping with a best friend's partner, a co-worker, or other person who should be off limits
Trying to cross the friend zone despite knowing it won't turn out well
Rioting during a celebration
Breaking the law
Pulling a dangerous prank where others get hurt
Abandoning friends to go off with strangers
The character revealing a secret—their own or one belonging to someone else

MINOR COMPLICATIONS
Being hurt
Embarrassment or humiliation
Making a bad impression on someone
Losing the trust or respect of someone the character cares about
Worrying loved ones
Letting someone down
Waking up in a compromised situation (alone in a sleazy hotel with no memory of what happened, the character's wallet being stolen, discovering they had unsafe sex or used drugs they normally wouldn't take, etc.)
Embarrassing their family, friends, or the company they work for

POTENTIALLY DISASTROUS RESULTS
Discovering their actions were filmed and are now on the internet
Losing their job
Destroying a relationship over a bad choice (being unfaithful, sharing another's secret and breaking trust forever, being caught in a big lie, revealing inappropriate feelings, etc.)
Getting a disease (through unsafe sex or drug use)
Doing something that cannot be taken back (like killing someone while driving impaired)
Being convicted of a crime and losing custody of one's children
Being sued
Being convicted of a crime and going to jail
Hurting someone and having no memory of it
Being attacked or robbed
The media grossly twisting a minor event into something grotesque or horrendous

RESULTING EMOTIONS: Anguish, Appalled, Denial, Depressed, Disbelief, Emasculation, Embarrassment, Guilt, Horror, Humiliation, Panic, Powerlessness, Regret, Self-Loathing, Shame

POSSIBLE INTERNAL STRUGGLES

Mentally berating oneself for the lapse in judgment while blaming those who encouraged the alcohol or drug use

Embracing responsibility while resenting the people who never seem to suffer consequences for bad behavior

Feeling terrible about one's actions but believing the resulting punishment was too severe

The character knowing they're at a crisis point but having no one to turn to

NEGATIVE TRAITS THAT MAY WORSEN THE SITUATION: Addictive, Cocky, Disloyal, Foolish, Gullible, Impulsive, Irresponsible, Jealous, Macho, Rebellious, Reckless, Rowdy, Self-Destructive, Tactless, Temperamental, Unethical, Vindictive, Violent, Volatile

IMPACT ON BASIC NEEDS

Self-Actualization: If the character does something while impaired that greatly damages their reputation or trustworthiness, they could miss out on an opportunity, lose access to something important, or relinquish an advantage that may cause lifelong regret.

Esteem and Recognition: Stupid decisions result in embarrassment and humiliation, not only causing other people to see the character differently but also affecting the way they look at themselves.

Love and Belonging: In the aftermath of an embarrassing action, loved ones may become enmeshed in the fallout. This can cause resentment and friction, damaging the character's core relationships.

POSITIVE TRAITS TO HELP THE CHARACTER COPE: Centered, Cooperative, Honest, Honorable, Humble, Mature, Obedient, Pensive, Persuasive, Proper, Responsible

POSITIVE OUTCOMES

Hitting rock bottom and being determined it will never happen again

Accepting responsibility and taking steps toward bigger life changes

Realizing one's drinking has become a problem and making a choice to seek help

The character realizing they're only human and letting go of perfectionist tendencies

A stiff or unapproachable character's ability to relax and be silly (providing no real harm is done) might humanize them, improving their relationships.

DROPPING THE BALL

NOTES: This entry explores scenarios where the character was specifically being counted on to perform well, but they dropped the ball. For more general information involving a character failing to meet the expectations of others, see DISAPPOINTING SOMEONE.

EXAMPLES
The character not following through on a promise to attend a child's concert, a parent-teacher meeting, etc.
A spouse forgetting their anniversary or their significant other's birthday
Being a no-show as a conference speaker because the character had the session's time wrong
A student not completing their portion of an important group project
An athlete making a critical mistake that results in a loss for the team
Working late and missing an important family celebration
A character who is part of a best friend's bridal party getting drunk and missing the whole thing
Not preparing enough for a crucial meeting and being unable to answer vital questions
A contractor failing to provide the level of quality that was promised in a product or service

MINOR COMPLICATIONS
Having to sit through an interrogation over what happened (reliving the failure)
Being criticized, yelled at, or threatened
The character and their group receiving a failing grade on a project
Losing an important client
Disappointing a child or spouse
The character earning a reputation for being flaky
Losing an important game that would have moved the character's team into the finals
The character enduring verbal abuse because of their mistake
Being constantly reminded about important events by family members who no longer trust the character's word that they'll be there
Being questioned constantly about future commitments: *Will you remember? Can you handle this? Is it written in your calendar?*

POTENTIALLY DISASTROUS RESULTS
People losing faith in the character—in their abilities, commitment level, or whatever else fits
Being given less responsibility, being demoted, or getting fired due to the misstep
Losing a scholarship when the student's GPA falls below an established level
Being cut from an athletic team
The important people in the character's life feeling like they're not a priority or aren't loved
Suffering financially because of a loss of a big client or account
Not being asked to be part of someone's team in the future
The character overcompensating for the mistake in ways that cause annoyance for others
Being given an ultimatum

RESULTING EMOTIONS: Anger, Anguish, Annoyance, Anxiety, Determination, Disbelief, Embarrassment, Flustered, Frustration, Guilt, Inadequacy, Nervousness, Regret, Uncertainty

POSSIBLE INTERNAL STRUGGLES
The character struggling to forgive himself for his mistake
Becoming overwhelmed with regret
Being tempted to shift the blame to someone else or manufacture an excuse
Replaying the mistake over and over, resulting in performance anxiety
The character worrying what others think about them
Developing an irrational fear of failure, making a mistake, or being late
The character being plagued with self-doubt about their ability to contribute meaningfully
Wishing they could do better but knowing the pressure placed on them means they are destined to keep failing

NEGATIVE TRAITS THAT MAY WORSEN THE SITUATION: Childish, Cocky, Dishonest, Disloyal, Forgetful, Inflexible, Insecure, Irresponsible, Macho, Nervous, Obsessive, Oversensitive, Paranoid, Perfectionist, Superstitious, Worrywart

IMPACT ON BASIC NEEDS
   Self-Actualization: If the character continually drops the ball, he might question his ability to prioritize and do what must be done. The fear of failure might cause him to settle rather than try for what he really wants in life.
   Esteem and Recognition: The character may struggle to forgive himself for letting others down. Being unable to let go of the mistake will lower his sense of self-worth, especially if he believes others would have handled the situation better than he did.
   Love and Belonging: In relationships, failing to show up and be present can only be tolerated for so long. If it continues to happen, eventually the character will face a difficult choice: to set other things aside and focus on the relationship or leave it all together.

POSITIVE TRAITS TO HELP THE CHARACTER COPE: Adaptable, Adventurous, Ambitious, Confident, Courteous, Diplomatic, Disciplined, Easygoing, Meticulous, Persistent, Proactive, Responsible

POSITIVE OUTCOMES
The event creating a chance for the character and their loved ones to air and resolve grievances
Becoming more reliable in the future
The character disappointing him or herself and being motivated to aim higher the next time
The character learning to let go of perfectionism and living a happier, more relaxed life
The character inventorying their aptitudes and finding activities or a career that better plays to their strengths
Shoring up areas of weakness so the same mistake isn't made down the road

FAILING AT SOMETHING

EXAMPLES
The character getting fired
Blowing an important business opportunity (failing to land a client or secure a partner, losing out on a promotion, doing or saying something that results in a demotion, etc.)
Having to file for bankruptcy
Having to file for divorce
Flunking out of school
Giving up on a venture before it has a chance to succeed, because it's risky, it's something the character has never done before, or it's more challenging than they expected
Losing an important race, contest, or competition
Failing at parenting (choosing not to be involved, being emotionally unavailable, always putting work first), resulting in estrangement or a broken relationship
Failing to overcome an addiction, unhealthy habit, or dysfunctional pattern of behavior
Failing to impress or win someone's favor (a baseball scout, a love interest, the in-laws, etc.)

MINOR COMPLICATIONS
Continuing to live in circumstances that are less than ideal
Living beneath one's true potential
A pattern of underachieving due to a fear of failure or change
Having to start over with a new job or goal
Fielding unwanted advice or commentary from friends and loved ones
People asking pointed questions, forcing the character to relive the failure
Enduring *I told you so* conversations with know-it-all family members, friends, or co-workers
Being gossiped about and pitied by others

POTENTIALLY DISASTROUS RESULTS
A drastic change in lifestyle due to a new financial situation
Losing the opportunity to make up for the past, right a wrong, or gain closure
The character's failure being made public
The failure triggering an addiction, negative thought pattern, or unhealthy response
Having to move or relocate (to find a new job, move into a cheaper home, etc.)
Giving up on a dream because it now seems out of reach
Being isolated, cast out, or estranged from loved ones
Overcompensating for perceived shortcomings (the character overspending and going into debt, overcommitting, agreeing to do things that are beyond their skills or knowledge, etc.)
Avoiding the pain of failure by rushing into a new opportunity
Pursuing risky or foolhardy ways to prove oneself after the failure
A loss of self-worth prompting the character to push people away
Becoming reactive, picking fights, and letting a *nothing to lose* attitude further damage the character's reputation and relationships

RESULTING EMOTIONS: Anguish, Denial, Devastation, Disappointment, Emasculation, Guilt, Humiliation, Inadequacy, Longing, Moodiness, Sadness, Self-Loathing, Self-Pity, Worthlessness

POSSIBLE INTERNAL STRUGGLES

Becoming obsessed with the failure; reliving it and being unable to let go or move on
Being consumed by one's failures; not being able to see one's strengths
Struggling with embarrassment despite knowing the failure wasn't one's fault
Feeling disappointed but resenting being put in the situation in the first place
The character knowing they did everything they could but still believing they deserve to be punished for their lack of success
Developing a martyr complex
Becoming paralyzed by indecision or fear of failure
Being secretly relieved by the failure (because it was a parent's dream rather than the character's or the pressure was too much) and shame at having disappointed others
Being torn between letting go and trying again

NEGATIVE TRAITS THAT MAY WORSEN THE SITUATION: Addictive, Controlling, Defensive, Impulsive, Insecure, Irresponsible, Reckless, Resentful, Self-Destructive, Vindictive

IMPACT ON BASIC NEEDS

Self-Actualization: If the consequences from the failure keep the character from being able to do more and reach higher, they may begin to feel as if they're stagnating rather than thriving.

Esteem and Recognition: Failures are personal, meaning they usually are tied to self-worth. If your character's failure comes with dire consequences (especially to a loved one or an innocent person), their self-worth might plummet to the point where it will require a lot of internal work for them to see their own value again.

Love and Belonging: If a character becomes afraid to connect because of a past relationship failure, they will miss opportunities to build rewarding friendships. And if they develop romantic feelings and are unable to act on them, this could lead to the pain of unrequited love.

POSITIVE TRAITS TO HELP THE CHARACTER COPE: Adaptable, Ambitious, Centered, Industrious, Mature, Objective, Perceptive, Persistent, Philosophical, Professional,

POSITIVE OUTCOMES

Learning from one's mistakes so they aren't repeated
Being able to see oneself realistically and accurately for the first time
Discovering inner strength while dealing with the repercussions or fallout
Channeling the experience into a teaching or coaching opportunity to help others
The character deciding to pursue their own wants and desires instead of catering to the unfair demands of others
Taking advantage of new opportunities that wouldn't have been possible without the failure, such as starting a new business, changing careers, or enjoying time on one's own instead of jumping into a new relationship

GETTING CAUGHT DOING SOMETHING WRONG

NOTES: There are many ways a character's mistakes can catch up with them. We've covered as many examples as possible here, but you can find information on more specific "getting caught" scenarios in the DOING SOMETHING STUPID WHILE IMPAIRED, A PRANK GOING WRONG, and ONE'S INFIDELITY BEING DISCOVERED entries.

EXAMPLES
The character getting audited for not paying their taxes
An employee being caught stealing from the cash register or giving product to friends
A neighbor discovering the character piggybacking on their utilities—splitting cable, using their Wi-Fi, or running appliances from the neighbor's power outlets
A co-worker being exposed for taking credit for someone else's good work
A student being caught with cheat notes for a test
Screenshots of the character's threatening or bullying text messages going public
A teenager getting caught sneaking out after curfew, skipping class, or being caught with drugs
Being charged for illegally downloading copyrighted music, books, or movies from the internet
Being pulled over for a traffic violation, such as speeding or running a red light
Someone in a position of authority being exposed for taking bribes
Being overheard saying unflattering things about a friend
A volunteer at a charity taking funds or goods that were intended for the needy
Getting caught in a lie
Setting someone up and getting caught
Being convicted of committing a crime

MINOR COMPLICATIONS
The character losing the respect of friends, family, or co-workers because of their transgression
The student being suspended due to their cheating
Having to pay for a lawyer
Time being spent attending court, hearings, or required disciplinary classes
Having to apologize to someone who was wronged
The character losing their driver's license and having to walk or take the bus everywhere
A loss of freedom—being grounded, surveilled, or unable to leave home because of reporters or protesters, for example
Living with increased scrutiny due to a loss of trust

POTENTIALLY DISASTROUS RESULTS
The character being fired or banned from practicing their profession due to their actions
Having to spend time in jail because of criminal activity
Losing one's parental custody because of illegal activities
A friend who was wronged wanting nothing to do with the character
Struggling financially because of reparations that need to be made

A nonprofit losing donations or having their charity status revoked due to the character's dishonesty

An employer losing business because of the character's unethical behavior

Trust being broken and other people distancing themselves because of a belief that the character's disappointing or unethical behavior is ongoing

The character making excuses for their behavior, ensuring more infractions will follow

Increased scrutiny that leads to more damaging wrongs being uncovered

RESULTING EMOTIONS: Anger, Anguish, Anxiety, Appalled, Apprehension, Betrayed, Bitterness, Certainty, Conflicted, Defensiveness, Denial, Desperation, Devastation, Dread, Fear, Frustration, Guilt, Humiliation, Nervousness, Panic, Powerlessness, Regret, Relief, Self-Pity

POSSIBLE INTERNAL STRUGGLES

Wanting to make amends for the wrongdoing but being too proud to apologize

The character believing they can't be a better person or make better choices

Resisting change because the character believes the rules are unreasonable

The character believing their circumstances warrant the behavior

Living with an undiagnosed or untreated mental health condition

NEGATIVE TRAITS THAT MAY WORSEN THE SITUATION: Apathetic, Childish, Compulsive, Confrontational, Cynical, Disloyal, Rebellious, Spoiled, Vindictive

IMPACT ON BASIC NEEDS

   Self-Actualization: If the character's actions result in a criminal record, it may limit their ability to pursue certain careers or paths in life that may have been fulfilling.

   Esteem and Recognition: Characters who know they've done wrong but continue in the misbehavior may come to loathe themselves for not making better choices.

   Love and Belonging: A character whose loved ones disapprove of their behavior may have to face the consequences alone, without the support system they desperately need.

   Safety and Security: Children being removed from the character's custody and placed in foster care, losing a job, going to jail … there are many ways the consequences for getting caught in wrongdoing can threaten the character's safety and that of their loved ones.

POSITIVE TRAITS TO HELP THE CHARACTER COPE: Alert, Ambitious, Appreciative, Cautious, Charming, Cooperative, Decisive, Diplomatic, Disciplined, Empathetic, Honest, Imaginative, Independent, Innocent, Obedient, Persuasive, Responsible

POSITIVE OUTCOMES

The character's family rallying around them with love and support to get them on the right track

The character making amends for their actions by starting a charity for those they've wronged

Learning that actions have consequences and making a change before a bigger mistake is made

Gaining empathy through those victimized by the character's behavior

GETTING CAUGHT IN A LIE

NOTES: Though most people believe lying is wrong and strive to avoid it, no one is 100% honest all the time. One factor that will dictate the repercussions of getting caught telling a lie is the reason behind it. Below are some examples of why your character might choose to be less than straightforward.

EXAMPLES
To save someone's feelings
To protect someone (from harm, from others discovering their involvement, etc.)
To keep from getting into trouble
So the character can hide their true opinions or feelings
So the character can get what they want
To tell someone what they want to hear
So the character can project or maintain a certain image
To impress others
As a way to keep the peace
To sabotage, manipulate, or control others
Because the character is a pathological liar
Because they don't believe lying is wrong

MINOR COMPLICATIONS
Having to quickly de-escalate the situation (especially if it's not the time or place to explain)
The character needing to buy someone's silence by making a promise, offering a bribe, or agreeing to their terms
The character's honesty being questioned in the future
People being reluctant to broach certain topics with the character
Revealing a "tell" in the moment that others will remember (and watch for)
Being accused of manipulation

POTENTIALLY DISASTROUS RESULTS
The character's reputation being damaged
Loved ones (a spouse, children, friends) questioning the character's honesty
Being called out publicly
Being fired or demoted for a lie that reflects badly on the character's employer
Important relationships being damaged or lost
The character using leverage to ensure silence, thereby revealing their true nature
People losing faith in someone or something important (if the character was influential)
The character losing their standing, platform, or connections
A company or organization (and those associated with it) suffering because of one person's lie
A hurtful stereotype or bias being reinforced
Conflict arising from the character digging in their heels and refusing to admit to the lie
Trying to save face or reverse the narrative (by telling more lies, discrediting the accuser, etc.)
Lashing out in anger instead of taking responsibility

RESULTING EMOTIONS: Anger, Apprehension, Defensiveness, Defiance, Desperation, Embarrassment, Fear, Guilt, Humiliation, Insecurity, Panic, Regret, Self-Loathing, Shame, Stunned, Tormented, Unease, Vengefulness, Worry, Worthlessness

POSSIBLE INTERNAL STRUGGLES
Struggling with insecurity, guilt, shame, or self-loathing
Being unable to share the reason behind the lie because it would hurt someone
The character believing the lie was justified
Misremembering or being blind to the facts; believing the lie was the truth
The character doubting herself
Feeling guilty for keeping certain people in the dark, even for good reasons
Having a hollow reason for lying but being too embarrassed to admit to it

NEGATIVE TRAITS THAT MAY WORSEN THE SITUATION: Apathetic, Callous, Cocky, Confrontational, Defensive, Hostile, Macho, Martyr, Self-Destructive, Stubborn, Tactless

IMPACT ON BASIC NEEDS
    Self-Actualization: If the character's lie results in professional or personal limitations, it could lead to lifelong regret.
    Esteem and Recognition: Shame and guilt can have a devastating impact on the psyche. If the character's esteem plummets because of his misstep, he may experience unwanted personality changes, such as struggling with insecurity or becoming an underachiever.
    Love and Belonging: If the lie isn't the first one (or it's a big one) for the character, it could be the final straw that ends a friendship or romantic relationship.
    Safety and Security: Characters who lose something they can never regain may seek to punish themselves. Risky behaviors, addictions, and other dysfunctional coping mechanisms can damage their health.

POSITIVE TRAITS TO HELP THE CHARACTER COPE: Cooperative, Diplomatic, Discreet, Friendly, Honest, Humble, Innocent, Loyal, Obedient, Persuasive, Proper, Protective

POSITIVE OUTCOMES
Recognizing the importance of always telling the truth
Realizing a person's reputation can be easily destroyed and vowing to protect that
Eventually becoming grateful for being called out because it led to important revelation and growth
The incident inspiring a moral status check, leading to growth and change
The uncovering of the lie bringing an injustice to light

HAVING A ONE-NIGHT STAND
WITH A CO-WORKER

EXAMPLES
The character hooking up with their boss on a business trip
Sleeping with a co-worker after having too much to drink at an office party
Celebrating a company win over dinner and letting things go too far
Running into a co-worker in an unexpected setting (such as a concert, club, or rodeo) and getting together when they realize they have a lot in common
Using a co-worker as a rebound from a recently ended relationship

MINOR COMPLICATIONS
Awkward interactions with the other party at work
Having to let the co-worker down easy afterward
Having to work closely with the other party while acting like nothing happened
Needing to follow the company's dating policy and confess the liaison to Human Resources
The character feeling like they've been taken advantage of
One party having stronger feelings than the other and not agreeing about how to move forward
The co-worker blabbing details to the whole office about their experience with the character
The co-worker changing their behavior toward the character after the incident, such as avoiding being alone with them or giving them the silent treatment
The character changing their schedule to avoid having to work directly with the other person
The co-worker later being promoted into a position of authority over the character

POTENTIALLY DISASTROUS RESULTS
Becoming a target of harassment at work
Finding out the co-worker was married
Getting pregnant or contracting a serious STD
The co-worker filing a sexual harassment claim against the character
Finding out the co-worker photographed or recorded the encounter
The interlude happening at work and being caught on security cameras
Being reprimanded for a poor work performance (caused by the character continually fantasizing about their co-worker)
Unfairly being moved to another department or store location because the character's manager doesn't want to be reminded of his or her lapse in judgment
The character passing up good career opportunities to avoid interactions with the co-worker
The co-worker or boss' spouse discovering what happened

RESULTING EMOTIONS: Adoration, Amusement, Anticipation, Anxiety, Conflicted, Confusion, Connectedness, Contempt, Dissatisfaction, Dread, Eagerness, Elation, Embarrassment, Excitement, Guilt, Hopefulness, Hurt, Indifference, Insecurity, Longing, Lust

POSSIBLE INTERNAL STRUGGLES

The character wanting to pursue a longer-term relationship with their co-worker but worrying about things ending badly, both professionally and personally

Experiencing temptation to get together with the co-worker again

Withholding legitimate criticism of the co-worker's job performance for fear of insulting them

Playing favorites by supporting the co-worker's ideas or praising their work

Becoming paranoid that the whole office knows about the indiscretion

The character receiving a promotion and wondering if it was earned or only granted because they slept with the boss

Regretting the one-night stand and wishing it had never happened

NEGATIVE TRAITS THAT MAY WORSEN THE SITUATION: Catty, Controlling, Gossipy, Gullible, Insecure, Jealous, Manipulative, Needy, Obsessive, Possessive, Pushy, Reckless, Self-Destructive, Sleazy, Suspicious, Vindictive

IMPACT ON BASIC NEEDS

Esteem and Recognition: If the one-night stand becomes public knowledge at the office, the character may become embarrassed and worry about what his colleagues think. If he slept with someone higher up the chain of command, co-workers might think he used sex to try and further his career, causing him scorn.

Love and Belonging: A character harboring unrequited feelings may struggle even more if the co-worker pulls away emotionally and the original friendship is lost.

Safety and Security: Personal interactions at work can have career blowback if the character's reputation is damaged, his opportunities are limited, or he's moved to an unwanted position to avoid a superior's discomfort. Any of these can have financial impacts if the character's work hours are cut or he is denied advancement because of the affair.

POSITIVE TRAITS TO HELP THE CHARACTER COPE: Adventurous, Affectionate, Ambitious, Bold, Centered, Discreet, Mature, Private, Professional, Protective, Spontaneous

POSITIVE OUTCOMES

Developing real feelings and pursuing a fulfilling romantic relationship with the co-worker

Gaining self-confidence from the encounter and becoming more assertive at work

The union producing a child that brings fulfillment to the character's life

Dissatisfaction with the experience informing the character of what they want and don't want, helping them to move toward fulfillment in the future

Deciding to find employment elsewhere and finding a better fit with more opportunities for advancement

Awakening to the need to create boundaries, which leads to a better work-life balance

HAVING POOR JUDGMENT

NOTES: Mistakes are mistakes because they're not intentional; many times they're the result of a character being shortsighted or not thinking things through, generating minor or moderate consequences. This entry explores these kinds of conflict scenarios. For ones that are more serious, possibly resulting in injury or death, see UNDERESTIMATING DANGER.

EXAMPLES
The character giving in to peer pressure and doing something thoughtless or destructive
Continuing to get involved romantically with the same kind of person who has hurt the character in the past
Choosing a college or moving across the country just to be near a love interest
Posting something on social media that harms the character's reputation
Getting a tattoo with a love interest's name early in the relationship
Sleeping with someone the character shouldn't
Getting drunk before an important event (a placement exam, an interview, a meeting with future in-laws, a championship game, etc.)
Making decisions in the moment; not thinking of the future or planning ahead
Cheating on an exam
Sharing sensitive information (account passwords, a credit card, etc.) with others
Participating in a foolish prank that goes terribly wrong
Responding to confrontation in a way that makes the character feel better initially but does more harm in the long run
Providing an alibi for a friend without thinking about possible blowback

MINOR COMPLICATIONS
Being taken advantage of
Losing money or possessions
The character offending others with their behavior or speech
Spending time or money to make retribution
Having to break off relationships with poor influences in the character's life
The character's reputation being damaged
Becoming the butt of a joke for doing something stupid
Increased rules or unwanted scrutiny by those in authority (an earlier curfew, probation, etc.)

POTENTIALLY DISASTROUS RESULTS
Being aligned with someone who is destructive, toxic, or a bad influence
Personal financial information or an incriminating secret being shared publicly
Losing the respect of family and friends
The character being unable or unwilling to see that their judgment was poor, resulting in them continuing to make similar mistakes
Other people no longer trusting the character to make responsible choices
Being sued
Serious injury or death, for the character or someone else

Having to serve jail time

Losing out on a promising opportunity because the character is seen as irresponsible, unreliable, or immature

Having one's fate tied to another person's—being charged as an accessory for providing an alibi or holding onto a package, for example

RESULTING EMOTIONS: Anger, Annoyance, Anxiety, Confusion, Defensiveness, Defiance, Despair, Devastation, Disbelief, Discouragement, Disillusionment, Embarrassment, Fear, Frustration, Guilt, Humbled, Regret, Remorse, Resignation, Self-Pity, Shame, Vulnerability

POSSIBLE INTERNAL STRUGGLES

The character struggling with self-blame, believing they deserve what happened

The character wanting to make better decisions but also wanting the freedom and instant gratification that comes from acting on impulse

Difficulty seeing how their actions were inappropriate or exhibited poor judgment

Being overwhelmed with shame or regret

Wanting to provide reparations for those affected but being too embarrassed to do so

Developing emotional wounds because the character trusted the wrong person or was taken advantage of by a friend

NEGATIVE TRAITS THAT MAY WORSEN THE SITUATION: Addictive, Apathetic, Callous, Compulsive, Defensive, Foolish, Frivolous, Gullible, Ignorant, Impulsive, Irresponsible, Mischievous, Perfectionist, Prejudiced, Reckless, Self-Indulgent, Weak-Willed

IMPACT ON BASIC NEEDS

Self-Actualization: If poor judgment becomes a pattern for the character, it may cost them opportunities for self-actualization, such as being asked to lead a sporting team or chair a nonprofit organization.

Esteem and Recognition: Poor choices can often lead others to look down on the character and think less of them, leading to a lower level of self-worth.

Love and Belonging: If a character's actions alienate people around them, they may pull away, excluding the character from groups, events, and social gatherings.

Safety and Security: Characters who don't think things through often fail to spot danger until it's too late.

POSITIVE TRAITS TO HELP THE CHARACTER COPE: Appreciative, Cautious, Disciplined, Focused, Inspirational, Mature, Obedient, Philosophical, Proper, Sensible, Studious

POSITIVE OUTCOMES

The character channeling their spontaneity and impulsivity into harmless pursuits

Learning from mistakes and making better decisions the next time around

Feeling gratitude that a bad situation didn't turn out worse

Realizing everyone makes mistakes and those mistakes shouldn't define a person

Being given a second chance and becoming more inclined to do the same for others

LOSING A BET

NOTES: People make bets all the time. Sometimes the wagers are friendly and other times … not so much. Typically, the bigger the bet, the higher the stakes—meaning, the loss will be more painful to bear.

EXAMPLES
The character being forced to do something humiliating that damages their reputation
A loss that requires the character to cater to or serve the victor
Having to do something mildly embarrassing, such as hitting on a stranger, singing in public, shaving one's head, having to wear a rival's sports jersey, or getting a tattoo
Being forced to support a competitor's goals, ambitions, or ideas
Agreeing to step aside or step down (in a competition, a relationship, etc.)
Having to forfeit something valuable, such as a car, a specialized piece of equipment, or an agreed-upon amount of money
Publicly having to admit to being wrong, apologize to an enemy, or beg for forgiveness
Having to take on an extra responsibility that requires time, costs money, or causes a hardship
Having to do something dangerous, such as participating in a risky social media challenge
Consenting to not get involved when something important is at stake
Having to share sensitive information that gives the winner an unfair advantage
Agreeing to leave (a job, a town, a group, etc.), giving up one's ties and connections

MINOR COMPLICATIONS
Being teased or becoming the butt of a joke
Losing esteem in the eyes of others
Missing out on an opportunity
Having to change plans, suffer a painful delay, or sacrifice something of importance
Having to ask for help to fix things, which increases the character's embarrassment
Dealing with critics who delight in the "I told you so" refrain (schadenfreude)

POTENTIALLY DISASTROUS RESULTS
Having one's humiliations filmed and uploaded to social media
Breaking the law to fulfill a punishment and being caught and charged
Someone being hurt as a result of the bet
A friendship being ruined in the process
The character having to betray someone or cross a moral line to keep their end of the bargain
Losing a job or a position when details of the bet are discovered by those in power
The character being forced to abandon a goal they care about
Being blackmailed by someone with inside information about the bet
The failure triggering a past wound which causes the character to devolve (falling back into an addiction, become caught in negative self-talk that ruins hard-won self-esteem, etc.)

RESULTING EMOTIONS: Anger, Apprehension, Bitterness, Defeat, Defensiveness, Defiance, Devastation, Disappointment, Disbelief, Dread, Emasculation, Embarrassment, Humiliation

POSSIBLE INTERNAL STRUGGLES

Berating oneself for making the bet in the first place

Moral struggles (if winning the bet requires the character to sacrifice their beliefs)

Second-guessing the choices that led to getting involved in the bet (hindsight being 20/20)

Weighing pride and honor against the harm the character will do if they follow through

Suspecting the other person cheated or manipulated the result but being unable to prove it

Anguish at knowing one's supporters will suffer to some degree and wanting to protect them

NEGATIVE TRAITS THAT MAY WORSEN THE SITUATION: Abrasive, Confrontational, Cowardly, Flaky, Foolish, Hostile, Impulsive, Irrational, Jealous, Melodramatic

IMPACT ON BASIC NEEDS

Self-Actualization: People in a heightened emotional state don't often think through the long-term consequences of their actions. If a character is forced to sacrifice something meaningful because they lost a bet, they may find themselves living a half-life, unable to be who they really want to be or do what they really want to do.

Esteem and Recognition: If a consequence for losing is humiliating, the character may become diminished in other people's eyes. Lost opportunities, a lack of support, professional distancing, and other fallout can lower the character's feelings of self-worth, as well.

Safety and Security: While some bets and their consequences are harmless, others are not. Those with an element of danger can threaten the character's safety.

Physiological Needs: It's all good fun until something goes too far. It's not unheard of for people to be killed acting out the foolish consequence of a lost bet.

POSITIVE TRAITS TO HELP THE CHARACTER COPE: Adventurous, Cautious, Discreet, Extroverted, Funny, Imaginative, Persuasive, Quirky, Resourceful, Uninhibited, Witty

POSITIVE OUTCOMES

Gaining a better appreciation for thinking before reacting

Becoming more astute to manipulation in the future

The character recognizing the fragility of their ego; resolving to understand why that is and how to change it

A loss prompting an epiphany where the character vows to not pressure others into taking stupid bets in the future

Using the fine art of interpretation to fulfill the bet in a way that costs the character very little

Uncovering proof of manipulation, thereby robbing the opponent of their ill-gotten victory

Recognizing not all bets are fair and those with dangerous or extravagant consequences shouldn't be honored

LOSING A PHONE

EXAMPLES
The character's phone being dropped and broken
Leaving the phone somewhere and not knowing where it is
The phone being stolen
A teenager's phone being confiscated as a consequence
Being without a phone while it's being repaired
Running out of battery and having no charger
A lack of signal, rendering most functions useless

MINOR COMPLICATIONS
The character being bored (while standing in line, as a passenger in a vehicle, etc.)
Being away from home and not being able to stay connected with loved ones
Losing the SIM card and having to start from scratch with a new phone (asking for phone numbers and addresses, resetting preferences, etc.)
Not having immediate access to emails, voicemail, and texts
Getting lost without the phone's GPS
Missing an appointment because of not having access to the calendar
The character being accused of ghosting when they don't respond to texts
Missing out on impromptu get-togethers that are set up via text message
Losing meaningful pictures that had not been backed up
Going without a phone because one can't afford the repair costs
Discomfort and anxiety arising from not having the phone

POTENTIALLY DISASTROUS RESULTS
The phone being stolen and the character's sensitive information being accessed
The thief using credit card information to make unwanted purchases
A stolen phone being connected to a crime
A loved one needing desperately to get in touch
The character experiencing an emergency (being carjacked, running out of gas in a deserted area, needing to call an ambulance, etc.)
Missing a vital work meeting
Having an occupation where missed calls have great impact—e.g., a lawyer missing a call from a friend who has been arrested and has used their one call to get help
Losing business opportunities because of not being able to receive and respond to emails quickly
Being stalked by the thief, who uses the character's calendar to track their location
A thief discovering inappropriate images on the phone and blackmailing the character
Suffering from a disorder that makes the loss much more difficult (anxiety, OCD, etc.)
Being in a situation where access to a phone would be lifesaving (being kidnapped, a child being in trouble with no way to contact their parent, etc.)

RESULTING EMOTIONS: Agitation, Anger, Annoyance, Anxiety, Disappointment, Embarrassment, Frustration, Impatience, Inadequacy, Panic, Unease, Worry

POSSIBLE INTERNAL STRUGGLES
Feeling stupid about having lost or misplaced the phone
Worrying a stolen phone could put loved ones at risk (due to the information that was on it)
Being afraid to tell others (a parent, a spouse) the phone is missing
Worrying about personal information (one's address, banking info, etc.) being compromised
Being terrified a friend has found the phone and will read through disparaging text messages about them

NEGATIVE TRAITS THAT MAY WORSEN THE SITUATION: Addictive, Compulsive, Controlling, Disorganized, Melodramatic, Needy, Perfectionist, Temperamental, Worrywart

IMPACT ON BASIC NEEDS
Esteem and Recognition: A character who already suffers from insecurity may blame themselves unnecessarily for losing a phone, believing it to be proof they are scatterbrained, irresponsible, or incapable.

Safety and Security: Phones provide legitimate security in many situations, so losing that resource can put the character's safety at risk.

Physiological Needs: There are situations where not having a phone can mean the difference between life and death: if the character becomes lost on a hiking trip and needs help, their car goes off the road in a snowstorm, or something happens to their sailboat while at sea, for instance.

POSITIVE TRAITS TO HELP THE CHARACTER COPE: Appreciative, Calm, Centered, Easygoing, Friendly, Imaginative, Independent, Nature-Focused, Simple, Tolerant, Whimsical

POSITIVE OUTCOMES
Learning to be present with others (rather than being glued to the phone)
Forging stronger face-to-face connections with other people
Being more efficient because less time is wasted on the phone
The character recognizing how much time they lose to social media and vowing to exercise restraint in the future
Recognizing the value in delayed gratification (not needing to see and respond immediately to everything that happens)
Learning to be more responsible
The character appreciating the luxuries and "extras" a phone affords them
Adopting a new perspective on what's important and necessary in life
The character seeing an improved mindset from their time away from the news and social media and determining to set healthier limits in this area

MAKING A BAD INVESTMENT

EXAMPLES

The character buying a rental property that ends up being a money pit, needing a ton of repairs

Lending money to a family member to start a business that doesn't get off the ground

Buying a painting, signed memorabilia, or a rare collector's item that turns out to be fake

Buying a used car that requires ongoing repairs

The character investing significant savings into a stock, product, or business and it crashing

Making a substantial financial investment without understanding the tax ramifications

Making an investment based on insufficient knowledge or experience

Starting a business and hiring a manager who robs the character blind

Going into business with a crooked partner

Making a bet that's supposed to be a sure thing and losing big

MINOR COMPLICATIONS

Losing money that will have to be re-earned

The character having to explain a financial loss to their spouse

Friction with the family member who owes the character money

Having to find a second job to get the money back quickly

Being stuck with unwanted goods the character can't resell

Having to make changes to save money, such as bringing lunch to work, giving up a gym membership, or walking instead of taking a cab

A strained relationship with the friend the character went into business with

The character lying to friends or family about the investment

The character blaming others for their misfortune

Having to put time and energy into reducing the fallout (stepping in to save a failing business, rebuilding trust with people caught in the crossfire, seeking advice on what to do, etc.)

Harboring anger toward the person who gave them the advice or pulled them into the investment

Having to take legal action against someone who has broken the law

POTENTIALLY DISASTROUS RESULTS

The character losing their life savings

A bad business deal causing a rift between family members or friends

Being obsessed with making the next big deal to make up for the bad investment

The character cutting corners when repairing a car or property and creating a safety hazard

The character turning to illegal activity, such as selling drugs or fencing stolen property, to earn back what they lost

The character violently confronting the person who wronged them

The character trying to save their investment and losing even more money

Having to file for bankruptcy

Having to move to a smaller home or less desirable neighborhood

RESULTING EMOTIONS: Anger, Anguish, Anxiety, Appalled, Apprehension, Betrayed, Bitterness, Defeat, Denial, Desperation, Determination, Devastation, Disappointment, Disbelief, Guilt, Hatred, Humiliation, Inadequacy, Overwhelmed, Panic, Rage, Remorse, Self-Pity, Shame

POSSIBLE INTERNAL STRUGGLES

The character facing a moral dilemma: report purchased goods as fakes or try to pass them off as genuine in a quick sale?
Resentment over a bad investment consuming the character, making everyday life difficult
Trying to reject thoughts of revenge, knowing it won't undo the financial loss
The character seeing themselves as a loser who can't be trusted to make sound decisions
Struggling with disappointment, depression, or feelings of failure

NEGATIVE TRAITS THAT MAY WORSEN THE SITUATION: Controlling, Cynical, Dishonest, Extravagant, Foolish, Greedy, Gullible, Ignorant, Impulsive, Know-It-All, Materialistic, Obsessive, Reckless, Self-Indulgent, Unethical

IMPACT ON BASIC NEEDS

Self-Actualization: A character facing a significant financial setback may end up with limited resources for pursuing the things that will make them truly happy. Alternatively, a character who wants to thrive in the business world might be too afraid of failure to try again.

Esteem and Recognition: A character who was swindled may view themselves as gullible, and their resulting self-doubt could make it hard for them to make big decisions moving forward.

Love and Belonging: When money and family mix, things can turn sour quickly. A cousin's investment tip that turns out to be worthless, an in-law's promise to double the character's money, or putting too much trust in a sibling's ability to manage retirement funds can all lead to regret and broken relationships.

Safety and Security: If a bad investment leaves the character bankrupt, they may lose their home or struggle to pay for basic necessities.

POSITIVE TRAITS TO HELP THE CHARACTER COPE: Adaptable, Analytical, Bold, Creative, Disciplined, Honest, Industrious, Intelligent, Patient, Resourceful, Studious, Wise

POSITIVE OUTCOMES

Realizing "get rich quick" schemes are red flags and avoiding them in the future
Persevering with a failing business and learning the skills needed to make it thrive
The character getting back on their feet thanks to a loved one's financial help and them wanting to pay it forward for someone else
The character seeking education to become a savvier investor in the future
Bringing a corrupt business partner to justice so they can't swindle or hurt anyone else

MAKING A CRUCIAL MISTAKE AT WORK

NOTES: So much time is spent at work; it makes sense that this environment is packed with opportunities for conflict. This entry explores the various ways a character might screw up professionally. For ideas on more general conflict scenarios due to a character's thoughtlessness or lapse in common sense, see HAVING POOR JUDGMENT.

EXAMPLES
The character being unprepared for an important interview or meeting
Misreading the room and saying something at a staff party that the character later regrets
Drafting a private email and accidentally hitting "Reply to All"
Missing the signs of a minor problem and it turning into a serious situation
Sending inappropriate photos to co-workers or fellow students
Sharing personal information that becomes fodder for the rumor mill
Leaving a job without having another plan in place
Hiring someone who robs the company or damages its reputation
Overestimating the company's growth and approving expenditures the business couldn't afford
Partnering with the wrong person
Getting romantically involved with a boss or employee
Not researching a vendor's reputation before engaging them on behalf of the company
The facility being robbed because the character forgot to set the alarm system
Behaving unethically or criminally
Taking a bribe to look the other way
The character overestimating their skills and committing to a project they can't complete
Getting caught sabotaging a rival within the company
The character stealing someone's idea and passing it off as their own

MINOR COMPLICATIONS
Having to take ownership of the mistake
Being removed from a prized or promising project
Having to extract oneself from an unhealthy relationship
Becoming the subject of office gossip
Being asked to step down from a committee for public relations purposes
Having to work with people the character has wronged
Putting in extra hours to make the situation right
Having to follow a new protocol or have certain decisions reviewed
The character having to tell loved ones about what they've done

POTENTIALLY DISASTROUS RESULTS
Losing one's job
The character's professional reputation being destroyed
The mistake leading to an injury or death
Incurring a financial loss that devastates the company
Facing a lawsuit or criminal charges

Being so humiliated that the character must leave the job and find another one
Participating in illegal activity and being blackmailed by someone who knows about it

RESULTING EMOTIONS: Anger, Anguish, Anxiety, Apprehension, Betrayed, Desperation, Determination, Disbelief, Dread, Embarrassment, Fear, Guilt, Humiliation, Panic, Regret, Remorse, Resentment, Self-Pity, Shame, Unappreciated, Wariness, Wistfulness, Worry, Worthlessness

POSSIBLE INTERNAL STRUGGLES
The character questioning their ability to make good decisions
Knowing a boss or administrator was responsible but being unable to speak up because of the confidential nature of the business
Reliving the mistake and imagining the character had made different choices
Being tempted to place blame elsewhere
Falling into depression
Feeling indebted to those impacted by one's mistake
Deliberating whether or not to quit and start over somewhere else
The burden of guilt being so overwhelming (because people were harmed or killed) the character begins entertaining suicidal thoughts

NEGATIVE TRAITS THAT MAY WORSEN THE SITUATION: Childish, Cocky, Defensive, Dishonest, Haughty, Hypocritical, Indecisive, Insecure, Irresponsible, Reckless, Resentful, Scatterbrained, Selfish, Sleazy, Unethical, Workaholic

IMPACT ON BASIC NEEDS
Self-Actualization: Making a crucial mistake at work can make a character feel paralyzed about life's big decisions. If they stay in their comfort zone, fear will prevent them from taking risks that could lead to achieving personal goals that bring them joy and fulfillment.
Esteem and Recognition: Shame, guilt, and other negative emotions may affect the way the character views herself.
Love and Belonging: A character who is ostracized at work because of their actions may lose their place in the group and their sense of connection with others.
Safety and Security: If the character's finances are depleted, they may have trouble paying the bills or keeping their home.

POSITIVE TRAITS TO HELP THE CHARACTER COPE: Ambitious, Analytical, Appreciative, Confident, Cooperative, Diplomatic, Disciplined, Focused, Honorable, Industrious, Persistent, Persuasive, Proactive, Professional, Resourceful, Responsible, Sensible, Talented

POSITIVE OUTCOMES
Learning to be better prepared or more cautious
The character recognizing their professional weaknesses (not being the best judge of character, not being great with numbers, lacking vision, etc.) and seeking to grow in these areas
The character hiring a mentor or coach to help them make better decisions at work
Drawing the admiration of peers for taking responsibility and making things right

SENDING A PRIVATE MESSAGE TO THE WRONG PERSON

EXAMPLES
The character sending a text or email to the wrong person
Accidentally hitting "reply all" to a work email
Replying to an email instead of forwarding the response to someone else
Responding to a group text instead of an individual recipient
Accidentally posting a private message to a public forum, discussion board, or social media page

MINOR COMPLICATIONS
Embarrassment over having made a stupid and public mistake
Feeling out the recipient to see if they're willing to delete the message and keep quiet about the contents
Relationship friction (if the message contained insulting or controversial material)
Time wasted having to do damage control
Distance created between the character and person being discussed when the latter realizes they were meant to be excluded from the conversation
Decreased productivity due to distraction and worry
A competitive co-worker learning of the character's plans or ideas and capitalizing on them
The character's capability and trustworthiness being questioned
Losing sleep and experiencing heightened stress over the situation
Conflict with the recipient, who is frustrated they've been involved in the situation

POTENTIALLY DISASTROUS RESULTS
Being fired for using work email for inappropriate purposes (sexting, propositioning a co-worker, harassing them, etc.)
Getting fired because the contents of the message resulted in lost revenue, lost clients, or public blowback for the company
Being arrested or sued (if the contents suggested illegal activity by the character)
A personal secret being shared widely rather than only with a trusted confidant
A relationship ending because of what was said in the message
A screen capture of the email being shared on social media, creating further damage
Being blackmailed by the recipient in exchange for their silence
Retaliation from the person who was maligned in the email (leaking personal information about the character, sabotaging their standing with a group, etc.)
Developing serious health problems, such as hypertension, an ulcer, or depression
Complaints arising about the content that was shared, such as people claiming they have been harassed or made uncomfortable by the character's jokes or actions
The content being taken out of context and blown out of proportion by a rival or ex looking to damage the character's reputation

RESULTING EMOTIONS: Anxiety, Disbelief, Dread, Embarrassment, Fear, Guilt, Humiliation, Insecurity, Nervousness, Paranoia, Regret, Self-Pity, Shame, Shock, Worry

POSSIBLE INTERNAL STRUGGLES

Shame over what the message revealed (prejudice on the character's part, a flaw such as cruelty or pettiness, etc.)
Feeling insecure around the involved parties
Worrying over possible long-term effects from what happened
Wanting to hide rather than confront or face those involved
Being tempted to lie about the circumstances to minimize the damage
Guilt over trouble the event has caused for loved ones or co-workers

NEGATIVE TRAITS THAT MAY WORSEN THE SITUATION: Catty, Cocky, Defensive, Melodramatic, Paranoid

IMPACT ON BASIC NEEDS

Self-Actualization: If the ramifications for the mistake are far-reaching enough to limit the character's ability to further a dream, they may begin to lose hope that the future will ever contain the fulfillment they're aiming for.

Esteem and Recognition: This is one of those mistakes that can make a person feel really stupid. In the aftermath, they will become their own biggest critic. It may take a significant amount of time to regain their self-esteem enough to trust their own judgment again.

Love and Belonging: This need could be threatened if the contents of the message are damaging enough to hurt a primary relationship (revealing infidelity, an indiscretion, secrets being kept from a spouse, etc.).

Safety and Security: If the contents of the message threaten or damage the interests of a powerful person, they may seek retribution against the character.

POSITIVE TRAITS TO HELP THE CHARACTER COPE: Charming, Generous, Persuasive, Proactive, Responsible, Unselfish

POSITIVE OUTCOMES

Learning to be more careful in the future about written communication
Seeing a blind spot in one's character (a flaw or ideology) and determining to change it
Recognizing gossip is hurtful and divisive and resolving to stop doing it
A necessary conversation being started that the character otherwise wouldn't have initiated
The object of the discussion hearing an important truth that would never have been purposely shared

TAKING ADVICE FROM THE WRONG PERSON

EXAMPLES
A character seeking advice from someone who is secretly working against them
Listening to someone whose top priority is themselves
Taking advice from someone with good intentions who doesn't know what they're talking about
Listening to a "yes" person who only tells the character what they want to hear
Asking for advice on social media instead of doing one's own research
Listening to an expert whose opinions are out of date (they've been out of the industry for a long time, they aren't current on their area of expertise, they believe the "old ways" are best, etc.)
The character following the first advice they hear because they're out of time and must make a decision quickly

MINOR COMPLICATIONS
Embarrassment at one's information being corrected by others
Having to re-check data and start the research process all over again
Relationship friction between the character and the advice-giver
Losing credibility in the eyes of others
The nature of the advice making the character complacent when time is of the essence
Having to apologize for the mistake
The misinformation causing embarrassment for co-workers, a spouse, one's child, etc.
The character being doubly embarrassed because they passed off the "expert advice" as their own Looking bad in front of one's worst critics (a rival professor, a father-in-law, etc.)

POTENTIALLY DISASTROUS RESULTS
Difficulty trusting others
Not being trusted in the future with important duties
Purposely not seeking the advice of others, which limits the character's knowledge
The misinformation causing the loss of an important ally or benefactor
The setback creating a ticking clock situation that makes the overall goal difficult to achieve
Someone being harmed or killed because the character acted on incorrect information
A rival swooping in to save the day with the correct information
Getting fired
The character becoming defensive and digging in their heels to support the bad advice
Losing a great deal of money on a bad investment
Unknowingly breaking the law or committing fraud
Hiring a friend of a friend and discovering they're stealing from the company, selling trade secrets, sabotaging the production line, etc.
Becoming obsessed with research and being overprepared with information
The advice leading to a big mistake with fallout that goes viral
Being reluctant to take advice from anyone; always having to be the expert on everything

RESULTING EMOTIONS: Anger, Confusion, Defensiveness, Denial, Embarrassment, Humbled, Humiliation, Hurt, Inadequacy, Resentment, Self-Pity, Skepticism, Surprise

POSSIBLE INTERNAL STRUGGLES

Doubting one's ability to read people and discern good advice from bad
The character worrying their gut instinct might be defective
Blaming oneself for trusting the wrong person or not being suspicious of the source
Being tempted to repay the humiliation in kind
Becoming paranoid about a possible setup
Conflicted feelings about the source (especially if the character values the relationship)

NEGATIVE TRAITS THAT MAY WORSEN THE SITUATION: Apathetic, Cocky, Defensive, Gullible, Insecure, Martyr, Melodramatic, Oversensitive, Perfectionist, Tactless, Volatile, Weak-Willed

IMPACT ON BASIC NEEDS

Self-Actualization: Taking bad life advice will likely cause problems for the character. Fulfillment won't be possible if they base major decisions on other people's input instead of investing time and energy into understanding their own preferences and desires.

Esteem and Recognition: It's very easy for a character who has trusted an untrustworthy person to feel gullible and easily led, generating crippling self-doubt in the process.

Safety and Security: If the character sacrifices common sense and solid research in favor of flimsy advice, they could overlook a danger that's right in front of them. This could end with them being hurt, being prosecuted for wrongdoing, or losing a great deal of money.

POSITIVE TRAITS TO HELP THE CHARACTER COPE: Diplomatic, Honest, Honorable, Innocent, Intelligent, Mature, Persuasive, Professional, Proper, Resourceful

POSITIVE OUTCOMES

Realizing the importance of doing one's own research
Being more careful about who one trusts in the future
Creating a checks-and-balances system by seeking out multiple people for advice
Being better able to spot inauthentic or unreliable people because of the experience
Being more inclined to trust one's gut (if the character didn't in this situation)
If the poor advice was deliberate, the character will gain insight about who can be trusted and who can't

UNDERESTIMATING DANGER

NOTES: This entry highlights conflict scenarios resulting from a character's misreading of a dangerous or life-threatening situation. For mistakes that aren't quite as serious, see HAVING POOR JUDGMENT.

EXAMPLES
The character accepting a ride from a stranger
Sustaining an injury because the character ignored danger signs while hiking, skiing, or boating
Venturing out to drive in unsafe conditions
Underestimating the number of drinks a friend has had and assuming they're fine to drive
Undergoing a risky elective surgical procedure that goes wrong
Deciding to ride out a hurricane or snowstorm that ends up being much more dangerous than anticipated
Opening the apartment building door to someone who claims to be visiting a neighbor but who actually has violent intentions
Meeting an online friend for the first time in a secluded place
Leaving one's children at home alone when they're not responsible or mature enough
The character believing they can manage their addiction
Attempting to break up a fistfight that becomes more dangerous when someone pulls a weapon
Jumping into a body of water without knowing its depth or what lies beneath the surface
Putting off critical medical care for oneself or a family member

MINOR COMPLICATIONS
Sustaining a minor injury, such as bruises or a broken arm
Getting a ticket or being fined
Having to go hungry because the character didn't stockpile enough resources to outlast a major weather event
Having to rely on strangers for assistance
A disruption in cell service making it difficult for the character to call for help
Initiating a lengthy legal battle against a medical practitioner
Getting into a minor car accident
Being stuck for a prolonged amount of time with people the character doesn't like
Having to be rescued by police, firefighters, or paramedics
Facing the danger alone, without any help

POTENTIALLY DISASTROUS RESULTS
The character suffering a serious injury that results in hospitalization or death
Someone dying in the character's care
Rescuers being injured while trying to save the character
The character being liable for other people's injuries
Losing a limb, one of the five senses, the ability to walk, etc.
The character putting her children in danger and losing custody of them
Paranoia about potential danger impacting the character's ability to enjoy life

RESULTING EMOTIONS: Anguish, Anxiety, Appalled, Defensiveness, Denial, Depressed, Despair, Desperation, Devastation, Dread, Fear, Grief, Guilt, Horror, Hysteria, Panic, Powerlessness, Rage, Regret, Remorse, Self-Loathing, Shame, Worthlessness

POSSIBLE INTERNAL STRUGGLES

Being overwhelmed with fear during the crisis but knowing it must be controlled to survive
Seeing others in danger but being tempted to only save oneself
Blaming oneself for underestimating the risk; not being able to let go
The character struggling in the aftermath with anger toward God

NEGATIVE TRAITS THAT MAY WORSEN THE SITUATION: Cocky, Controlling, Cowardly, Cynical, Dishonest, Disloyal, Flaky, Foolish, Ignorant, Impulsive, Inattentive, Indecisive, Inflexible, Irrational, Irresponsible, Know-It-All, Lazy, Oversensitive, Reckless

IMPACT ON BASIC NEEDS

Esteem and Recognition: Characters who blame themselves for underestimating a danger may believe their gut instinct is defective and think less of themselves.

Love and Belonging: Others may find it hard to forgive a character who endangered their loved one, creating strain within the relationship.

Safety and Security: Underestimating a threat could lead to injuries and financial hardship in the form of medical or legal bills.

Physiological Needs: If the character is unable to free himself or be saved from the dangerous situation, they could perish.

POSITIVE TRAITS TO HELP THE CHARACTER COPE: Adaptable, Adventurous, Alert, Analytical, Calm, Cautious, Courageous, Curious, Decisive, Disciplined, Efficient, Honest, Humble, Objective, Observant, Persistent, Proactive, Resourceful, Uninhibited, Unselfish

POSITIVE OUTCOMES

A romance blooming between the character and a rescuer who nurses them back to health
Developing better instincts for predicting danger in future
Educating others so they know what to do when they're facing the same danger
Gaining confidence from surviving the life-threatening ordeal
Becoming a more cautious and observant person, which helps them in a myriad of ways
The character learning to think about others and not only about him or herself
The character discovering new qualities or strengths they didn't know they had

UNKNOWINGLY SHARING INCORRECT INFORMATION

EXAMPLES
The character stating as fact information that turns out to be false
Quoting something online that is proven to be fake news
Misquoting statistics
Gathering and passing along information from disreputable sources
Sharing old information that has since been refuted
Passing along written numerical facts that contain a critical typo
The character guessing incorrectly when asked a question they should know the answer to
Stating an opinion as fact
Passing on instructions that are incorrect
Passing along information from a higher-up that turns out to be erroneous

MINOR COMPLICATIONS
Being laughed at
People bringing up the gaffe later, reawakening the embarrassment
Being corrected publicly
People no longer taking the character seriously
Being called out on social media for peddling fake news
Having to issue a retraction or apology for sharing the wrong information
Trying to explain how the mistake happened and having people assume the character is just making excuses or trying to avoid repercussions

POTENTIALLY DISASTROUS RESULTS
The character doubling down and arguing their erroneous point, refusing to see or admit the truth (especially if it aligns with a long-held political belief or bias)
The misinformation being used in decision making, resulting in far-reaching impacts for many people
Losing an important client
Someone's identity being exposed when anonymity was crucial
The character losing credibility at work and not being trusted with important projects anymore
Friends, business contacts, and acquaintances distancing themselves from the character online
Being labeled a conspiracy theorist or part of a fringe political group
A larger organization (a business, nonprofit organization, etc.) experiencing bad PR because they're associated with the character
Believing no source is unbiased and no information shared by others can be trusted
Becoming disillusioned when the person responsible for the misinformation doesn't step up and take responsibility

RESULTING EMOTIONS: Appalled, Confusion, Defensiveness, Denial, Disillusionment, Embarrassment, Flustered, Frustration, Guilt, Humiliation, Indignation, Insecurity,

Intimidation, Nervousness, Panic, Regret, Reluctance, Remorse, Uncertainty, Unease, Vulnerability, Worry

POSSIBLE INTERNAL STRUGGLES
Struggling with self-doubt and becoming consumed with what other people think
Hesitating to share information in the future for fear it will also be wrong
Becoming bitter toward people and how quickly they can turn on someone for making a mistake
Becoming soured on social media, which the character used to enjoy
Berating oneself for not double-checking facts before passing them on even though it wasn't one's job to do so
The character appreciating the supportive emails or direct messages they receive but wishing they were more public in nature, so others could see or hear them

NEGATIVE TRAITS THAT MAY WORSEN THE SITUATION: Confrontational, Controlling, Cynical, Defensive, Foolish, Hypocritical, Ignorant, Impulsive, Inflexible, Insecure, Irrational, Martyr, Melodramatic, Oversensitive, Perfectionist, Stubborn

IMPACT ON BASIC NEEDS
Esteem and Recognition: One of the biggest problems with this form of conflict is that it causes people to lose respect for the character. The character can then become resentful if the error was an honest mistake or if others who were responsible for the fact-checking somehow escape the same judgment.

Safety and Security: The character's safety may be threatened if the erroneous information hurts those who are vengeful or whose power is threatened.

POSITIVE TRAITS TO HELP THE CHARACTER COPE: Calm, Cooperative, Courteous, Honest, Just, Loyal, Patient, Patriotic, Persuasive, Professional, Responsible

POSITIVE OUTCOMES
Learning from the mistake and more thoroughly checking facts in the future
The character choosing not to weigh in on topics they're unfamiliar with
Recognizing opinions are not facts and don't always need to be shared
More carefully checking written memos for typos before sending them
Deciding to be grateful (rather than defensive or stubborn) when a mistake is pointed out
Using the situation to change a faulty process so a mistake like this doesn't happen again

Moral Dilemmas and Temptations

BEING GIVEN AN OPPORTUNITY TO CHEAT

EXAMPLES
The character being given a fake ID by a friend
An instructor offering a passing grade if the character does them a favor in return
A friend offering the character a copy of the exam to study
Being tempted to claim the credit for someone else's work
An athlete taking steroids to unfairly increase their advantage
A contest entrant being provided access to information the other contestants don't have
Receiving intel that a judge or city official will rule a certain way if they're financially incentivized
Receiving insider information that could be used to make an investment
A company or program offering to waive certain requirements because the character is connected
Having friends or family who have no issue with (or may even encourage) cheating to get ahead

MINOR COMPLICATIONS
Being a terrible liar and worrying about getting caught
Embarrassment over being caught
Having to hide (from parents or a spouse) where the bribery money is going
Friction with friends who find out about the cheating and don't like it
Watchful security guards, organizers, referees, or others tasked with upholding fairness for all
A rival suspecting the character might be cheating
Choosing not to cheat and having to accept the result (a failing grade, not winning a race, not being viewed as the best, being denied entry into a friendship group, etc.)
Taking the high road and having to watch other people cheat and get away with it

POTENTIALLY DISASTROUS RESULTS
Getting caught
Being expelled, removed from the team, ejected from the competition, etc.
Being blackmailed by someone who found out about the cheating
Losing the trust of others; people always suspecting the character is cheating
The character having to continue to cheat to maintain their standing
Family members seeing a discrepancy in the character's finances and demanding an explanation
Losing the respect of a valued mentor, coach, teacher, or friend
Dreams being dashed when the cheating is discovered (the character not getting into their dream college, being kicked off an athletic team, losing a scholarship, etc.)
Being prosecuted (if the cheating was illegal)
The character making the right choice and excelling on their own merit but still being accused of cheating
Choosing not to cheat and being vilified by teammates or friends

RESULTING EMOTIONS: Appalled, Concern, Conflicted, Contempt, Curiosity, Desire, Desperation, Eagerness, Elation, Excitement, Guilt, Hopefulness, Nervousness, Pleased, Relief, Reluctance, Skepticism, Uncertainty, Unease, Wariness

POSSIBLE INTERNAL STRUGGLES

Not wanting to cheat but feeling like it's the only way to succeed
Being driven to cheat to live up to the demands and expectations of others
Believing that cheating evens the playing field because of ongoing unfairness in other areas of life—e.g., the character lacking the political connections others have
Not wanting to cheat but knowing if a rival wins, many will suffer under their authority
Struggling with feelings of inferiority that birthed the temptation to cheat
Feeling guilty about even wanting to cheat

NEGATIVE TRAITS THAT MAY WORSEN THE SITUATION: Addictive, Antisocial, Controlling, Cowardly, Cynical, Devious, Dishonest, Disloyal, Greedy, Hypocritical, Insecure, Irresponsible, Jealous, Know-It-All, Macho, Manipulative, Perfectionist, Reckless, Self-Indulgent

IMPACT ON BASIC NEEDS

Self-Actualization: The temptation to cheat may seem like a fast-track solution to achieving a meaningful dream or personal goal, but if the character's morals kick in, the decision will haunt them, stealing their joy.

Esteem and Recognition: While cheating can affect this need, the temptation itself can also cause problems. Characters who want to take the easy path may think less of themselves for it, despising their moral fragility. Or the desire to cheat may highlight their weaknesses and vulnerabilities, leading to more self-doubt.

Love and Belonging: A character whose important relationships are built on conditional love may feel cheating is the only way to be loved or accepted by those people.

POSITIVE TRAITS TO HELP THE CHARACTER COPE: Cautious, Centered, Confident, Courageous, Decisive, Disciplined, Honest, Honorable, Idealistic, Independent, Industrious, Inspirational, Just, Optimistic, Professional, Spiritual, Studious, Talented, Wise

POSITIVE OUTCOMES

Pride and an increased sense of self at being strong enough to say no to the opportunity
Being reminded of the importance of trust in significant relationships
The character developing the ability to think about the long-term effects of their decisions
The character being reminded of the importance of their personal values and ethics
Regret over cheating causing the character to value effort, not results, moving forward
An overly competitive character giving up their need to always win

BEING OFFERED AN EASY WAY OUT

EXAMPLES
The character being offered a solution in exchange for a favor down the road
Someone offering to take over a difficult situation the character is struggling with
A powerful connection offering to pay someone off to make one's sticky situation go away
A friend being willing to lie so the character can escape repercussions
Having an inside man offer to fast-track a process or application
Being offered a position because of a connection, not because the character earned it
Someone offering to ensure evidence against the character gets "lost"
An insider offering to alter records to get the character out of trouble
Being offered a bribe or donation to look the other way after making a discovery that could be hazardous to one's job, health, etc.
Discovering incriminating evidence against a competitor and being tempted to use it to take them out of the running
A friend providing a fake alibi that will allow the character to avoid unwanted consequences
A romantic partner the character has lost interest in breaking things off before the character has a chance to

MINOR COMPLICATIONS
Accepting the offer and being forced to lie about it to the people one cares about
Accepting the offer and having to lie on the record
Giving in to temptation and later regretting it
Deciding to resist temptation and deal with the fallout
Turning down the offer and being threatened or bullied
Disappointing others when the truth comes out
Being unable to enjoy the victory or achievement because it wasn't earned

POTENTIALLY DISASTROUS RESULTS
Owing the wrong sort of person a favor
Problems escalating when the person acting on one's behalf does something unconscionable
Being blackmailed
The truth getting out and one's reputation or standing being ruined
Losing the trust of someone the character cares deeply about
Having to live a lie
Being forced to do something uncomfortable (dangerous, morally wrong, etc.) in return
The people who solved the problem using their leverage to control the character in the future

RESULTING EMOTIONS: Anxiety, Conflicted, Dread, Fear, Gratitude, Guilt, Panic, Paranoia, Powerlessness, Regret, Relief, Reluctance, Self-Loathing, Shame, Tormented

POSSIBLE INTERNAL STRUGGLES
Being paranoid about someone finding out but trying to act like nothing's amiss
Having an identity crisis from crossing a moral line

Wanting to find the courage to be honest about a failure but not wanting to disappoint the people who have invested so much in the character's success

Guilty feelings over the fallout to others that resulted from one's actions

Self-hatred for being weak (if one took the easy way out)

Trying to make up for what one did in a way that doesn't reveal what truly happened but finding it doesn't erase the guilt or shame

Wanting to confide in someone about the mistake but being too ashamed

NEGATIVE TRAITS THAT MAY WORSEN THE SITUATION: Cocky, Cowardly, Foolish, Gossipy, Gullible, Paranoid, Self-Destructive, Weak-Willed, Whiny, Worrywart

IMPACT ON BASIC NEEDS

Self-Actualization: If the character gives in to a temptation they believe is ethically or morally wrong, the resulting guilt or shame can weigh on their conscience and make them doubt who they are at their core.

Esteem and Recognition: Taking the easy way out can erode the character's self-esteem as they doubt whether they can succeed on their own merits. Moving forward, they may continue to seek unfair advantages because they're afraid of someone discovering they're a fraud. On the flip side, if others know the character was "helped," it can lower their opinions about the character and generate contempt.

Safety and Security: If taking the easy way out includes cutting corners meant to keep the character safe, they (and others) could end up hurt. Another danger lies with the one offering to help. If the person who encourages the character to let them fix the problem has questionable motives, rejecting the offer of help could be dangerous for the character.

POSITIVE TRAITS TO HELP THE CHARACTER COPE: Analytical, Cautious, Courageous, Disciplined, Honorable, Intelligent, Perceptive, Professional, Proper, Wise

POSITIVE OUTCOMES

Resisting temptation and accepting responsibility

The character declining the offer and winning or succeeding on their own merits, growing in confidence

Learning the value of being prepared

Being determined to not make the same mistake that landed the character into trouble

Redoubling one's efforts to be ethical, moral, or honest in the days ahead

Gaining respect for people who accept responsibility, even when it hurts the character

Becoming wiser regarding the difference between shortsighted wins and harder-to-reach yet deeply satisfying long-term goals

BEING OFFERED DIRTY MONEY

NOTES: "Dirty" money is money or a gift that is tainted in some way. Sometimes it's the person giving it who makes it repugnant but often it has more to do with the way it was obtained or what it represents. For characters reluctant to take and benefit from a dirty gift, the offer would create a moral dilemma. Some specific examples of these conflict scenarios can be found below.

EXAMPLES

A person convicted of drunk driving wanting to pay for a wheelchair that the character's child needs after the accident
An absentee parent reentering the character's life and offering to pay for their upcoming wedding
An abusive spouse or parent buying gifts for the character out of remorse
An absentee parent trying to make up for past disappointments with expensive trips
Regular income being generated for the character through a parent or partner's objectionable career (prostitution, the sale of drugs, human trafficking, etc.)
An inheritance from a mafia boss or lifelong criminal
Being given a raise or bonus for completing a horrible task
Receiving settlement money from a thriving organization that still engages in the unethical practices that hurt the character

MINOR COMPLICATIONS

Losing sleep over whether to take the money or not
The character's life being harder if they don't take what's being offered
The character feeling guilty every time they use the money or see the gift
Having to keep the source of the gift a secret from loved ones
Lying about where the money is coming from
Feeling indebted to the person (if the money is a gift or donation)
Hocking the gift for necessary money, incurring the giver's anger
Accepting a gift that comes with inconvenient or unexpected conditions

POTENTIALLY DISASTROUS RESULTS

The character rejecting the gift and the family suffering financially
Not accepting the gift as a way of withholding forgiveness from the other person and being consumed with bitterness and anger
The character taking the gift and letting an imbalanced or controlling person into their life
Confusing acceptance of a gift with acceptance of the person or their behavior
Being triggered into an anxiety attack at the sight of the person or their gift
Family members finding out the character accepted the gift and cutting them off
The giver using the gift to control the character or force their way into their life

RESULTING EMOTIONS: Anger, Anguish, Appalled, Apprehension, Betrayed, Bitterness, Conflicted, Contempt, Desperation, Disbelief, Fear, Flustered, Guilt, Hatred, Horror,

Intimidation, Irritation, Nervousness, Panic, Rage, Reluctance, Scorn, Shame, Shock, Suspicion

POSSIBLE INTERNAL STRUGGLES
Being paralyzed with indecision; not knowing what to do
Needing the money but not wanting to take it
Making an effort not to think about the money or where it came from
Being consumed with worry that other people will find out where the gift originated
The character not feeling reluctant about taking the gift, then wondering what's wrong with them
Taking the gift out of a desire to placate an abuser, then hating the sight of it
Feeling self-blame and loathing for considering take the money
The character's heart softening toward the person and them worrying they've lost their moral compass by accepting the gift
Other people seeing the giver as a benefactor rather than the monster he is and the character being bothered by that

NEGATIVE TRAITS THAT MAY WORSEN THE SITUATION: Confrontational, Controlling, Forgetful, Frivolous, Greedy, Gullible, Judgmental, Materialistic, Self-Destructive, Self-Indulgent, Spoiled, Stubborn, Suspicious, Tactless

IMPACT ON BASIC NEEDS
Self-Actualization: This can be a no-win situation in the self-actualization department. If a reluctant character takes the money, they could end up living a life of regret. But if the character declines the money despite needing it to achieve certain goals, they may have to settle for less.

Esteem and Recognition: Characters who are morally opposed to taking the gift but do so anyway may lose respect for themselves. And if others despise a character for taking (or declining) the gift, they also could lose the respect of others.

Love and Belonging: A character struggling to make this decision may experience friction with loved ones or family members who see a clear path forward.

Safety and Security: The character's safety could be threatened if their decision offends a dangerous "benefactor" or allows a toxic or controlling person into their life.

POSITIVE TRAITS TO HELP THE CHARACTER COPE: Analytical, Centered, Decisive, Efficient, Focused, Honorable, Independent, Industrious, Objective, Resourceful

POSITIVE OUTCOMES
The character's quality of life being improved because of the money
The character taking the money and using some of it to help others in need
The gift opening the door to repairing a broken relationship
The offer cementing in the character's mind their decision to maintain healthy boundaries
Learning to forgive and realizing people can change
Recognizing good things can come from bad circumstances

BEING PRESSURED TO COVER FOR A FRIEND

EXAMPLES
Being asked to lie by providing a glowing character reference or referral for a friend
Being pressured to claim responsibility for a friend's misdeeds at work
A friend wanting the character to provide an alibi for their whereabouts
Being asked to be someone's backup in a dangerous situation (accompanying them on a drug buy, coming with them to collect a debt, driving a getaway car, etc.)
A co-worker asking the character to cover their shift so they can do something they're not supposed to do
A student being bullied into completing a school assignment for someone else
Being coerced to lie under oath
Being asked to take a drug test for a friend
Being encouraged to loan money to someone who is always mismanaging their funds
Discovering a friend has hidden something illegal or questionable (drugs, a stolen item, a fake ID) in the character's house

MINOR COMPLICATIONS
Having to create a cover story and lie to people
Putting oneself out financially to help a friend
Having to nudge the friend to pay the money back
Being scolded for something the character didn't do
Having to work a friend's shift or cancel personal plans to accommodate them
Having to avoid getting caught (cheating, lying, etc.) to cover for the friend
Upsetting the friend by refusing to cover for them
Putting oneself on the line and the friend not showing proper appreciation
Inconveniencing family members by covering the friend's work shifts
Upsetting a spouse for showing up late time and again because the friend needed rescuing

POTENTIALLY DISASTROUS RESULTS
Getting caught lying to someone important
The character giving money to the friend against their spouse's wishes and them finding out about it
Facing criminal charges
Being suspended or expelled from school
The character being viewed as guilty by association for the part they played
Being fired or reprimanded at work
The friendship falling apart under the strain
The friend expecting the character to continue covering for her in the future
The friend asking for more dangerous coverage the next time
The character's reputation being ruined
The friend backstabbing the character by letting them take the fall for a misdeed

RESULTING EMOTIONS: Anger, Annoyance, Anxiety, Apprehension, Concern, Conflicted, Connectedness, Disappointment, Disbelief, Eagerness, Empathy, Fear, Flustered, Frustration, Nervousness, Pity, Powerlessness, Reluctance, Resentment, Unappreciated, Unease, Worry

POSSIBLE INTERNAL STRUGGLES
Not knowing what to do
Feeling backed into a corner
Questioning the friendship
Feeling taken advantage of and used
Wanting to help the friend but resenting having to betray others by lying to them
The character questioning their morals: *Is this really such a big deal?*
Struggling between competing loyalties
Caring for the friend but resenting them for putting the character in this position
Secretly enjoying the unpredictability and sense of danger while fearing where it will lead

NEGATIVE TRAITS THAT MAY WORSEN THE SITUATION: Disloyal, Flaky, Gossipy, Gullible, Insecure, Lazy, Martyr, Needy, Nervous, Resentful, Stingy, Subservient, Timid, Uncooperative, Unethical, Weak-Willed, Worrywart

IMPACT ON BASIC NEEDS
   Esteem and Recognition: If the character loves to be needed, coming to someone's rescue will fill them with a high level of esteem. But if their actions and sacrifices are not being adequately appreciated, they may experience diminished self-worth for letting themselves be used.
   Love and Belonging: The character may feel as though the relationship is imbalanced if they're always being asked to take risks to cover for someone else. But if the friendship is an important one, they may fear losing it if they don't comply. Either way, a relationship steeped in stress and uncertainty could fall apart, leaving the character feeling bereft.
   Safety and Security: Covering for a friend might pose great risk for the character, leading them to lose their job, academic standing, or their own financial security.

POSITIVE TRAITS TO HELP THE CHARACTER COPE: Adventurous, Bold, Cautious, Charming, Confident, Empathetic, Honorable, Independent, Just, Loyal, Obedient, Objective, Playful, Protective, Sensible, Sentimental, Spiritual, Supportive, Traditional, Trusting, Unselfish

POSITIVE OUTCOMES
The character learning to recognize the difference between helping and enabling
The character becoming more self-reliant, determining never to put a friend in the same situation
A bad experience helping the character to choose friends more wisely
Learning to set healthy boundaries
The act of covering for the friend reinforcing positive traits of the character's, such as loyalty, dependability, or generosity
The friend appreciating the character's involvement and helping them out down the road
The bonds of friendship being strengthened because the character chose to help out

BREAKING THE LAW FOR A GOOD REASON

EXAMPLES

The character breaking the speed limit to get an injured person to the hospital

Stealing essential supplies for someone who is starving or suffering

Hunting to obtain food when it's not allowed

Engaging in activist work to further social justice or rights for marginalized groups

Harboring an innocent fugitive from a corrupt regime

Lying under oath to protect someone who is being framed

The character escaping a closed country to gain a better life

Leading a rebellion to overturn an oppressive government

Citizens arming themselves to fight against a tyrannical monarchy

Holding onto banned materials, such as books or a radio

People meeting in secret to worship

Spreading truth the government considers to be propaganda

Refusing to obey a law that goes against the character's moral beliefs (reporting someone to authorities based on their religion or sexual preference, euthanizing the elderly, etc.)

MINOR COMPLICATIONS

The character having to explain their actions to a loved one

Minor health issues due to worry over being caught (insomnia, stomach upset, etc.)

Having to keep up a charade, such as a sham marriage or hiding people in your home

Being chastised by friends and co-workers who don't understand the character's choice

Receiving a reprimand at work

Making financial sacrifices to help others

Knowing if the character is caught, their family will suffer

Hiding one's beliefs and actions from loved ones who are blind supporters of a corrupt government or religion

Being questioned by police and having to lie convincingly

POTENTIALLY DISASTROUS RESULT

Going to jail for breaking the law

The character losing access to an important resource and being unable to help

Someone finding out about the character's actions and threatening to make the whole thing public if they don't stop

Being blackmailed by someone who finds out

Being seriously injured (being attacked at a violent protest, getting into a car accident after speeding, etc.)

Being villainized by family members, co-workers, and people in the community who don't agree with the character's actions

The character having to make financial recompense for their actions

Making a mistake that causes the character and the people they're protecting to get caught

Being betrayed by a family member or friend and turned over to arresting officers

RESULTING EMOTIONS: Anguish, Annoyance, Anxiety, Apprehension, Bitterness, Defiance, Determination, Doubt, Dread, Elation, Excitement, Fear, Guilt, Loneliness, Moodiness, Nervousness, Overwhelmed, Pride, Reluctance, Resignation, Satisfaction, Schadenfreude

POSSIBLE INTERNAL STRUGGLES

Being caught between wanting to do the right thing and not wanting to break the law
The character weighing the benefits of their actions for others against the consequences for himself
The character knowing they're doing the right thing but struggling with guilt for breaking the law or lying to others
Trying to hold onto courage as the likelihood of being caught grows
Being resentful of friends and family who won't support the character's choices
The character loving their country but hating some of the things they allow

NEGATIVE TRAITS THAT MAY WORSEN THE SITUATION: Abrasive, Childish, Disrespectful, Flaky, Foolish, Impatient, Impulsive, Nervous, Paranoid, Reckless, Scatterbrained, Tactless, Uncooperative, Volatile, Weak-Willed

IMPACT ON BASIC NEEDS

Self-Actualization: Morality is an important part of self-actualization, so a character facing this situation will struggle with dueling beliefs: do the right thing or uphold the law.

Esteem and Recognition: A character who yearns for recognition may chafe at being secretly put at risk and never being thanked or lauded for their good works.

Love and Belonging: If a character's viewpoint goes against others in their family, they'll be forced to hide their actions. Depending on the danger and risk, they may feel isolated and resentful that they can't trust loved ones to support them when the stakes are so high.

Safety and Security: Characters who break the law set themselves up against those in authority, which often results in a loss of freedom or personal safety.

POSITIVE TRAITS TO HELP THE CHARACTER COPE: Adventurous, Bold, Calm, Centered, Courageous, Decisive, Diplomatic, Disciplined, Discreet, Honorable, Idealistic, Inspirational, Merciful, Passionate, Persuasive, Socially Aware, Uninhibited, Unselfish

POSITIVE OUTCOMES

Laying the groundwork for fair legislation and a positive shift in public opinion
Gaining a better understanding of a marginalized or misunderstood people group
The character showing their kids it's more important to stand up for what's right than what's popular
Experiencing great satisfaction from having done the right (if difficult) thing
The character's demonstration of courage helping to win other people over to a noble cause

DISCOVERING AN OUTCOME HAS BEEN FIXED

EXAMPLES

A contestant winning a talent show because of their romantic involvement with a producer, judge, or other person of influence

A student getting a solo, scholarship, or leadership position because they're a teacher's favorite

The character applying for a coveted job that's eventually offered to one of the boss's relatives

An athlete "throwing" a match so their opponent will win

Biased referees determining who wins a championship game

A civic election being decided by widespread fraud (voting machines being hacked, a name being "left off" of the ballot, certain people not being allowed to vote, etc.)

A candidate winning a high school election because students were bribed or intimidated into voting for him

MINOR COMPLICATIONS

Losing the benefit that would have come with the win (getting the job, being the best, being elected to a position that would allow good to be done, etc.)

A lengthy investigation of an election that postpones the final result

The character having to sue the organization to achieve justice

The character complaining about the unfair outcome and being labeled a sore loser, trouble-maker, or conspiracy theorist

Dwindling passion and increased apathy

The character losing respect for a person or organization they once idolized

Wasted time and money pursuing a dream that was never going to happen

A loyal friend or family member going on a public tirade, bringing unwanted attention to the character

Dealing with disappointment, both in the loss and the fixed outcome

The character betting on the outcome and losing money

Wanting to go public with the information but being dissuaded by family members

POTENTIALLY DISASTROUS RESULTS

Ending up with a tyrannical or unstable leader and having no recourse to remove them

Swathes of people losing faith in the electoral process

The character's reputation being attacked when they try to speak out

Speaking out against favoritism at work and being blackballed, demoted, or cold-shouldered

The responsible party and their family members being targeted with death threats

The character being reluctant to compete in any situation where someone else will decide their fate

Losing a scholarship that would enable the character to attend college

Losing a job that would improve the character's financial situation or allow them the freedom to care for an ailing family member

The character giving up on a dream because they believe the outcome will always be fixed, so why bother?

RESULTING EMOTIONS: Anger, Appalled, Betrayed, Bitterness, Confusion, Denial, Devastation, Disappointment, Disbelief, Disgust, Disillusionment, Frustration, Hatred, Paranoia, Powerlessness, Rage, Resentment, Resignation, Sadness, Scorn, Self-Pity, Skepticism, Stunned

POSSIBLE INTERNAL STRUGGLES
Wanting to go public but not wanting to make waves
Wanting to do something but being paralyzed, feeling the situation is too big
Becoming discouraged, feeling everything is rigged and it's pointless to try for anything
Being tempted to give up and not participate, vote, or get involved
Becoming jaded; seeing unfairness and bias in situations where it doesn't exist
The character doubting their abilities despite knowing the outcome was fixed; believing if they were good enough, they should have overcome the opposition

NEGATIVE TRAITS THAT MAY WORSEN THE SITUATION: Apathetic, Catty, Childish, Cocky, Confrontational, Cynical, Dishonest, Fanatical, Hostile, Macho, Martyr, Paranoid, Prejudiced, Vindictive, Whiny

IMPACT ON BASIC NEEDS
   Self-Actualization: A character who becomes discouraged by a rigged decision may be reluctant to compete again in the future, which would limit their ability to do the things they are individually gifted to do.
   Esteem and Recognition: A character who internalizes the loss may irrationally feel they should have been able to win if they were more talented, smart enough, etc.
   Love and Belonging: If a disillusioned character walks away from a sport, career, or group of people that had been part of their community, they may keenly feel that loss.
   Safety and Security: The character's safety may become jeopardized if their attempts to bring injustice to light make them the target of powerful or motivated people.

POSITIVE TRAITS TO HELP THE CHARACTER COPE: Adaptable, Ambitious, Bold, Charming, Confident, Cooperative, Decisive, Disciplined, Honorable, Idealistic, Just, Organized, Passionate, Patient, Patriotic, Persistent, Persuasive, Socially Aware, Talented

POSITIVE OUTCOMES
Bringing attention to the situation so it doesn't happen again
Being able to spot similar injustices in the future
The character tempering their idealism with the proper amount of realism to stave off disillusionment and despair
The character redoubling their efforts to excel in the face of injustice

FACING A DIFFICULT DECISION WITH NO EASY SOLUTION

EXAMPLES
The character having to reveal hurtful information to a loved one
A child having to choose which parent to live with
An employee having to following a boss's unethical command or be fired
The character having to decide if they should move away to attend college or stay home to work and care for a relative
Being forced by someone in authority to reveal incriminating information about a friend
Choosing between a risky dream job or a stable job that won't bring fulfillment
A family member having to decide whether or not to pull the plug on a relative
Having to lay off loyal, high-performing employees
Only having the time or resources to save the life of one person and having to choose which one
Having to sacrifice one person so many more can be saved
The character sacrificing their morals to survive
Being forced to pick the lesser of two evils

MINOR COMPLICATIONS
Having to share upsetting information with someone
Making an agonizing choice and not being appreciated for it
Becoming embroiled in drama with people who are affected by the decision
Being criticized by people who disagree with the character's choice
Being pushed or bullied by people to make a certain decision
Having to adjust to changes because of the decision (starting over in a new place, a child seeing one parent less than the other, etc.)
Procrastinating and making things worse
Over-researching the options and potential outcomes and becoming more confused
Needing more time or information to make an informed decision and having neither

POTENTIALLY DISASTROUS RESULTS
Being ostracized by loved ones, kicked out of a community, or otherwise rejected because of the decision
Following an unethical command at work, then getting caught and being prosecuted
Choosing a job that leads to a joyless, unfulfilled life
Mental anguish, anxiety attacks, or depression arising from having to make the decision
The character suffering serious health issues from the stress, such as hypertension, migraines, and weight loss
Agonizing over a decision, then circumstances changing for the worse—e.g., giving up a college scholarship to care for an ailing relative, then the relative passing away
The aftereffects being much worse than anticipated, doubling the character's guilt

RESULTING EMOTIONS: Agitation, Anger, Anguish, Anxiety, Apprehension, Bitterness, Conflicted, Defeat, Despair, Discouragement, Dread, Fear, Guilt, Horror, Inadequacy, Nervousness, Overwhelmed, Panic, Reluctance, Resentment, Uncertainty, Unease, Worry

POSSIBLE INTERNAL STRUGGLES
Weighing the benefits and disadvantages of each side but still not knowing what to do
Feeling guilt for wanting to make the more "selfish" decision
The character wanting to stay true to their morals but not seeing a way to do so
Being torn between loyalty to numerous loved ones
Second-guessing oneself
Feeling paralyzed by indecision and being unable to make a decision
Dreading the outcome because the character feels that, either way, the wrong decision will have been made
Being privy to information that could help others understand one's decision but being unable to share it
A war between logic and intuition making the choice impossible to make

NEGATIVE TRAITS THAT MAY WORSEN THE SITUATION: Cowardly, Disorganized, Flaky, Foolish, Frivolous, Gullible, Ignorant, Impatient, Indecisive, Insecure, Nervous, Obsessive, Perfectionist, Reckless, Selfish, Timid, Unintelligent, Weak-Willed

IMPACT ON BASIC NEEDS
   Self-Actualization: Characters can struggle when it comes to putting their needs before others, especially when it comes to their own fulfillment. If guilt or an inflated sense of duty causes them to sacrifice their biggest desires for the needs of others, regret will usually follow.
   Esteem and Recognition: In the aftermath of the decision, the character may be unfairly hard on themselves, believing they somehow should have known better and chosen differently.
   Love and Belonging: Controlling, toxic family members can feel betrayed if their advice is not heeded and may retaliate by withholding love.
   Safety and Security: Struggling with a decision like this can take a toll on the character's mental and physical health.

POSITIVE TRAITS TO HELP THE CHARACTER COPE: Analytical, Calm, Cautious, Centered, Confident, Creative, Decisive, Diplomatic, Disciplined, Easygoing, Efficient, Independent, Just, Mature, Objective, Patient, Perceptive, Persistent, Persuasive, Responsible

POSITIVE OUTCOMES
The character taking a risk and learning they're more capable than they thought
Loved ones showing appreciation for the difficulty of the character's situation
The character growing in confidence as they realize they did well in a hard situation
Gaining wisdom from the experience that helps make future decisions easier
The character gaining a clearer vision of what their priorities should be
Helping to improve someone's life, even if they initially resent the character's involvement
Learning to give oneself grace in challenging circumstances

HAVING FEELINGS FOR
SOMEONE ONE SHOULDN'T

EXAMPLES

The character falling for their enemy, opponent, or jailer

Desiring a family member's spouse

Wanting a relationship with a friend's significant other

A professor having feelings for a student (or vice versa)

An employer wanting to be with their employee

Having feelings for a co-worker who is attached to someone else

A married person developing feelings for someone else (who may also be attached)

Having feelings for someone who is much older or much younger

An officer wanting to be with a subordinate

Wanting a friendship to become something more when that friend has other romantic interests

Being attracted to someone of a specific gender, religion, or culture and the character thinking they will not be accepted for it (hence, believing they shouldn't have those feelings)

MINOR COMPLICATIONS

Embarrassment if their feelings are made known and not returned

Friction in their other relationships (caused by guilt, shame, and secrets)

Disrupting their routine so they can spend more time around the other person

Having to answer questions about their odd behavior when it's noticed by a friend (leading to evasiveness, denial, or lying)

Rumors starting to fly

Damage to the character's reputation

Being unable to focus properly on other things

Losing sleep to uncertainty and worry over what to do

POTENTIALLY DISASTROUS RESULTS

A spouse's heartache at discovering these hidden feelings

A marriage breaking down in the wake of an affair being discovered

Losing one's job if the character takes action on their feelings and is discovered in an inappropriate relationship

Ruining a friendship or relationship once feelings are out in the open

Losing an opportunity (for a promotion, a scholarship, admission to a special sorority, etc.)

Being kicked out of an organization or group to avoid a conflict of interest

Being cast out of a church, community, or family

Being demoted or reassigned to a new department or job posting

Developing an emotional wound (unrequited love) and being unable to move on

Family relationships fracturing due to differences of opinions about the situation

RESULTING EMOTIONS: Adoration, Anguish, Anticipation, Apprehension, Conflicted, Connectedness, Desire, Desperation, Disappointment, Eagerness, Elation, Embarrassment,

Envy, Euphoria, Excitement, Fear, Flustered, Guilt, Hopefulness, Longing, Love, Lust, Panic

POSSIBLE INTERNAL STRUGGLES
The character experiencing guilt or shame for what they feel, even while allowing themselves to fantasize about fulfilling their desires

Struggling with questions about monogamy and whether it's natural or not

Agonizing over the idea that one's desires might make one a deviant

Trying to rationalize one's feelings and failing

The character examining their interactions with the person, looking for signs that they feel the same way

Feeling angry at oneself for having the desires

Questioning the role of fate and if the attraction was "meant to be," as it would explain their difficulty controlling what they feel

Vacillating between wanting to tell the other person and staying silent

Moral questions over loyalty to familial or societal beliefs vs. loyalty to one's heart

NEGATIVE TRAITS THAT MAY WORSEN THE SITUATION: Addictive, Compulsive, Disloyal, Foolish, Impulsive, Jealous, Needy, Nervous, Obsessive, Possessive, Reckless, Selfish

IMPACT ON BASIC NEEDS
Self-Actualization: A character who gives in to this desire may find doors closing if they're caught. Being ousted from an organization, being denied a dream job, or losing access to something that brings them joy may be devastating, especially if their feelings for the person dim over time.

Esteem and Recognition: Being caught in a relationship that is forbidden or taboo is a fast way to lose standing in the eyes of others.

Love and Belonging: If the character's feelings are discovered and not returned, this can lead to them being rejected and the relationship in its current form (friendship, professional, etc.) being severed.

POSITIVE TRAITS TO HELP THE CHARACTER COPE: Cautious, Disciplined, Discreet, Kind, Nurturing, Patient, Perceptive, Playful, Private, Proper, Uninhibited, Wise

POSITIVE OUTCOMES
The character recognizing unhappiness is at the root of their wandering eye and making the choice to work on that

Discovering what one really wants (to stay in an existing relationship or move on)

Realizing a truly inappropriate desire isn't okay and seeking help before they act on those feelings

HAVING TO DECIDE TO HELP OR DO NOTHING

NOTES: Your character will likely encounter situations where they're able to come to someone's aid. But it's not always easy deciding whether or not they should. Scenarios that include an element of danger for the character—or for others—and those that involve moral implications can cause them to pause, uncertain whether or not to act.

EXAMPLES
Deciding whether or not to intervene in a physical fight between strangers on the street
Witnessing discrimination or racism at work and deciding whether to say something or not
Suspecting a child is being trafficked but not being certain or having proof
Wavering about telling the truth in a legal investigation that implicates a friend
Suspecting illegal activity may be happening next door and struggling with the decision to get more involved and discover the truth
Trying to decide if one should stage an intervention for a family member who will not appreciate the attention
The character not knowing if they should tell their parents about a sibling's secret that involves self-destructive thoughts or behaviors
Wanting to aid a homeless person but having too many responsibilities as it is
The character having to decide if they should relocate their family to remove their child from a dangerous situation or if they're fine staying where they are
Seeing an animal in distress but not wanting to endanger oneself to help it
Being asked for money by a friend whose poor financial decisions result in constant need

MINOR COMPLICATIONS
The situation worsening while the character tries to make up their mind
Trying to help someone who doesn't want help
The person in need being upset at the character's reluctance to do what was asked
Making sacrifices that cause problems for the character
An unexpected complication that requires more effort or sacrifice
Choosing to help, then being overwhelmed with similar requests from others
Helping someone who expects the character to continue providing aid
The character learning they're being scammed
Family members pressuring the character into ignoring the situation because they don't want to be inconvenienced
Choosing not to help, then regretting the decision

POTENTIALLY DISASTROUS RESULTS
The character being injured while attempting to help
Misreading the situation; making a decision based on false information or preconceived ideas
Providing help that ends up enabling or belittling the person in need
Loved ones being angry with the character for having made sacrifices that impact them
The character choosing to help but changing their mind in the middle, thereby dashing the requester's hopes

Choosing not to help and being seen as someone who is uncaring or selfish
Believing someone else will help and something awful happening when no one does
Offering false hope; agreeing to help without having the ability or resources to do so
The character helping but their lack of expertise makes the situation worse

RESULTING EMOTIONS: Agitation, Anger, Anguish, Annoyance, Anxiety, Concern, Conflicted, Defensiveness, Dread, Fear, Flustered, Guilt, Inadequacy, Nervousness, Overwhelmed, Pity, Reluctance, Resentment, Resignation, Self-Pity, Skepticism, Suspicion

POSSIBLE INTERNAL STRUGGLES
The character wanting to help but not feeling qualified or capable of doing so
Struggling to do what's best for everyone (especially if other people would suffer from the character's involvement)
Being reluctant to help because it would require personal sacrifices and feeling guilty about it
Not helping and feeling responsible for the person's worsening situation
Thinking badly of oneself because the decision is so difficult
Being resentful at being put in the situation
Procrastinating in the hopes someone else will step up to help in the meantime

NEGATIVE TRAITS THAT MAY WORSEN THE SITUATION: Apathetic, Callous, Controlling, Cruel, Cynical, Defensive, Gossipy, Gullible, Indecisive, Judgmental, Lazy, Prejudiced, Resentful, Scatterbrained, Selfish, Stingy, Suspicious, Vindictive

IMPACT ON BASIC NEEDS
Self-Actualization: If the character's value system includes helping others or putting others first, their difficulty at deciding what to do may cause them to question their morality.
Esteem and Recognition: Being unwilling to help someone in need if a sacrifice is involved may cause the character to question their self-worth.
Love and Belonging: A friend who has asked for help could be hurt if the character doesn't jump to their aid. But loved ones who don't want the character to intervene might be angry if they do so. A character in either situation could end up damaging those important relationships.
Safety and Security: Providing aid in a perilous situation could put the character in danger, and they would need to balance their desire to help against the need for self-preservation.

POSITIVE TRAITS TO HELP THE CHARACTER COPE: Adventurous, Analytical, Decisive, Empathetic, Generous, Idealistic, Objective, Passionate, Perceptive, Wise

POSITIVE OUTCOMES
The situation resolving itself without the character having to make a decision
Learning to read people and their motivations to be able to make better and quicker decisions in the future
Confiding in someone about the weight of the choice and gaining an ally who decides to help
The character recognizing the difficulty of the situation they're in and determining not to feel bad about struggling to make a decision

HAVING TO STEAL TO OBTAIN SOMETHING VITAL

EXAMPLES
The character being forced to steal essential supplies, such as medicine or food, to survive
Needing to steal an item to build a machine or piece of technology that will save many lives
Having to steal documents to create false papers so the character can flee oppression
Needing to "borrow" someone's keys, password, or access codes to gain necessary information
Having to procure weapons or munitions to even the playing field and enable a rebellion to succeed
Appropriating a car to get somewhere quickly before a critical deadline expires
Taking resources from the wealthy and redistributing them to the poor (a *Robin Hood* scenario)
Needing to procure an item to trade for something even more vital

MINOR COMPLICATIONS
Conflict with other characters over the necessity of the theft
Encountering unforeseen issues (a security system in the form of a three-headed dog, the items not being where they're supposed to be, etc.) that complicate the plan
Receiving minor injuries during the process
The character getting caught and having to talk their way out the situation
Accidentally stealing the wrong items or not enough of them
Being partnered for the job with an impulsive, clumsy, or scatterbrained accomplice
Having to keep the plan a secret from others
Discovering a competitor is trying to collect the same resource
Additional responsibilities being added to the mission (transporting refugees, taking a kid brother along and showing him the ropes, procuring other items that increase the risk, etc.)

POTENTIALLY DISASTROUS RESULTS
Nerves or inexperience causing the character to fumble the job
Being seriously injured or harmed in the process of trying to get away with the stolen goods
Being arrested
The character getting caught and losing their job
Damaging or losing vital supplies in the rush to escape the scene
A bounty being put on the character's head, forcing them into hiding
Becoming lost, trapped, or captured during the mission
The character's involvement bringing unwanted attention to other family members
Circumstances worsening and the item being needed immediately
A widespread need for the item that shortens the supply even further

RESULTING EMOTIONS: Acceptance, Anger, Annoyance, Anxiety, Apprehension, Bitterness, Conflicted, Determination, Doubt, Dread, Eagerness, Excitement, Fear, Guilt, Inadequacy, Reluctance, Schadenfreude, Unease, Vulnerability, Worry

POSSIBLE INTERNAL STRUGGLES

Feeling guilty about having to steal

Not wanting to steal but realizing there's no alternative

The character being tempted to keep the stolen goods rather than pass them on

Internal conflict when the character realizes they're stealing from someone who needs the resources as much as they do

Anger or resentment toward those who don't have to deal with this situation

Weighing the need for the resources against the possibility of getting caught

Wanting to do this important job but worrying about what will happen to dependent loved ones if the character is caught

The character recognizing the need to steal but doubting their ability to do so successfully

NEGATIVE TRAITS THAT MAY WORSEN THE SITUATION: Disloyal, Foolish, Greedy, Impatient, Impulsive, Mischievous, Reckless, Timid

IMPACT ON BASIC NEEDS

Self-Actualization: A character whose basic needs are threatened to the point that they must steal to survive won't be able to achieve self-actualization until those needs are met.

Esteem and Recognition: A character who sees himself as a provider or savior may have a hard time looking himself in the eye if he's unable to give his loved ones what they need to survive.

Safety and Security: If the resource is highly valued or well protected, anyone trying to steal it will be risking their physical safety.

Physiological Needs: Lives could hang in the balance if resources necessary to survival aren't obtained.

POSITIVE TRAITS TO HELP THE CHARACTER COPE: Adventurous, Cautious, Charming, Confident, Cooperative, Courageous, Discreet, Empathetic, Nurturing, Passionate, Persuasive, Protective, Socially Aware

POSITIVE OUTCOMES

Being able to meet the basic needs of loved ones or large groups of people

The character keeping track of what was taken so they can pay it back later

Learning a new (if questionable) trade

The character being able to navigate the ethical minefield of stealing to obtain vital supplies and emerging with their values intact

Building bonds of friendship and respect with those involved in the procurement mission

Hating the feeling of being dependent on others and vowing to reach a point of self-reliance

Shining a light on the crooked system that makes stealing to survive a necessity

A growing shortage of a vital resource leading to the discovery of a suitable (and plentiful) substitute

INDULGING WHEN ONE SHOULD NOT

EXAMPLES
The character overindulging in cake or other sweet treats during a diet
Using performance-enhancing steroids when there's a chance of being randomly tested
Bingeing on food
Drinking heavily while taking prescription medicine
Accepting tempting food or drink from a character with suspicious motives
Heavy alcohol or drug usage the night before an important event
Eating indulgent foods while knowing they will exacerbate allergies or other health conditions
Excessive or unnecessary spending
Repeatedly skipping class to play video games or binge-watch a favorite TV show
Drinking heavily when the character knows they need to drive home
Bringing home yet another pet—one the character can't afford to care for
The character responding to sexual impulses with someone when they shouldn't
Smoking, using drugs, or drinking too much while pregnant
Returning to the casino cash machine for more money despite finances being tight

MINOR COMPLICATIONS
Being hungover at an interview, church meeting, or during a standardized test
Oversleeping due to a binge and being late to work
Slipping grades or work performance
Gaining weight
Suffering when the character's food interacts with their medication
Feeling bloated and nauseous after overindulging
Minor allergic reactions or other food-related distress, such as IBS (Irritable Bowel Syndrome)
The character reaching the spending limit on their credit card
Romantic complications with a partner who wants to pursue a long-term relationship

POTENTIALLY DISASTROUS RESULTS
Suffering from alcohol poisoning
Overdosing on drugs
Getting pregnant
Being ticketed or losing a license for driving under the influence
The character harming someone while driving impaired
Oversleeping and missing an important event (like picking up in-laws from the airport)
Severe allergic reactions requiring hospitalization and medical intervention
Racking up debt the character can't pay back
Fighting with parents or a spouse over the irresponsible behavior
The character's partner finding out about their infidelity
Alcohol interfering with the character's necessary medication, causing it not to work

RESULTING EMOTIONS: Appalled, Conflicted, Embarrassment, Euphoria, Guilt, Indifference, Regret, Relief, Sadness, Satisfaction, Self-Loathing, Shame, Unease, Worthlessness

POSSIBLE INTERNAL STRUGGLES
Wanting to indulge even if the consequences could be problematic or dangerous
Knowing the right thing to do but struggling with peer pressure
Feeling guilty or ashamed about indulging
The character experiencing regret when their actions produce fallout for others
Knowing the behavior is a problem but being too self-destructive to stop it

NEGATIVE TRAITS THAT MAY WORSEN THE SITUATION: Addictive, Childish, Hypocritical, Impulsive, Irresponsible, Nervous, Perfectionist, Rebellious, Self-Destructive, Self-Indulgent, Selfish, Spoiled, Weak-Willed

IMPACT ON BASIC NEEDS
Self-Actualization: If indulging at the wrong time results in consequences that sideswipe a meaningful goal, the character's future may be sabotaged.

Esteem and Recognition: Choosing to indulge, then behaving in an embarrassing or irresponsible manner, could change how others view the character. The character may also think less of himself if he knew the choice was wrong but felt too week or unable to stop—especially if it wasn't an isolated event.

Love and Belonging: If the indulgence is an unhealthy compulsion or addiction that family and friends are concerned about, shame may cause the character to pull away from the people they need the most.

Safety and Security: The character's personal safety and health could become threatened if their indulgence leads to poor decisions and an inability to spot dangers.

Physiological Needs: Indulging in dangerous substances, foods that will cause allergic reactions, or risky activities, could result in loss of life.

POSITIVE TRAITS TO HELP THE CHARACTER COPE: Appreciative, Disciplined, Honest, Humble, Mature, Obedient, Observant, Optimistic, Proactive, Protective, Responsible, Sensible, Socially Aware, Spiritual, Wise

POSITIVE OUTCOMES
Learning to say no to temptation
Learning to indulge in moderation
Deciding to tackle the root problem rather than avoid it by indulging in harmful distractions
Recognizing the situations where temperance is needed and indulgence should be avoided
Recognizing an addiction and seeking help for it
Frank discussion about the behaviors allowing old pain to be aired and released, leading to emotional healing and a fresh start in a relationship

LEAVING SOMEONE TO THE CONSEQUENCES OF THEIR ACTIONS

EXAMPLES

The character letting their unmotivated or irresponsible teenager fail at school

Not loaning money to someone whose poor decisions keep them in constant financial distress

Leaving a failing company after one's advice on how to turn things around was repeatedly refused or scorned

Not posting bail for a son or daughter who has been arrested

Allowing the justice system to decide a guilty loved one's fate

No longer paying for rehab or staging interventions for an addicted loved one

Letting a loved one who refuses to acknowledge or treat a mental health diagnosis make their own choices

Not giving in to a loved one's request to lie for them, cover for them, or provide an alibi

MINOR COMPLICATIONS

The character having to explain their actions to loved ones who disagree or don't understand

Confrontations with the other person

The person trying to manipulate the character for "abandoning" them

Being saddened by reports the person is not doing well

Other people taking the character's place in enabling the person to continue making the same choices

POTENTIALLY DISASTROUS RESULTS

The person incurring a terrible consequence for their actions (being sent to prison, contracting a lifelong disease, etc.)

Innocent people being dragged into the wake of the person's actions

The person continuing in their unhealthy behaviors and suffering harm

Being threatened or verbally abused by the person

The person attacking the character publicly (on social media, at church, at a family gathering, etc.)

Being at odds with a spouse who wants to handle things differently

Being ostracized by family members who are angry about the character's choice

The person turning to bad influences or toxic people for help

The person being unable to keep a job

The person becoming homeless

A suicide attempt

RESULTING EMOTIONS: Anger, Anguish, Anxiety, Bitterness, Concern, Conflicted, Defeat, Depressed, Devastation, Fear, Grief, Guilt, Panic, Pity, Powerlessness, Regret, Relief, Reluctance, Remorse, Resentment, Resignation, Sadness, Shame, Uncertainty, Worry

POSSIBLE INTERNAL STRUGGLES

The character wanting desperately to save someone and worrying that maybe they can't
Feeling guilty when the person suffers devastating consequences
Resenting the constant conflict
Being validated when things turn out the way the character said they would and experiencing guilt over feeling that way
Constantly battling the temptation to go back and try to help the person
The character feeling shame and remorse over negative thoughts about the other person
The character wishing they had taken action sooner
Knowing that stepping back is the right choice to maintain one's personal well-being but feeling like an awful person for doing so

NEGATIVE TRAITS THAT MAY WORSEN THE SITUATION: Abrasive, Addictive, Controlling, Cowardly, Flaky, Gullible, Hostile, Hypocritical, Impulsive, Insecure, Nagging, Needy, Nosy, Obsessive, Possessive, Pushy, Vindictive, Weak-Willed, Worrywart

IMPACT ON BASIC NEEDS

Self-Actualization: It's hard for a character to pursue dreams and high aspirations when they're worried about a loved one's basic survival. While it's not impossible, it will be difficult for the character to be personally actualized unless they're able to fully release responsibility for the person in question.

Esteem and Recognition: A character who feels responsible for someone else's difficulties (because they enabled the person, didn't deal with them effectively, or took too long to make the right decision) will blame themselves, at least in part, for the other person's unhappiness.

Love and Belonging: Choosing to leave someone to the consequences of their own actions will very likely result in a rift with that person.

Safety and Security: The character's mental and physical well-being can be depleted if she's unable to distance herself from an unhealthy preoccupation with a loved one's choices.

POSITIVE TRAITS TO HELP THE CHARACTER COPE: Analytical, Calm, Confident, Courteous, Decisive, Diplomatic, Disciplined, Friendly, Just, Nurturing, Optimistic, Patient, Persistent, Persuasive, Supportive, Unselfish, Wise

POSITIVE OUTCOMES

The other person hitting rock bottom and turning their life around
The character recognizing when they're being manipulated or played
Creating distance from the constant drama and conflict and experiencing peace
Gaining confidence from being able to stand up for oneself
The character accepting they're not responsible for other people's actions and choices
Letting go of what other people think
Being appreciative of the nurturing and supportive people in the character's life

MAKING A DISCOVERY THAT THREATENS THE BOND OF FRIENDSHIP

EXAMPLES

Discovering a secret from a friend's past that colors the character's view of them, such as his role as a bully, abusive behavior toward animals, or reckless behavior that endangered others

Learning a friend is cheating on their partner—perhaps with the character's own spouse

Finding out the friend holds extreme political or social views, such as racism or sexism

Learning the friend was responsible for a major blunder that impacted others—a blunder they denied playing a part in

Discovering a friend is secretly competing with the character for a job, a romantic partner, a prize, etc.

The friend being involved in something that runs counter to the character's values, such as embezzling funds or harassing others

Overhearing the friend speaking badly about the character

Learning the friend has shared the character's secrets or struggles with others

MINOR COMPLICATIONS

Having to confront the friend

The friendship becoming awkward because the character is pulling back

Not knowing what to do and having to act in the meantime like nothing is wrong

Telling someone else about the situation and them taking the friend's side

Frustration with the friend for their underhanded dealings

Learning that others knew about the issue and didn't tell the character

Conflict with other friends who feel they have to take sides and can't stay neutral

The character's reputation being questioned because of their association with the friend

POTENTIALLY DISASTROUS RESULTS

Severing the friendship and losing the friend entirely

Not saying anything and becoming complicit in the friend's criminal or unethical behavior

Supporting the wrongdoer and being rejected by other friends

The friend responding to the character's confrontation in a volatile or violent way

Seeking vengeance against the friend that causes pain, isolation, or physical harm

Being targeted with vengeance by the friend, leading to physical injury, social isolation, property damage, or wrecked relationships

Facing backlash when the friend denies the accusation, bringing the character's reputation into question

The character sticking with the friend out of convenience instead of doing what's right

Choosing to continue the toxic relationship in hopes the other person will change

Forgiving a transgression only to be betrayed again

RESULTING EMOTIONS: Agitation, Anger, Anguish, Annoyance, Appalled, Apprehension, Betrayed, Conflicted, Contempt, Denial, Determination, Disappointment, Disbelief, Dread, Hurt, Nervousness, Overwhelmed, Reluctance, Resentment, Sadness, Shock, Skepticism

POSSIBLE INTERNAL STRUGGLES

Wanting to maintain the friendship but finding it difficult to forgive the friend
Wanting to be a good friend but not being able to bear the truth of the discovery
Forgiving the friend but seeing them differently now
Needing to confront their friend but not knowing how to go about it
Not knowing if they should address the situation or turn a blind eye
Feeling betrayed by the friend, even if their actions were not against the character personally

NEGATIVE TRAITS THAT MAY WORSEN THE SITUATION: Catty, Confrontational, Controlling, Disloyal, Disrespectful, Evasive, Fanatical, Gossipy, Haughty, Hypocritical, Indecisive, Inflexible, Judgmental, Melodramatic, Needy, Pushy, Resentful, Subservient

IMPACT ON BASIC NEEDS

Esteem and Recognition: A character who feels duped or manipulated may feel a jolt to their self-esteem, wondering how they didn't see this coming.

Love and Belonging: A severed friendship, even for good reason, can leave the character feeling as if they have no one to confide in or connect with. If the character's been betrayed, they may struggle to trust others in the future and stick to more distanced relationships.

Safety and Security: If their friend has done something dangerous or illegal, knowing about it could threaten the character's safety. The situation could become even more tenuous if the character chose to speak out about it.

POSITIVE TRAITS TO HELP THE CHARACTER COPE: Bold, Calm, Cautious, Diplomatic, Discreet, Easygoing, Empathetic, Humble, Independent, Inspirational, Kind, Loyal, Mature, Objective, Optimistic, Patient, Protective, Unselfish, Wise

POSITIVE OUTCOMES

Being able to work through the situation and creating a deeper bond with the friend
Recognizing everyone makes mistakes and being able to offer forgiveness
The character ending the relationship, freeing them to make new, more compatible friends
The character's circle of friends becoming stronger once the negative influence is removed
The character learning to follow their intuition about people
Having frank conversations in which the characters can exchange views and grow as people
The friend seeing the error of their ways
Seeing similarities between oneself and the friend (how they treat others, behaving self-destructively, etc.) and deciding to make a change

NEEDING TO SABOTAGE SOMEONE TO WIN

NOTES: The character's outer motivation is everything, and their number one goal is to reach that milestone. This need can be so great that when someone or something comes along and threatens that objective, the character may be tempted to do whatever it takes to win. The act of sabotaging someone can generate inherent conflict, but the prior mental struggle, the *Do-I-Or-Don't-I?* inner turmoil, can pose intriguing questions and add rich layers to a scene.

EXAMPLES
The character spiking a rival's drink or food prior to an interview or big game
A politician digging up dirt on an opponent
Entrapping a romantic rival to set them up and gain "evidence" against them
Giving someone the wrong answers to an important exam
Holding back useful information
Badmouthing an ex to win a child over to one's side
Leaking an unflattering story about the rival to the press
Knowingly sharing information about a rival that can be used against them
Creating an emergency for the rival's family to distract him or remove him from the competition
Hiring someone to physically take out the competition

MINOR COMPLICATIONS
Trying to make plans without getting caught
The character having to be subversive and sly when they're not good at it
Trouble finding dirt on a rival
The character having to cozy up to people they're just using as a source of information
Time and energy being diverted from the character perfecting their skills to sabotaging a rival
Having to hire shady individuals to do the character's dirty work
Financial expenses (to hire a private detective, pay off informants, etc.)
Increased self-doubt, since the character knows they can't beat the opponent through fair means
Interacting with the competitor on a daily basis and having to act like everything is normal

POTENTIALLY DISASTROUS RESULTS
The character being in denial about the wrongness of this course of action (believing it to be justified), meaning, they completely discard their moral beliefs in pursuit of the goal
Someone finding out and threatening to expose the character
The plan going wrong and blowing up in the character's face
Someone innocent getting caught in the crossfire
The character being removed from the running (being kicked off a team, expelled from school, removed from a contest, etc.)
Getting fired
The situation going public and shining an unwelcome spotlight on the character's misdeeds
Loved ones abandoning the character when the truth is made known

The character succeeding with their plan and being empowered to do it again when other competitors come on the scene

Engaging in addictive behaviors, either to cope with the stress or as a method of self-punishment

The character sabotaging the rival and then losing to someone else

RESULTING EMOTIONS: Bitterness, Conflicted, Desperation, Determination, Doubt, Dread, Embarrassment, Envy, Fear, Frustration, Guilt, Hatred, Inadequacy, Insecurity, Intimidation, Jealousy, Remorse, Resentment, Schadenfreude, Scorn, Self-Loathing, Shame

POSSIBLE INTERNAL STRUGGLES
The character hating to break their own moral code but being desperate to win
Knowing deep down that even if they win, they didn't earn it and don't deserve it
Feeling they will never be good enough
Struggling with self-loathing

NEGATIVE TRAITS THAT MAY WORSEN THE SITUATION: Cocky, Compulsive, Controlling, Foolish, Impulsive, Jealous, Nervous, Reckless, Unethical, Unintelligent, Violent

IMPACT ON BASIC NEEDS
Self-Actualization: If the character feels badly about their attempt to undermine a competitor, any euphoria at winning will be short-lived. Because their morals and actions didn't align, a crisis of identity may follow.

Esteem and Recognition: If the character knows a win was not deserved, this will only deepen underlying self-esteem issues and insecurities.

Love and Belonging: If the character's actions are condemned by others, he may find himself ousted from an organization or community he cares about.

Safety and Security: A character doing something like this risks a lot and, if caught, could lose everything—including his job, profitable endorsement deals, and other sources of income.

POSITIVE TRAITS TO HELP THE CHARACTER COPE: Appreciative, Centered, Confident, Cooperative, Empathetic, Gentle, Honorable, Industrious, Inspirational, Kind, Nurturing, Objective, Optimistic, Spiritual, Talented, Unselfish

POSITIVE OUTCOMES
Improved self-esteem gained from deciding not to go through with it
The competitor being removed, clearing the way for the character to win
A moral reality check causing a change of heart where the character learns that winning isn't everything
The moral crossroads leading the character to become a better person
Discovering and revealing dark information about the competitor that saves people from being victimized.

PULLING THE PLUG ON SOMEONE

EXAMPLES
The character making a medical choice for a loved one on life support
Not taking measures to prolong life for the person who wants to die
Abandoning someone to their fate because it is the only choice
Putting a cherished pet down
Not intervening as someone is dying
Making a decision that will result in another person's death
Choosing between two people because only one can be saved
The character assisting someone in suicide

MINOR COMPLICATIONS
Dealing with angry relatives who don't agree with the character's decision
Having to temporarily set aside all other responsibilities and commitments
Having to explain the decision repeatedly to justify it to others involved
Rushing to take care of any red tape
Fast-tracking the individual's last wishes (setting up an appointment with a lawyer, bringing loved ones in to visit, making funeral arrangements, etc.)
Carrying the burden of guilt
Being made to feel guilty by the one making the request (if the character is reluctant)
Having to do things a certain way to avoid prosecution
Emotional discomfort at being present for the person's final moments

POTENTIALLY DISASTROUS RESULTS
Threats and violence from those who opposed the decision
Discovering after the fact there was another option
Finding out there was a clerical error and the DNR (Do Not Resuscitate) order wasn't valid
Creating a rift in the family
Being sued or cast out of the family
The character discovering they were used as a pawn by those who wanted the patient to die
Supporters, allies, or family of the one who died coming for revenge
Nightmares, anxiety, depression, and other aftereffects of PTSD (Post-Traumatic Stress Disorder)
False accusations surrounding the action that ruins the character's reputation or career
Discovering a caregiver's mistake after the fact (the diagnosis was wrong or a typo in the dosage caused a false appearance of terminal deterioration, etc.)

RESULTING EMOTIONS: Anguish, Anxiety, Conflicted, Connectedness, Despair, Desperation, Disillusionment, Dread, Grief, Guilt, Overwhelmed, Powerlessness, Reluctance, Remorse, Resignation, Sadness, Somberness, Tormented, Vulnerability

POSSIBLE INTERNAL STRUGGLES
Overwhelming guilt, even though it was the right decision
Second-guessing the decision and actions in the aftermath
The character worrying about being judged spiritually for their actions
Feeling stupid and worthless for being duped (if this was the case)
Struggling with regret and remorse
Feeling shocked, betrayed, and angry at the reactions of others to the no-win situation
Feeling anger at the one who passed, followed by shame for being angry
Anguish at not being able to make the passing less painful for others
Experiencing regret for not offering or asking for forgiveness, trying to repair a rift, or otherwise making things right before the end

NEGATIVE TRAITS THAT MAY WORSEN THE SITUATION: Addictive, Cowardly, Defensive, Disrespectful, Insecure, Morbid, Needy, Self-Destructive, Withdrawn

IMPACT ON BASIC NEEDS
Self-Actualization: In the case of close relationships where the character is the protector (such as a mother and child), helping to end their loved one's life may cause them to believe they failed in their role, leading to an identity crisis.

Esteem and Recognition: Being forced to participate in someone's death could erode a character's sense of self-worth, even if they believe they had no other option.

Love and Belonging: Loved ones who opposed the character's choice may cast them out, leaving them without family or home.

Physiological Needs: When someone dies unexpectedly, loved ones who were not there to see what happened can make accusations and lay blame unfairly. If this is taken to the extreme, family members could come after the character to make them pay for what they took … an eye for an eye.

POSITIVE TRAITS TO HELP THE CHARACTER COPE: Calm, Centered, Courageous, Decisive, Empathetic, Gentle, Honorable, Kind, Merciful, Perceptive, Spiritual, Wholesome

POSITIVE OUTCOMES
Being relieved by seeing an end to someone's suffering
The character realizing they are strong enough to make exceptionally hard decisions
A greater appreciation for life and the importance of living it in full
Having a closer relationship with people who were supportive throughout the process
Working through a fear of death by being exposed to the peace it brought the one dying
The death serving as a wake-up call, pushing the character to change their habits and attitudes, let go of past pain, and pursue meaningful goals

SACRIFICING ETHICS OR MORALS FOR THE GREATER GOOD

EXAMPLES

The character cheating to win an election and prevent a despot from assuming power

A narcotics officer sampling drugs to maintain his cover so he can bust a drug ring

The character sleeping with someone to gain their trust and find damning evidence against them

Voting for a despicable politician because his policies or ideals are better than his rival's

Beating someone up to get information from them to solve a crime or save a life

Stealing from a corrupt employer to provide essential supplies for suffering people

Allowing one person to die to save a city full of people

Framing a corrupt employee to save the company from ruin

Planting evidence or lying under oath to make sure a guilty person doesn't go free

Murdering a known child abuser or rapist

Spiking an enemy's drink to get them temporarily out of the way so the bigger plan can proceed

Breaking a promise to never again be involved with certain activities or people (because doing so allows the character to right a wrong)

Pretending to like or agree with despicable people so the character can avoid scrutiny and continue with their underground operation

MINOR COMPLICATIONS

The character needing to cozy up to people they despise

The character having to become intimately involved with the people they're working against

The enemy becoming suspicious of the character

Being insulted or criticized by those who don't know about the character's ulterior motive

Needing to sneak out at unusual hours without raising suspicions

Having to dodge questions about what the character is doing and why

The character being confronted by a beloved friend or family members about their actions

Being questioned by the police

Having to keep the plan secret and go through it all alone

POTENTIALLY DISASTROUS RESULTS

Going to jail for breaking the law

Losing access to resources, money, or a powerful ally that is necessary for the mission to succeed

The character's reputation being trashed

The enemy coming after the character's family in retribution

The character being gravely injured or killed

The character's morals shifting along the way

Making the sacrifice and the enemy winning anyway

Making the sacrifice, then learning all was not as it seemed

The character learning they've been a pawn for someone else

The people who benefited from the character's actions never appreciating what he did
Developing a panic or anxiety disorder from the stress
The character becoming hardened; losing empathy and only caring about the mission

RESULTING EMOTIONS: Anxiety, Apprehension, Conflicted, Determination, Disillusionment, Dissatisfaction, Doubt, Dread, Fear, Guilt, Loneliness, Paranoia, Reluctance, Remorse, Resignation, Self-Loathing, Shame, Unappreciated, Vulnerability

POSSIBLE INTERNAL STRUGGLES
The character worrying they won't achieve their goal and any sacrifices are in vain
Being tempted to give up before they get in too deep
Becoming paranoid; believing the enemy knows about the character's agenda
Coping with guilt or shame over the sacrificed morals
A religious character worrying about their eternal fate and whether or not they'll be forgiven
The character experiencing a crisis of doubt as they begin to see things from the enemy's perspective
Wanting to explain to loved ones what's really going on but being unable to
Struggling with self-loathing over their actions
Worrying that something deep and fundamental is being damaged as they maintain their cover

NEGATIVE TRAITS THAT MAY WORSEN THE SITUATION: Cynical, Haughty, Judgmental, Nervous, Paranoid, Reckless, Subservient, Timid, Volatile, Weak-Willed, Worrywart

IMPACT ON BASIC NEEDS
   Self-Actualization: A character with a clearly defined view of right and wrong may never be able to fully justify going against their moral code, even for a good cause.
   Esteem and Recognition: The character may despise himself for doing things he believes to be immoral, even if it means righting a wrong. He also might deal with criticism and a lack of respect from loved ones who don't understand his motivation or actions.
   Love and Belonging: By embracing nefarious methods, the character risks losing dear friends or a whole community of people who don't agree with his course of action.
   Safety and Security: If the character's methods are ones that could land them in jail or raise the ire of dangerous people, their safety and security will be at risk.

POSITIVE TRAITS TO HELP THE CHARACTER COPE: Adaptable, Centered, Confident, Decisive, Diplomatic, Discreet, Independent, Industrious, Objective, Organized, Resourceful, Responsible, Socially Aware, Uninhibited, Unselfish

POSITIVE OUTCOMES
Saving many people from harm
Solving a crime or bringing a criminal to justice
Making society a safer place for a particular group of people
The character gaining great personal satisfaction from having done the right thing despite the sacrifices that were made
Great injustice or a flaw in the system being brought to light so others can take up the cause

SOMEONE WITNESSING ONE'S MISBEHAVIOR

NOTES: It's a sad fact of human nature that people don't always feel remorse for wrongdoing; very often, they only express regret for getting caught. When a character trying to keep their actions secret discovers that someone knows about their behavior, they may experience conflict in the form of what to do about the witness.

EXAMPLES
The character being caught in the act of doing something wrong
Realizing a security camera may have recorded the character's misbehavior
Receiving an anonymous email or text from someone claiming to have witnessed the act
The character seeing someone in the vicinity who may have witnessed the act
Being confronted by someone who witnessed the misbehavior
Being blackmailed by someone with details about the event
Someone asking specific questions that indicate they already know the answers

MINOR COMPLICATIONS
Being confronted by the witness
Feeling embarrassed about being caught or guilty about the wrongdoing
Needing to convince the person they didn't see what they thought they did
Having to quickly manufacture a convincing cover story
Having to do favors for the witness to prevent them from telling anyone
Not knowing what exactly the person saw or heard
Living on pins and needles; constantly expecting to be confronted and accused
Spending time doing damage control
Having to surveil the witness to see who they talk to
Investigating the witness to find leverage that can be held over them if needed
Having to falsify evidence or secure an alibi (in case the witness speaks out)
The witness telling someone else—meaning more people the character must neutralize
Trouble sleeping and eating
Being distracted at work or school
Having to lie convincingly by remaining calm, controlling one's body language, and speaking in an unrushed and unconcerned tone
Having to figure out what the witness knows and if anything should be done

POTENTIALLY DISASTROUS RESULTS
The witness speaking to the character's spouse, teacher, boss, etc.
The character being brought in for questioning
Getting caught and facing repercussions for the action (being arrested, being suspended from school or work, being sued, etc.)
Trusting the witness with the truth and being betrayed when they go to the police, tell the enemy, or use the information to their advantage
Being blackmailed by the witness

Going to extreme measures to silence the witness, such as threatening, kidnapping, or killing them
A shaky marriage falling apart under the stress
Family members and friends pulling away when they find out what the character did
A partner-in-crime blaming the character for being seen and deciding to take them out
Word getting out in the criminal community, triggering a lack of trust and the character not being able to get work (if the behavior was illegal)

RESULTING EMOTIONS: Agitation, Anger, Anxiety, Apprehension, Desperation, Determination, Fear, Flustered, Insecurity, Self-Pity, Shock, Unease, Vulnerability, Worry

POSSIBLE INTERNAL STRUGGLES
Wanting the witness to stay quiet so nothing more permanent needs to be done but having too much experience to believe that will be the case
Being mad at oneself for not hiding the misbehavior better
Wanting to neutralize the witness but being opposed to doing what would have to be done
Blaming the witness for putting the character in this situation

NEGATIVE TRAITS THAT MAY WORSEN THE SITUATION: Confrontational, Controlling, Cruel, Hostile, Irrational, Nervous, Paranoid, Unethical, Vindictive, Volatile

IMPACT ON BASIC NEEDS
   Self-Actualization: A character who is ashamed or remorseful because they know they were caught in a compromising position may find it hard to move on and live life at their best. This can result in them settling for less than what they're capable of.
   Esteem and Recognition: If the character regrets their misbehavior, knowing someone witnessed it would exacerbate the embarrassment, making the character feel even worse.
   Love and Belonging: A character who is always on edge can become a nightmare to live with, driving away the people closest to them.
   Physiological Needs: If the character was acting on behalf of someone else and word gets out that they left behind a witness, the character could be taken out to tie up loose ends.

POSITIVE TRAITS TO HELP THE CHARACTER COPE: Bold, Cautious, Decisive, Diplomatic, Honest, Just, Loyal, Merciful, Observant, Patient, Persuasive, Protective, Spunky

POSITIVE OUTCOMES
Being able to put things right, thanks to the intervention of the witness
Convincing the witness there was nothing underhanded going on, causing them to let it drop
Discovering the witness is sympathetic to the character's behavior—in the case of politically-motivated vandalism, for instance
The character coming clean about the misbehavior and clearing their conscience
The character's willingness to cross moral lines to silence the witness being a wake-up call

WITNESSING ABUSE

EXAMPLES
The character seeing someone mistreat, neglect, or physically harm their pet
Hearing screaming matches in a neighboring apartment or house
Watching a stranger hit or verbally abuse their child
Suspecting someone is being trafficked
Witnessing a neighbor gaslighting their spouse
Seeing a friend regularly abuse a co-worker by belittling or making fun of them
A child witnessing an adult harming a sibling
Seeing the neglect of a nursing home patient
Witnessing sexual abuse at a party
Seeing others being abused in a prisoner-of-war, internment, or refugee camp

MINOR COMPLICATIONS
The character not being sure if what they've witnessed is considered abuse
Time spent speaking with the police, signing papers, attending court, etc.
Sustaining minor injuries from attempting to intervene
Others wanting to gossip with the character about the situation
Facing threats and intimidation from the abuser
Bringing up the situation with someone and being ignored or dismissed
Other people reinforcing the idea that nothing serious is going on

POTENTIALLY DISASTROUS RESULTS
Not intervening, then being held liable
Feuds erupting when others find out the character did nothing
Going to the authorities and having them refuse to investigate
The character not stepping in because they believe someone else will (the bystander effect) but no one else does
Waffling over what to do and something horrible happening in the meantime
The character's heart hardening over time due to them consistently turning a blind eye to abuse
Intervening to stop the abuse and being seriously injured or harmed
The character's intervention infuriating the abuser, resulting in escalated abuse or retaliation
Developing PTSD from repeatedly witnessing the abuse of others
A child who consistently witnessed violence growing up to be an abuser
Taking matters into one's own hands and being charged for assault, trespassing, or another crime

RESULTING EMOTIONS: Anger, Anguish, Appalled, Concern, Conflicted, Denial, Desperation, Determination, Disgust, Disillusionment, Dread, Fear, Horror, Indifference, Intimidation, Moved, Nervousness, Pity, Powerlessness, Rage, Shock, Uncertainty, Vengefulness

POSSIBLE INTERNAL STRUGGLES
The character wanting to intervene but fearing for their own safety

The character wanting to do something but doubting their capabilities
Intervening, then worrying about how the victim fared later at the hands of their abuser
Being paralyzed with indecision over what to do
Choosing to do nothing and feeling guilty about it
Suffering from survivor's guilt
A long-term victim being relieved they're not the one being abused this time, then suffering from shame or self-loathing for feeling that way

NEGATIVE TRAITS THAT MAY WORSEN THE SITUATION: Apathetic, Cowardly, Cruel, Disloyal, Evasive, Evil, Inattentive, Indecisive, Inhibited, Lazy, Nervous, Prejudiced, Selfish, Timid, Uncooperative

IMPACT ON BASIC NEEDS
   Esteem and Recognition: If the character witnessing abuse doesn't intervene or provide any kind of assistance, it could impact both their own self-esteem and how others view them.
   Love and Belonging: Not intervening on behalf of a friend or loved one could undermine their status as part of a social group since they enable the abuse to continue by not getting involved.
   Safety and Security: Standing up for someone in an emotionally charged situation could endanger the character or result in greater harm for the victim.
   Physiological needs: In extreme situations where emotions are high and the people involved are unstable, a character trying to save someone from being abused could be killed.

POSITIVE TRAITS TO HELP THE CHARACTER COPE: Alert, Bold, Courageous, Decisive, Diplomatic, Empathetic, Honorable, Idealistic, Just, Kind, Mature, Nurturing, Observant, Passionate, Perceptive, Protective, Responsible, Socially Aware, Spontaneous

POSITIVE OUTCOMES
Helping the abused character escape a dangerous situation
Building a relationship with the victim, providing strength and support in their situation
Testifying against the abuser and ending the mistreatment
A business or organization being made aware of the abuse and creating a plan to keep it from happening
Reporting animal abuse to the authorities and saving mistreated pets
The character feeling good about doing the right thing in a difficult situation

WITNESSING CORRUPTION

EXAMPLES

The character witnessing someone accepting a bribe

Knowing that someone benefited from cronyism or nepotism

Witnessing an abuse of authority (police brutality, evidence being planted, etc.)

Seeing someone skim money from a business

Watching a certain agenda being pushed via unethical means (biased media coverage, censorship, intimidation, etc.)

Learning a powerful lobby has illegally influenced government officials to pursue legislation that suits its purposes

Discovering an "impartial" company or establishment is owned by an individual or corporation with a clear agenda

Jurors being bought off, intimidated, or influenced

Seeing an obviously guilty party go free because of their wealth, position, or political connections

MINOR COMPLICATIONS

Being told that what was seen was different than what it appeared

Not knowing who to inform about the corruption

Being "leaned on" by people who don't want the character to go public with what they've seen

Speaking out and facing unfair reprisals, such as losing a perk or lucrative account

Being investigated by the offending party in an effort to discredit the character

Having to be available for interviews by reporters, investigators, or detectives

Being "advised" (intimidated) by others to drop the complaint

Nosy neighbors, relatives, and co-workers giving unhelpful advice about what to do

Losing respect for the individual involved (if they were known to the character)

The corrupt party applying a guilt trip about how their life will be ruined if the character says anything

Having to change a routine to avoid the guilty party

POTENTIALLY DISASTROUS RESULTS

The character's faith in a trusted organization, institution, or individual being destroyed

Not reporting the corruption and becoming implicated by association

The character allowing himself to be convinced what he witnessed wasn't corruption

Acting as a whistleblower and being fired or demoted

Informing authorities about the corruption and becoming a victim of violent reprisals

The character being doxed as a form of punishment, endangering them and their family

The character's name and reputation being ruthlessly tarnished

A past discretion the character desperately wants to remain hidden being brought to light to discredit them

Family members being targeted (their private information being given to nefarious parties, a vehicle being repossessed through a mysterious error, etc.)

Confiding in a manager or senior colleague about the corruption, then learning the trusted person is also involved

RESULTING EMOTIONS: Anger, Annoyance, Anxiety, Appalled, Betrayed, Bitterness, Contempt, Denial, Determination, Devastation, Disappointment, Disgust, Disillusionment, Excitement, Fear, Frustration, Intimidation, Powerlessness, Rage, Resignation, Shock, Worry

POSSIBLE INTERNAL STRUGGLES

Wanting to do something but being afraid to get involved

Struggling with apathy; the character knowing they should act but believing it will accomplish nothing

Choosing not to act, then feeling guilty when the corruption continues

The character struggling over what to do because they're involved in their own unethical activities and don't want to draw unwanted scrutiny

The character knowing the corruption is wrong but not wanting to speak out because they're also benefiting from it

The character being fear-driven because they're close to the people involved

Difficulty trusting similar institutions or organizations

NEGATIVE TRAITS THAT MAY WORSEN THE SITUATION: Antisocial, Apathetic, Confrontational, Controlling, Dishonest, Fanatical, Hypocritical, Nervous, Paranoid, Timid

IMPACT ON BASIC NEEDS

Self-Actualization: A character who sees corruption in a system may choose not to engage with it, but if that organization or institution is needed to achieve certain dreams, the decision could sacrifice other meaningful goals.

Esteem and Recognition: A character who doesn't take action due to insecurity or inferiority may find those feelings exacerbated.

Love and Belonging: Not reporting the corruption could weaken close relationships if those people think the character should have taken action.

Safety and Security: If the corrupt individuals know their behavior was witnessed, the character or their family could become targeted.

POSITIVE TRAITS TO HELP THE CHARACTER COPE: Ambitious, Calm, Courageous, Decisive, Diplomatic, Discreet, Honorable, Idealistic, Just, Observant, Passionate, Protective, Responsible, Uninhibited, Unselfish

POSITIVE OUTCOMES

Doing the right thing and feeling more confident because of it

Knowing which companies or organizations not to support because of the corruption

Becoming more determined to fight against corruption and stop it from getting started

The character trusting their instincts when it comes to reading other people

Informing the authorities and seeing the corrupt parties face justice for their actions

Being able to help form a stronger and more ethical workplace

Reporting the wrongdoing and exposing an entire network that can then be taken down

Discovering a friend's true moral stance by their support of the character or their efforts to dissuade them from acting

WITNESSING DISCRIMINATION

NOTES: While being a victim of discrimination is its own form of conflict, the situation is slightly different for those seeing it happen. Below are some examples of the kinds of discrimination your character might witness.

EXAMPLES
An employer favoring one person over another because of ethnicity, gender, or sexual preference
A parent habitually disciplining one sibling more severely than the other
An employee being promoted because they're related to the boss
Someone being given a job because they belong to a certain club, church, or organization
Journalists skewing their reporting toward one side of the story
A customer being treated differently because of the way they look
Service being denied to someone because of a mental disability, skin color, etc.
Learning male and female employees with the same job description, experience, and education are being paid vastly different salaries
A landlord refusing to rent their home to a same-sex couple
An employee being let go for being pregnant
A patient being denied medication or health care because of racial bias
Criminals of a certain race, religion, etc. being given harsher sentences
Neighbors not being invited to a block party because they speak a different language
An assumption being made about someone's preferences (what they like to eat, what kind of music they prefer, etc.) based on certain factors

MINOR COMPLICATIONS
Wondering how to bring the inequity up when an employer is discriminating—say, in the case of a nanny observing one child being loved unconditionally while the other is not)
Trying to stand up for those maligned and being shot down
Not knowing how to bring up the behavior with relatives who are touchy about criticism
Being ridiculed for not being able to "take a joke"
Trying to talk about discrimination with people who immediately go on the offensive
Conversations escalating to arguments
The character being asked to leave or told to mind their own business
Strained relationships becoming unstable when the behavior is brought up
Not being sure who to talk to about the inequity, especially when bias is widespread
Trying to support the person who experienced the discrimination but saying something that reveals a similar bias

POTENTIALLY DISASTROUS RESULTS
The character's ignorance causing them to see nothing wrong with the behavior, resulting in them doing nothing and tacitly encouraging it
Bias and discrimination becoming more widespread because no one is speaking against it
A child developing behavioral or emotional disorders from a parent or teacher's bias

Losing a job for speaking out against discrimination in the workplace
Losing friends who believe the character is overreacting
Not doing enough to speak out against a wrong and something terrible happening (a mob attacking an individual, the royal guard destroying property and a child being hurt, etc.)
The character recognizing biased thinking in their own mind but instead of dealing with it, they ignore it—along with the discrimination going on around them
Being mistreated for standing up to those who are discriminating others

RESULTING EMOTIONS: Anger, Annoyance, Anxiety, Appalled, Conflicted, Defensiveness, Denial, Determination, Disappointment, Discouragement, Disillusionment, Frustration, Hatred, Indifference, Pity, Rage, Resentment, Resignation, Satisfaction, Schadenfreude, Scorn, Shock

POSSIBLE INTERNAL STRUGGLES
Wanting to speak up but fearing retribution
Struggling to process newfound personal bias in the wake of the discrimination
Feeling guilty for sharing characteristics with the biased person (being of the same race, gender, religion, etc.)
Worrying that speaking up will escalate the discriminatory behavior rather than prevent it
Feeling incapable of bringing about change because the task is so enormous

NEGATIVE TRAITS THAT MAY WORSEN THE SITUATION: Abrasive, Cowardly, Disloyal, Fanatical, Inhibited, Insecure, Melodramatic, Paranoid, Prejudiced, Timid, Violent

IMPACT ON BASIC NEEDS
Self-Actualization: Confronting discrimination in hostile or closed-minded environments can result in the character being punished and her goals being pushed out of reach.
Esteem and Recognition: A character who knows the right thing to do but struggles to take action can begin to think badly about herself.
Love and Belonging: Discrimination (and what defines it) is an emotional topic for many people. Whether the character speaks out or remains silent, she may find herself isolated from friends in her circle who disagree with her decision.

POSITIVE TRAITS TO HELP THE CHARACTER COPE: Bold, Confident, Courteous, Decisive, Honorable, Idealistic, Just, Nurturing, Persuasive, Protective, Socially Aware

POSITIVE OUTCOMES
Creating a space for discussion where real change and progress can be made
Forming stronger relationships with those being discriminated against, providing support and partnerships
Creating a better understanding between groups of people, leading to less friction
Committing to unlearn personal biases and be a better ally

Duty and
Responsibility

A CHILD GETTING SICK

NOTES: A child falling ill can be a temporary inconvenience that disrupts the character's schedule when time is of the essence, or it can be a devastating event that turns their entire world upside down.

EXAMPLES
Developing an infection (sinusitis, pneumonia, strep throat, etc.)
Having a severe allergic reaction
Getting food poisoning
Coming down with something contagious (pink eye, the flu, scarlet fever, etc.)
Suffering from motion sickness on a long car ride
Being diagnosed with in incurable disease (HIV, epilepsy, Muscular Dystrophy, diabetes, etc.)
Being stricken with cancer
Having an asthma attack

MINOR COMPLICATIONS
Having to miss work to care for the child
Feeling guilty for having to work and leave a slightly ill child at home alone
Difficulties arising from the child missing school
Having to administer medication on a set schedule
The child crying or complaining
Being unable to obtain a medical appointment in a timely manner
The child refusing to take their medication or get a shot
Having to launder soiled bedding or clothing
Adjusting a child's diet or environment to improve their illness
Figuring out the needs or pain of a nonverbal child
Managing other children while caring for the one who is sick
Having to isolate a contagious child from other family members
Others in the household catching the child's cold or flu

POTENTIALLY DISASTROUS RESULTS
Doctors being unable to diagnose the illness (or diagnosing it incorrectly)
Experiencing the death of a child due to the illness
Being unable to pay for medication, medical care, or equipment
The character missing so much work they lose their job
A severe allergic reaction that results in the throat closing up
Medication being ineffective in treating the child
An insurance company refusing to cover medical care
Having to re-home a pet that is the source of an allergy
Having to travel long distances for treatment or to see a specialty doctor
The child having permanent injuries as a result of the illness
The illness becoming a chronic one that recurs often
Needing to relocate to better meet the child's needs

Dealing with a stigma associated with the illness
Having to explain a severe illness to the child

RESULTING EMOTIONS: Annoyance, Anxiety, Apprehension, Disbelief, Dread, Empathy, Fear, Frustration, Impatience, Overwhelmed, Panic, Powerlessness, Resentment, Resignation, Sadness, Unease, Worry

POSSIBLE INTERNAL STRUGGLES
Feeling guilty for making decisions that unknowingly contributed to the illness
Having to trust others with the critical care of the child
Struggling to accept the new "normal" of a long-term illness
Being tempted to obtain money or care in an unlawful or unethical way
Resenting the child for the difficulty they're causing and hating oneself for feeling that way
Feeling incapable and powerless in the wake of a serious diagnosis or a terrifying element of the illness (severe pain, frequent seizures, etc.)
Worrying others will discover the true cause of the illness (Munchausen syndrome by proxy)

NEGATIVE TRAITS THAT MAY WORSEN THE SITUATION: Apathetic, Compulsive, Cruel, Disorganized, Forgetful, Impatient, Inattentive, Irresponsible, Martyr, Melodramatic, Possessive, Pushy, Selfish, Stubborn, Uncooperative, Workaholic, Worrywart

IMPACT ON BASIC NEEDS
   Self-Actualization: Caring for a seriously ill child may require other goals to be put on hold, especially those tied to meaningful personal development.
   Esteem and Recognition: If the character feels guilty for unknowingly contributing to the illness (or if others blame her), she may begin to despise herself.
   Love and Belonging: Caring for a child with a severe illness may mean the character will not have much time and energy for other family members. Younger children in the household may have difficulty understanding this and feel resentment or act out.
   Safety and Security: An overworked, distraught character may have a hard time keeping up with her own mental health. As well, if finances become strained, the child's safety may be threatened from not receiving needed medications or care.
   Physiological Needs: Sleep deprivation is a real problem for someone providing round-the-clock care for a sick child.

POSITIVE TRAITS TO HELP THE CHARACTER COPE: Adaptable, Appreciative, Centered, Easygoing, Empathetic, Honorable, Industrious, Kind, Loyal, Nurturing, Optimistic, Organized, Patient, Persistent, Protective, Resourceful, Unselfish

POSITIVE OUTCOMES
The character becoming aware of their own strength and capability
Being able to educate others or raise awareness about the illness
The character recognizing their priorities are out of order and taking steps to fix that
Seeking out healthy ways to handle life's difficulties (faith, meditation, exercise, etc.)
Learning to accept help from others

A PROBLEM AT A CHILD'S SCHOOL

NOTES: Every parent wants their child to do well—for a variety of reasons, from desiring what's best for them to not wanting to be personally inconvenienced. So when the character gets a call from the school, tensions automatically rise. Consider the following scenarios that could cause conflict for your character should their child be involved.

EXAMPLES
Getting into a fight
Bullying others or being bullied
Getting caught with drugs, alcohol, a weapon, pornography, or some other forbidden item
Sending or receiving inappropriate text messages at school
Posting something inappropriate about another student on social media
Being truant or repeatedly tardy to class
Failing to complete assignments or participate in class
Disrupting the learning environment
Disrespecting a teacher or another staff member
Violating the dress code policy
Leaving the classroom or campus without permission
Getting caught being intimate with another student
Using school technology inappropriately
Failing to demonstrate mastery of curricular objectives
Sharing information that forces the school to summon child protective services

MINOR COMPLICATIONS
Missing work to meet with the school or stay home with a suspended child
Having to drive the child to and from school
Having to punish a child for their behavior at school
Difficulty getting the child to go to school (if they're a victim of bullying or are fearful)
Trying to get to the bottom of a child's misbehavior
Struggling to be able to pay for formal evaluations and testing
Having to find helpful resources to support the child
The parent being embarrassed by their child's behavior
Facing criticism from other parents

POTENTIALLY DISASTROUS RESULTS
The child being reassigned to another classroom or school, increasing the parent's commute
The school not protecting the child from bullying or physical harm and them being hurt again
The parent ignoring that their child is at fault for breaking rules or hurting others
The parent blaming the teacher for the child's failing grades
Administration responding punitively, not supportively, to a child's emotional or psychological event
A teenage child facing legal charges (due to drug possession, hurting another student, sexual harassment, etc.)

A disability or condition going undiagnosed and untreated

The child being retained an additional year or having to repeat classes

The child being hospitalized for physical, mental, or emotional reasons

The child refusing to attend school or complete assigned work, creating a problem for the parent

A child being victimized at school (cyber bullying, extortion via sexual images, etc.), leading to their suicide

RESULTING EMOTIONS: Anger, Annoyance, Anxiety, Apprehension, Confusion, Defeat, Defensiveness, Denial, Desperation, Disappointment, Discouragement, Dread, Embarrassment, Frustration, Guilt, Hurt, Overwhelmed, Reluctance, Resentment, Resignation, Surprise, Unease

POSSIBLE INTERNAL STRUGGLES

Feeling tempted to blame someone else

Dealing with resentment toward the child, school staff, or a spouse

Fighting a loss of control over the child's behavior or academic performance

The character doubting their parenting abilities

Wanting to intervene instead of letting the child handle the problem on their own (when appropriate)

Difficulty knowing if the child's actions are simply poor choices or are stemming from an underlying problem

NEGATIVE TRAITS THAT MAY WORSEN THE SITUATION: Abrasive, Apathetic, Confrontational, Controlling, Defensive, Inattentive, Judgmental, Nagging, Perfectionist

IMPACT ON BASIC NEEDS

Esteem and Recognition: Characters who internalize their child's choices may blame themselves. Likewise, they may receive criticism from others that erodes their confidence in their ability to parent well.

Love and Belonging: If a "difficult" child is shunned by other families, the parent may find herself bereft of the community she once belonged to.

Safety and Security: Constant worrying over the child and how they'll turn out can cause emotional distress and even physical health issues for the parent.

POSITIVE TRAITS TO HELP THE CHARACTER COPE: Calm, Cooperative, Diplomatic, Discreet, Loyal, Nurturing, Observant, Persistent, Protective, Supportive

POSITIVE OUTCOMES

The school, family, and community coming together to meet the child's needs

A correct medical or psychological diagnosis that helps the child significantly

Addressing a minor behavioral issue before it escalates into something serious

The parent giving greater attention to their child, improving their relationship

The child learning how to ask for help

Finding a new school that is a better fit for the child

AN ELDERLY LOVED ONE REQUIRING CARE

EXAMPLES
The character's mother being diagnosed with cancer and needing immediate surgery
A grandfather with Alzheimer's or dementia who requires constant monitoring
A godparent who suffered a stroke and needs help to recover
Having to drive an elderly parent to and from appointments
A stubborn uncle with a medical condition (like diabetes) who isn't managing it properly
An elderly neighbor needing one's support because they have no one else
An estranged parent with a terminal illness reaching out to the character and needing help
Taking in an adopted "aunt" who has fallen on hard times and lacks the financial resources to care for herself

MINOR COMPLICATIONS
Employers who aren't sympathetic when the character has to take a parent to the doctor
Being unable to afford in-home support
Moving the loved one into one's home and creating friction with existing family members
A loss of freedom
Being unappreciated by the loved one, who is bitter about needing help
A loss of sleep
Financial distress
Having no time or energy to socialize or pursue hobbies
Other relationships suffering because they aren't being looked after
Extended family members disagreeing with the character's way of caring for the individual

POTENTIALLY DISASTROUS RESULTS
Arguments with siblings over a lack of shared responsibility, causing a falling out
A stubborn parent who refuses home health assistance falling and being injured
Resentment creeping into the character's life at having to trade freedom for caretaking
Having to travel for work and being unavailable to the parent at a critical time
Mounting medical bills
Developing a habit or addiction (to sleeping pills, drinking too much, etc.) to cope with trying to do it all
Discovering evidence that family members have been taking financial advantage of the parent
Learning the previous caretaker was neglectful (finding bed sores, rashes, injuries, improper medication dosing, etc.)

RESULTING EMOTIONS: Anxiety, Concern, Conflicted, Connectedness, Depressed, Frustration, Gratitude, Grief, Guilt, Hopefulness, Impatience, Moodiness, Pity, Powerlessness, Resentment, Resignation, Sadness, Self-Pity, Shame, Unappreciated, Wistfulness, Worry

POSSIBLE INTERNAL STRUGGLES
Resenting the burden of care, followed by shame for those feelings
Being tempted to try and pass the responsibility to someone else

Anger at a parent who is being difficult but knowing if the character were in their shoes, they would behave the same

Grieving at having to transition from a daughter or son to a caretaker, yet knowing it has to be done

Experiencing a personal crisis that forces a choice about the character continuing to care for their loved one

Being torn between loved ones who need different things—e.g., a physically ill parent who needs care and a child with special needs who requires extra attention

NEGATIVE TRAITS THAT MAY WORSEN THE SITUATION: Cowardly, Disloyal, Disorganized, Impatient, Inattentive, Irresponsible, Oversensitive, Pessimistic, Worrywart

IMPACT ON BASIC NEEDS

Self-Actualization: If a character is in a situation where their parent requires constant care, this can limit their ability to devote time to their own meaningful goals. They may have to leave school to be available for the parent, give up passions they have no time for, or feel their identity is becoming that of a caregiver rather than who they were meant to be.

Love and Belonging: As a loved one declines, their mental state might grow volatile, their moods turning bitter and resentful. This can cause them to lash out at caregivers, making the character feel abandoned or rejected by the person who should love them most.

Safety and Security: If your character is struggling to make ends meet because they must assume their loved one's medical bills and living expenses, this can cause financial hardship.

POSITIVE TRAITS TO HELP THE CHARACTER COPE: Affectionate, Calm, Courteous, Efficient, Empathetic, Funny, Gentle, Hospitable, Kind, Loyal, Merciful, Nurturing

POSITIVE OUTCOMES

Building a closeness with a loved one that has been lost over time

Rediscovering compassion and grace

Gaining a deeper appreciation for one's parent that causes the character to seek out stronger connections with their own children

Having an opportunity to make up for lost time (or past mistakes)

Reflecting on one's life and the sum of it and being encouraged to avoid regret by making meaningful changes

Gaining perspective about past hurts and slights and working through them as needed so they can be put to rest

BEING ASSIGNED AN UNDESIRABLE PARTNER

EXAMPLES
The character being saddled with the boss' entitled, clueless kid as an intern
A police officer getting stuck with a new recruit
Being told by one's parents to buddy up with the new kid next door
Having to work on a school project with someone who is unmotivated
Having a slob for a desk mate at work
Having to work with someone the character can't stand
Partnering with someone who has a poor work ethic
Being assigned to a "poor performer" to try and turn them around
Having to work with someone who is not a personality match
Working with a control freak who won't let the character contribute
Being assigned a partner on a sports or fine arts team who isn't up to the character's level
An arranged marriage proposal that disappoints

MINOR COMPLICATIONS
Power struggles
Personality clashes
Arguments or uncomfortable silences
An imbalance in responsibility, workload, and accountability
Wasting time checking the other person's work to ensure it's correct
Having to repeat instructions
Having to micromanage to ensure something is done properly
Time lost having to document problems to take to a manager
Trying to help the other person and unintentionally hurting their feelings

POTENTIALLY DISASTROUS RESULTS
Starting a feud that brings out the worst in both people
Talking behind the person's back and being overheard
Being reprimanded for not being a "team player"
Getting fired for inter-office sabotage
Being demoted for bad behavior
An audit that uncovers fraud or illegal activity for which the character is unfairly blamed
Breaking ties with family (in the case of a bad marriage match)
Being pressured into "making it work," leading to deep unhappiness
Having one's performance tied to the partner's, resulting in reprimands or lower bonuses
Losing a game, contest, client, or other important opportunity because of the partnership

RESULTING EMOTIONS: Bitterness, Contempt, Determination, Dread, Frustration, Impatience, Irritation, Powerlessness, Resentment, Schadenfreude, Self-Pity, Unappreciated

POSSIBLE INTERNAL STRUGGLES
Wanting to succeed but being angry that the incompetent partner will benefit, too

Wanting to give the benefit of the doubt but finding it hard when too many things go wrong

Being torn between acting professional and giving in to childish behavior as friction escalates

Looking for someone to blame when, really, there isn't anyone

An unfair situation shaking the character's belief in and loyalty to a beloved company

Resenting having to cover up a partner's actions but needing to do so to keep the situation from blowing back on the character

Wanting to respect the loved ones responsible but harboring anger and betrayal for them not placing a higher value on the character's happiness

NEGATIVE TRAITS THAT MAY WORSEN THE SITUATION: Abrasive, Confrontational, Disloyal, Grumpy, Gullible, Hostile, Inflexible, Perfectionist, Tactless, Temperamental, Uncommunicative, Uncooperative

IMPACT ON BASIC NEEDS

Self-Actualization: A character whose path to success is tied to another person may grow disillusioned and decide to pivot to something that's less fulfilling but is within their power to obtain.

Esteem and Recognition: If having the esteem of others is vital to your character and their partner is someone who is looked down upon, this will likely impact their self-worth.

Love and Belonging: In the case of an arranged marriage or family partnership, if your character is unhappy with the match, it will leave them longing for the freedom to choose someone who is a fit for them and their relationship needs.

Safety and Security: If your character is saddled with a partner who takes dangerous risks, this could place your character in harm's way, too.

POSITIVE TRAITS TO HELP THE CHARACTER COPE: Alert, Ambitious, Charming, Diplomatic, Industrious, Inspirational, Organized, Persistent, Persuasive, Proactive, Wise

POSITIVE OUTCOMES

The parties setting differences aside and coming to appreciate each other's uniqueness

Learning strategies for getting along with difficult people

The character reclaiming their power by standing up to whoever is responsible for the mismatch (parents, a boss, etc.) and refusing to participate

The character learning to view situations objectively while keeping their emotions separate

The other person's negative qualities prompting the character to inventory herself and take steps to overcoming any undesirable traits

The character being able to mentor the partner and help them make personal improvements

BEING ASSIGNED AN UNPLEASANT TASK

NOTES: For entries in a similar vein, see BEING ASSIGNED AN UNDESIRABLE PART-NER, BEING THE BEARER OF BAD NEWS, HAVING TO PUNISH SOMEONE, and BEING SADDLED WITH UNEXPECTED RESPONSIBILITY.

EXAMPLES
The character having to reprimand an employee who happens to be their friend
Being assigned an impossible-to-please client
Having to clean up someone else's bodily fluids
Being the executor for someone with feuding family members
Cleaning the home of a hoarder
Having to be a juror in a drawn-out trial
Confronting someone about an addiction or another difficult topic
Searching for survivors or human remains at the site of a disaster
Serving a warrant, divorce papers, subpoena, or other legal document
Executing or assassinating someone
Assisting someone with personal care tasks (bathing, using the restroom, removal of lice, etc.)
Removing children or pets from an unsafe home
Carrying out an unpleasant medical procedure
Having to inform someone about the death of their loved one
Having to give a patient a devastating diagnosis

MINOR COMPLICATIONS
Procrastinating and therefore compounding the problem
The character shirking their responsibility so someone else has to take care of it
Facing fear, anxiety, and pressure
Key details being left out, making the task more difficult
Dealing with ailments brought on by stress (nausea, stomach pain, loss of appetite, etc.)
Giving bad news to someone who doesn't take it well
Preparing oneself to take on the unpleasant task only to have it postponed
Worrying about not knowing what to say or having the right answers

POTENTIALLY DISASTROUS RESULTS
Refusing to do the task and facing repercussions
Developing PTSD from an emotionally traumatizing task
Failing to remain objective; becoming emotionally involved
Rushing to get the job over with and botching it
An unpleasant task dragging out
The character knowing their actions or words are hurting the other person but being unable to do anything about it
Being blamed or attacked, even though the character is just the messenger

RESULTING EMOTIONS: Anger, Anguish, Annoyance, Anxiety, Defiance, Disappointment, Dread, Fear, Frustration, Inadequacy, Irritation, Overwhelmed, Panic, Reluctance, Resentment, Resignation, Self-Pity, Suspicion, Worry

POSSIBLE INTERNAL STRUGGLES

Wanting to refuse the task but not wanting to face the consequences
Feeling uncertainty over being able to handle the task
Struggling to separate the character's personal and professional lives
Being asked to do something that goes against one's moral beliefs
Weighing the need to do what's best with the anguish it will cause others
Struggling to be patient and respectful in the moment
Afterward, the character second-guessing the way they handled the situation

NEGATIVE TRAITS THAT MAY WORSEN THE SITUATION: Abrasive, Childish, Confrontational, Cruel, Disrespectful, Haughty, Impatient, Irresponsible, Lazy, Nervous, Pessimistic, Rebellious, Selfish, Spoiled, Stubborn, Tactless, Temperamental, Uncooperative

IMPACT ON BASIC NEEDS

Self-Actualization: A character who is frequently stuck doing undesirable tasks will never be fulfilled.

Esteem and Recognition: A character doing work she believes to be beneath her station may suffer a drop in self-esteem.

Love and Belonging: If a character is asked to do something that doesn't sit well with her morally, she may refuse, which can strain the relationship between her and the one asking.

Safety and Security: If the unpleasant situation is dangerous is some way (due to dealing with bodily fluids, hazardous chemicals, or unstable people), the character's safety may become undermined on the job.

POSITIVE TRAITS TO HELP THE CHARACTER COPE: Adaptable, Ambitious, Appreciative, Bold, Confident, Cooperative, Diplomatic, Easygoing, Enthusiastic, Focused, Honorable, Humble, Industrious, Obedient, Responsible, Sensible, Simple, Unselfish

POSITIVE OUTCOMES

Helping someone see the error of their ways and chart a new course
Removing additional worry from others during a time of pain or loss
Intervening in time to save someone's life
Giving dignity to someone needing basic care
Fulfilling a necessary role others are not suited to handle
Helping those who cannot help themselves
Becoming intrinsically motivated instead of seeking affirmation and value from others
Being on hand to help someone navigate a difficult life situation, such as the loss of a loved one, a terminal diagnosis, a crisis of faith, or being charged with a crime

BEING THE BEARER OF BAD NEWS

EXAMPLES
The character having to tell friends and family of their plans to relocate
Notifying tenants they must vacate a home
Explaining to someone that they have been the victim of a crime
Diagnosing a serious health condition
Notifying someone of a loved one's death
Revealing the loss of a pregnancy
Sharing the news of one's own serious health condition with loved ones
Letting family members know about a job loss
Telling a friend or family member their spouse is cheating
Notifying a parent or guardian about their child being held back in school
The character admitting they no longer love their spouse and want to end the marriage
Notifying someone of a lawsuit or legal charges against them
Having to tell a client about setbacks, increased costs, or decisions that won't make them happy
Delivering a jury's unfavorable decision
Sharing unpopular news or updates at a press conference

MINOR COMPLICATIONS
Being emotionally attached to the recipient (because they're a friend or family member)
Struggling to find the right place and time to share the news
Being unable to locate the recipient of the bad news
The recipient becoming shocked, upset, or angry
Having to provide comfort and support to a stranger
Being nervous about not saying the right thing
Being put on the spot for additional information or answers
Difficulty getting the recipient alone to share the news privately
Having to navigate a language barrier
Being asked for proof that may or may not be in the character's possession
The receiver attacking the messenger instead of responding to the news itself
Putting the confrontation off until the last minute

POTENTIALLY DISASTROUS RESULTS
Irreparably damaging the relationship with the recipient
Notifying the wrong person
Not sharing the news in a timely manner
Delivering the incorrect medical diagnosis or test results
Exacerbating grief by getting the facts wrong
Being blamed for the bad news
Someone overhearing the news and using it for their own gain
The recipient of the news becoming violent
Delivering the news poorly or insensitively
The news being made public before the recipient is notified

The character being threatened or scorned publicly because they're the "face" of the bad news
Failing to hide one's schadenfreude and being called out for it (when the character believes the recipient deserves what they're getting)

RESULTING EMOTIONS: Agitation, Anguish, Anxiety, Apprehension, Concern, Determination, Dread, Empathy, Fear, Flustered, Guilt, Inadequacy, Nervousness, Overwhelmed, Regret, Resentment, Resignation, Sadness, Schadenfreude, Unease, Worry

POSSIBLE INTERNAL STRUGGLES
Being tempted to pass the duty along to someone else
Struggling to balance personal fears with dutiful needs
Questioning whether the recipient needs to know the news at all (or all of it)
The character doubting their ability to handle the situation properly
Resentment at being given a duty others passed on or refused to do
Being triggered about a moment in the past when the character was the recipient of bad news

NEGATIVE TRAITS THAT MAY WORSEN THE SITUATION: Abrasive, Apathetic, Confrontational, Cowardly, Cruel, Disrespectful, Flaky, Gossipy, Morbid, Nosy, Tactless, Timid, Uncommunicative, Verbose, Vindictive

IMPACT ON BASIC NEEDS
Self-Actualization: Serving people in difficult moments can help the character achieve self-actualization if they feel called to those duties.
Esteem and Recognition: A character who can't handle this sensitive situation with the utmost dignity and care may find public opinion turning against him.
Love and Belonging: Friends may be unable to separate the bearer from the bad news, associating him with this intensely painful moment in their life. As a result, they may blame him or pull away, leaving him isolated and lonely.

POSITIVE TRAITS TO HELP THE CHARACTER COPE: Ambitious, Analytical, Appreciative, Calm, Cautious, Courteous, Diplomatic, Discreet, Empathetic, Hospitable, Humble, Kind, Nurturing, Objective, Perceptive, Wise

POSITIVE OUTCOMES
The character learning new life skills, like discernment, objectivity, and tact
Delivering impossible news in a way that makes things easier for the recipient
New relationships emerging as a result of the shared experience
The bad news improving the recipient's life, such as encouraging them to seek life-saving care, obtain a better job, or leave a bad relationship
Feeling satisfaction at having done a thankless job well

BUREAUCRACY TYING ONE'S HANDS

NOTES: Bureaucracy, in the context of this entry, is a system of unrelenting rules or regulations that make it difficult for the character to complete a task.

EXAMPLES
Having to coordinate across government agencies in a time of emergency
Obtaining necessary certifications and licenses to start a business
Being required to report on friends or family (for suspected abuse, use of hate speech, etc.)
Red tape with the insurance company keeping one from receiving necessary medical care
Having to fire an employee, even if one empathizes with the reasons for their actions
Not being able to fire an employee because of all the regulations and rules
Not being able to change or bypass requirements associated with training for a degree, designation, or licensure
A legal case dragging out interminably because of due process
A health care provider being unable to deviate from the terms of their policy
Having to assign a particular punishment based on written law or policy
Homeowner Association rules limiting a property owner's rights
Being unable to act as a whistleblower due to losing one's security clearance

MINOR COMPLICATIONS
Losing productivity
Dealing with impatience, frustration, and aggravation
The character's creativity being diminished or restricted
Having to spend money on certifications and licenses
Other people farther down the chain of command becoming frustrated by the wait
Employees losing morale
Time wasted filling out forms and collecting required data to secure the next steps in a process
Experiencing delays
Having to pay fines or penalties for not adhering to standard practices
Being stuck in limbo while an appeal is filed
The character feeling like they're at the mercy of an uncaring system

POTENTIALLY DISASTROUS RESULTS
Being unable to help someone in desperate need
Losing one's employment because of a minor misstep
Serving or receiving unfair criminal charges
Trying to cheat the system or take shortcuts and getting caught
Lives being lost because of a slow emergency response
A business owner giving up their dream because it's just too hard
Having to fire someone for a small transgression
Legally being prevented from speaking out about injustice or mistreatment
Facing imprisonment or criminal charges
Complaining about the process and making things worse

Spotting a discriminatory practice within a policy and being unable to change it
Being unable to charge someone with abuse, fraud, or another crime because they're exempt from prosecution for political reasons

RESULTING EMOTIONS: Anger, Annoyance, Bitterness, Contempt, Desperation, Determination, Disbelief, Disillusionment, Frustration, Impatience, Indifference, Intimidation, Irritation, Powerlessness, Rage

POSSIBLE INTERNAL STRUGGLES
Considering giving up on a meaningful goal because of unfair, restrictive measures
Questioning whether or not to challenge the status quo
Being tempted to circumvent the system to get what one wants
Struggling with apathy
Having to contain one's rage so the situation isn't made worse
Feeling disillusioned that racism, discrimination, and inequity is still happening in society (and is protected by policy)
Being tempted to break the law and one's moral code to do the right thing
Fighting hopelessness during a long battle that yields slow headway

NEGATIVE TRAITS THAT MAY WORSEN THE SITUATION: Abrasive, Apathetic, Cynical, Dishonest, Disorganized, Fussy, Hostile, Impatient, Impulsive, Inhibited, Nagging, Needy, Rebellious, Reckless, Scatterbrained, Temperamental

IMPACT ON BASIC NEEDS
   Self-Actualization: Being forced to follow bureaucratic policies may severely limit the character's ability to freely create and think critically.
   Esteem and Recognition: A character who is unable to do the right thing in this situation may blame herself, thinking if only she was smarter, more capable, stronger, etc., she could have gotten the job done.
   Love and Belonging: Bureaucracy can cause undue stress and strain on relationships between employees, employees and management, and businesses and their clients.

POSITIVE TRAITS TO HELP THE CHARACTER COPE: Calm, Confident, Cooperative, Creative, Diplomatic, Easygoing, Efficient, Idealistic, Industrious, Just, Organized, Persistent, Persuasive, Proactive, Resourceful, Spunky, Uninhibited

POSITIVE OUTCOMES
Patience and hard work producing a helpful outcome
The character persevering and earning recognition for affecting positive change
Seeing in hindsight that the bureaucratic system actually worked
Thinking creatively and finding acceptable ways around the red tape
The character realizing in the middle of the wait that they were taking the wrong course of action

CHAFING UNDER POOR LEADERSHIP

EXAMPLES
The character having to implement a leadership directive they don't agree with
Being coerced to lie to cover for someone higher up the ladder
Having to usurp one's boss in order to avert disaster
Following an unpredictable or irresponsible leader
Lacking the resources or direction needed to do the job
Being held responsible for the poor decisions of one's leaders
The character's hard work not being recognized
Being more informed than those in management
Leadership being closed to input or feedback
Dealing with a disorganized leader
Not being supported
Failing to be empowered to act
Having one's time wasted with meaningless meetings or tasks
Poor communication from the boss
Being evaluated through unrealistic expectations
The employees' needs not being understood by management
Leadership putting a personal agenda ahead of the business's goals
Being assigned a task that does not match one's skill set or experience level

MINOR COMPLICATIONS
Dealing with tension in the workplace
Losing sight of one's purpose
Not feeling heard or valued
Being overwhelmed by limited resources
Receiving an unfair evaluation
Not wanting to go to work
Appearing incompetent due to others' missteps
Dealing with frustration and anger
Being stuck professionally, unable to move up the ladder
Leaders with no vision producing stagnation and frustration among employees

POTENTIALLY DISASTROUS RESULTS
Work projects falling apart
Losing clients or the company's public reputation
Being so frustrated the character has to leave their job
Being unable to retain or recruit talented employees
Getting caught covering for the boss
A higher-up taking credit for the character's discovery so they'll look good in the media
People being endangered (physically, financially, mentally, and emotionally) by a leader's ineptitude
Being perceived as disrespectful, disobedient, or insubordinate

Speaking up about the issue and getting fired

Being told by leadership to do something the character doesn't know is illegal and being prosecuted as an accessory

Discontent leading to a strike, mutiny, or other uprising

A scandal at the leadership level sinking the company and the character's career

RESULTING EMOTIONS: Agitation, Anger, Annoyance, Anxiety, Apprehension, Contempt, Defeat, Depressed, Despair, Discouragement, Dissatisfaction, Dread, Frustration, Indifference, Intimidation, Irritation, Neglected, Powerlessness, Resentment, Resignation, Unappreciated

POSSIBLE INTERNAL STRUGGLES

Being forced to compromise one's values for the sake of earning an income

Facing temptation to disobey directives from above

Having to handle conflict without support

Having to provide one's own source of self-worth where work is concerned

Constantly battling the temptation to leave and find work elsewhere

Wanting to do something about the poor leader but not knowing who's safe to talk to

NEGATIVE TRAITS THAT MAY WORSEN THE SITUATION: Compulsive, Confrontational, Controlling, Cowardly, Disrespectful, Foolish, Impulsive, Insecure, Know-It-All, Nagging, Needy, Oversensitive, Perfectionist, Rebellious, Resentful, Tactless, Worrywart

IMPACT ON BASIC NEEDS

Esteem and Recognition: A character who isn't appreciated or encouraged will lose confidence in their abilities.

Love and Belonging: Stress from the job can be brought home and create tension in relationships, especially if the character seeks to control loved ones to make up for a lack of control at work.

Safety and Security: A character who is afraid of losing their job may not feel safe to disclose unethical or abusive behavior by a company's leadership.

POSITIVE TRAITS TO HELP THE CHARACTER COPE: Adaptable, Ambitious, Appreciative, Confident, Cooperative, Decisive, Enthusiastic, Imaginative, Industrious, Inspirational, Loyal, Optimistic, Passionate, Persistent, Proactive, Professional, Resourceful

POSITIVE OUTCOMES

Earning the respect of one's colleagues despite poor leadership

Identifying creative ways to get the job done regardless of circumstances

Building a relationship and opening up communication with leadership

The work environment being improved from the character's efforts and positive attitude

The investigation resulting from the character coming forward causing the problematic leader to be ousted

Becoming the visionary, encourager, or inspirational figure in the office

CHILDCARE FALLING THROUGH

EXAMPLES
A babysitter flaking out and forgetting they were supposed to work that day
The nanny quitting, calling in sick, or going on vacation
The school or daycare closing due to inclement weather, illness outbreaks, or a maintenance issue
The caregiver getting into an accident on their way to the house
The daycare canceling their before- or after-school program

MINOR COMPLICATIONS
Having to make alternate childcare arrangements
Having to pay for otherwise free services or having to pay a higher fee than expected
Being late for one's intended destination
Having to work from home to care for one's child
Being forced to take unplanned leave from work
Having to reschedule or cancel plans such as an appointment, social outing, meeting, etc.
Needing to bring one's child to work
A delayed departure leading to increased traffic or missing a train or flight
Incurring fees to change previously arranged transportation
Lost wages due to a canceled shift
Needing to juggle work and homeschooling
Dealing with the emotional distress associated with a disrupted routine
Having to ask for help from friends, family, or neighbors
Embarrassment when one's personal life bleeds into the professional realm

POTENTIALLY DISASTROUS RESULTS
It taking longer than anticipated to find a replacement
Having to request a change of work hours to accommodate a new caregiver
Missing a job interview or an important work engagement
Losing one's job
Missing a court hearing
Risking the welfare of one's child by leaving them without appropriate supervision
Being overlooked for promotion due to being perceived as unreliable at work
Missing a loved one's important event or last moments
Losing a romantic relationship due to an impatient or selfish love interest
Being left out from plans with friends in the future
Strain being added to an already unstable spousal relationship because the new responsibility isn't being shared equally
Having to request help when it's painful to do so (asking an estranged grandparent to step up, requesting a favor from an ex with whom the character doesn't get along, etc.)

RESULTING EMOTIONS: Anger, Annoyance, Anxiety, Disappointment, Disbelief, Frustration, Overwhelmed, Panic, Rage, Stunned, Worry

POSSIBLE INTERNAL STRUGGLES

Feeling guilty about having to choose between one's family and career

Not feeling right about the new caregiver but not knowing what else to do

Experiencing resentment toward one's significant other for not being available

Feeling indebted for asking a favor from someone else

The character organizing social events, then being sad because they can't enjoy them

Being terrified the same thing will happen again

Struggling to achieve a balance between work and family life

Fighting to hide one's anger and frustration

Stress increasing from the changing routine and financial impact

Feeling torn between feeling sorry for the caregiver and angry about the cancelation

Resenting having to care for one's child and feeling guilty about it

NEGATIVE TRAITS THAT MAY WORSEN THE SITUATION: Confrontational, Controlling, Fussy, Inflexible, Irrational, Martyr, Resentful, Worrywart

IMPACT ON BASIC NEEDS

Esteem and Recognition: The fear of appearing incompetent at work coupled with struggling to balance one's personal and professional duties may cause a decline in self-esteem.

Love and Belonging: Imposing on others for help with childcare can strain those relationships or change the dynamic in negative ways.

Safety and Security: Financial hardship due to lost wages may result in the character's inability to support himself or his family.

POSITIVE TRAITS TO HELP THE CHARACTER COPE: Adaptable, Charming, Cooperative, Creative, Diplomatic, Friendly, Organized, Persuasive, Resourceful

POSITIVE OUTCOMES

Saving money on childcare fees and transportation-related fees

Having additional time at home with one's child

Having an unexpected day off from work

The situation creating an opportunity to work from home and the character being happy with the new arrangement

Avoiding an unforeseen transportation disaster, such as a car accident in inclement weather

Hosting social contacts at one's house instead of going out

The character being relieved because they've been unhappy with the child's caregiver and the situation forces them to take action

The situation leading to a rift being mended when a loved one or ex-spouse comes through at a much-needed time

HAVING TO BREAK A PROMISE

EXAMPLES

The character breaking off their engagement

Having to betray someone's confidence so a worse disaster may be prevented

Breaking a promise to be present for a loved one's event due to work or another constraint

Deciding to leave one's marriage

Being unable to financially support someone (through tuition, assisted living, alimony, child support, etc.)

Forfeiting parental rights due to an inability to care or provide for a child

Having to set aside religious beliefs to uphold the law (or vice versa)

Failing to meet an agreed-upon professional deadline

Having to cancel a trip or a plan with a friend

Exiting a work-related contract or verbal agreement

Discontinuing medical treatments after vowing to fight an illness

Breaking a professional oath

Deciding to take a different career path than what the character promised loved ones

MINOR COMPLICATIONS

Causing others disappointment and upset

Fines or interest accruing for being late on a payment

Being hit with penalty fees for canceling travel plans

Experiencing guilt for letting others down

Having to ask for extra time, understanding, or forgiveness

Losing trust from others

Missing out on coveted family time or an important event

Being ghosted or given the silent treatment by a friend or loved one

Having to sit through criticism or tirades

POTENTIALLY DISASTROUS RESULTS

Facing a lawsuit for failure to uphold a contract

Having to file bankruptcy

Losing one's job

Filing or being hit with a divorce

Having to pull a child out of school due to not being able to afford it or having to move

A loved one being unable to receive care in their home or through an assisted living facility

Facing criminal charges and jail time

Irrevocably breaking a relationship

Losing a professional license or certification

Experiencing depression

Having to fire or lay off employees due to unforeseen business difficulties

Getting caught making excuses or lying about why the promise was broken

RESULTING EMOTIONS: Agitation, Anguish, Anxiety, Apprehension, Conflicted, Defensiveness, Despair, Determination, Dread, Embarrassment, Fear, Flustered, Guilt, Overwhelmed, Regret, Relief, Reluctance, Unease, Worry

POSSIBLE INTERNAL STRUGGLES

Anguish at being caught in a no-win situation
The character struggling to forgive herself
Being tempted to do something unethical or unlawful to keep the promise
Regretting choices that led to the broken promise
The character questioning their ethics or morality
Feeling like a failure as an employee, manager, friend, family member, or love interest
Wanting forgiveness but feeling undeserving of it

NEGATIVE TRAITS THAT MAY WORSEN THE SITUATION: Apathetic, Cowardly, Defensive, Dishonest, Disloyal, Forgetful, Impulsive, Irresponsible, Manipulative, Martyr, Self-Indulgent, Selfish, Stubborn

IMPACT ON BASIC NEEDS

Esteem and Recognition: Letting others down may lead to a character's poor self-image and the inability to forgive himself.

Love and Belonging: Relationships with others may suffer due to the lost trust that accompanies a broken promise.

Safety and Security: The inability to keep a promise can lead to significant losses in employment, residence, finances, or other means of security.

POSITIVE TRAITS TO HELP THE CHARACTER COPE: Charming, Confident, Cooperative, Diplomatic, Empathetic, Generous, Honorable, Industrious, Kind, Loyal, Persuasive, Professional, Responsible, Unselfish

POSITIVE OUTCOMES

The character increasing their understanding of their own limits, beliefs, or allegiances
Receiving grace and understanding from others
Exercising caution when making future promises
Successfully navigating what felt like an unrecoverable situation
Breaking a promise that was detrimental for the character, resulting in a brighter and healthier future
The character recognizing their circumstances are the problem and taking steps that allow them to make independent decisions and follow through on them

HAVING TO PUNISH SOMEONE

EXAMPLES
The character punishing their child for poor choices or inappropriate behavior
Removing a student's in-school or extracurricular privileges, such as recess or being president of a club, due to misbehavior
Assigning failing grades to a student who neglected to turn in assignments
Issuing a ticket or arresting someone who broke the law
Demoting an employee for flouting authority
Suspending or expelling a student
Barring an athlete's participation in a game due to poor sportsmanship or a rule violation
Removing someone from their home because they violated a contract or didn't pay their rent
Closing someone's account (social media, bank, etc.) due to a terms of use violation
Firing an employee or putting them on forced leave because they violated workplace policies
Closing a business due to health code violations or failure to obtain permits or licenses
Administering physical punishment to a convicted criminal
Removing someone's children or animals because of neglect

MINOR COMPLICATIONS
The recipient of the punishment lashing out verbally
Being berated by others who were impacted by the decision (members of a sports team, a client, etc.)
A sports match, tournament, or game being lost because the character couldn't participate
The parents of the student or athlete contesting the decision
A lessening of morale on the team or in the workplace
Other involved parties going unpunished
Receiving threats from the one being punished
The recipient refusing to take responsibility for their actions, making things difficult for the character

POTENTIALLY DISASTROUS RESULTS
The one being punished lobbying upper management to have the punishment (which was justified) removed
The character punishing the wrong person
Trauma arising from having to remove children or pets from a home
People acting out violently because of the punishment
Being unable to find or catch the person who should be punished
The character being sued
The guilty party quitting their job or committee or dropping out of school in protest
The character being physically targeted in an act of revenge
A public outcry against the character for enacting the punishment
A victim going to the press because the punishment was too light for the crime
The person being punished committing suicide

RESULTING EMOTIONS: Agitation, Anger, Anguish, Annoyance, Anxiety, Concern, Conflicted, Contempt, Disillusionment, Dread, Eagerness, Fear, Guilt, Indifference, Intimidation, Nervousness, Pity, Regret, Reluctance, Schadenfreude, Sympathy

POSSIBLE INTERNAL STRUGGLES

Knowing the punishment must be given but being afraid of damaging the relationship
The character hating their job (because it requires them to issue punishments like this one)
Second-guessing whether the recipient is deserving of the punishment
Feeling as though the violation of rule, law, or policy was justified
Uncertainty as to whether the chosen punishment is appropriate and/or effective
Wondering if something could have been done differently to avoid the offense in the first place
Discomfort delivering the punishment on behalf of someone else or a larger governing body
Struggling to punish one's child because of the fallout that will ensue
The character worrying they don't have all the facts about the case
Struggling with guilt over how the punishment will impact the recipient (financially, relationally, emotionally, etc.)

NEGATIVE TRAITS THAT MAY WORSEN THE SITUATION: Abrasive, Controlling, Cruel, Disrespectful, Gossipy, Hypocritical, Indecisive, Irrational, Prejudiced, Pretentious, Tactless, Unethical, Vindictive, Weak-Willed

IMPACT ON BASIC NEEDS

Esteem and Recognition: A character who is forced to enact punishments he disagrees with could end up viewing himself as a coward for not challenging the rulings.
Love and Belonging: Being the punisher can cause damage to the character's relationships, sowing resentment and driving wedges.
Safety and Security: The character's well-being may become threatened if the recipient reacts in a volatile way.

POSITIVE TRAITS TO HELP THE CHARACTER COPE: Analytical, Calm, Cautious, Confident, Courageous, Courteous, Discreet, Efficient, Just, Persuasive, Professional, Supportive

POSITIVE OUTCOMES

The relationship between the character and the guilty party growing stronger
The punished individual experiencing growth and improved behavior
The character being able to root out the cause of the other party's bad choices, helping them to change for the better
Justice being served
The punished individual avoiding a worse outcome
The character advocating for reform to keep unfair or ineffective punishments from happening
The situation acting as a cautionary tale, encouraging others to make better choices
The affected business thriving from the removal of toxic or underperforming workers

HAVING TO WORK WITH AN ENEMY

EXAMPLES
The character having to work with someone whose personality traits clash with their own
The character having to co-parent with a difficult ex-spouse during a challenging time (a daunting health diagnosis, a child struggling with depression, etc.)
The character joining forces with an estranged family member to save a family business
The character needing to work with an enemy to protect a cover-up that will ruin both their lives if it's discovered
The character joining up with someone they can't stand to escape a mutual threat
Working with a hated sibling to fight back against abusive or neglectful parents
Having to plan a mutual loved one's funeral with a relative the character has never liked
The character pooling resources and talents with an opponent to bring down a corrupt organization, union, or government
The character teaming up with her husband's girlfriend to take the cheater down

MINOR COMPLICATIONS
Flaring tempers and arguments
Other people being made to feel uncomfortable
Having to swallow one's pride for the greater good
Having to monitor one's tone and words to avoid splintering the group
Being distracted by resentment and negativity
Having to ignore small digs and references to past conflicts to keep the peace
Wasting mental energy on questioning the other's motives
Struggling with mistrust
The discomfort of waiting for things to go wrong

POTENTIALLY DISASTROUS RESULTS
Holding back resources or information to maintain an advantage, leading to self-sabotage
Revealing secrets that will have repercussions after the crisis is over
Unintentionally giving an enemy intel they can use later
Being manipulated into giving up an advantage that wasn't necessary
The character letting their guard down only to be burned again
Revealing techniques, trade secrets, strategies, and processes that help the enemy in the long run

RESULTING EMOTIONS: Agitation, Anger, Bitterness, Certainty, Conflicted, Contempt, Defensiveness, Defiance, Dread, Frustration, Irritation, Jealousy, Paranoia, Powerlessness, Reluctance, Resentment, Schadenfreude, Scorn, Skepticism, Smugness, Suspicion, Wariness

POSSIBLE INTERNAL STRUGGLES
The character discovering likable qualities about someone they should hate
Resentment warring with appreciation (hating to need help but being glad to have it)
Wanting to hang onto knowledge or a strength to keep the advantage but knowing it must be

shared to solve the current situation

Worrying about what others will think about the collaboration

Worrying about what will happen after the crisis has ended

Receiving feedback or advice from the enemy and not knowing if it can be trusted

Discovering commonalities with the other person and not being comfortable with that

The character feeling begrudging admiration of the enemy's skills, abilities, or behavior under pressure and resenting the fact that they could probably learn a few things from them

Wanting to dismiss a great idea because of its source

NEGATIVE TRAITS THAT MAY WORSEN THE SITUATION: Abrasive, Catty, Childish, Cocky, Confrontational, Controlling, Dishonest, Inflexible, Jealous, Oversensitive, Paranoid, Stubborn, Tactless, Temperamental, Uncommunicative, Uncooperative, Vindictive

IMPACT ON BASIC NEEDS

Esteem and Recognition: Losing control of a situation and having to work with an enemy to regain that control can be a huge blow to the characters' ego. She may see herself differently moving forward, having less self-worth than before.

Love and Belonging: If the enemy is dangerous enough or there's a significant history of bad blood, the character's alliance with him may be a non-negotiable situation for loved ones, leading them to pull away for their own well-being.

Safety and Security: Not every story has a happy ending. Should the enemy be unable to set aside animosity, your character may be betrayed and put in harm's way.

POSITIVE TRAITS TO HELP THE CHARACTER COPE: Calm, Confident, Courteous, Discreet, Efficient, Funny, Hospitable, Observant, Patient, Professional, Tolerant, Wise

POSITIVE OUTCOMES

Self-confidence blossoming from overcoming difficult circumstances

The character achieving awareness of their flaws because the enemy isn't afraid to point them out The character being better equipped to work with difficult people in the future

Working out past issues that really needed to be dealt with

The characters realizing more can be gained by working together than against each another

Shifting from enemies to rivals or competitors because a bond of mutual respect has allowed both to let go of their animosity

The adversity forcing each character to deal with internal hang-ups that are holding them back

Discovering common ground that helps both characters gain a better perspective

LOSING A JOB

EXAMPLES

The character being fired

Having to leave a beloved job due to personal circumstances beyond one's control—needing to relocate, having to care for a sick relative, or sustaining an injury that causes mobility issues

Being laid off due to budget cuts or a merger

Being intimidated into quitting (through discrimination, harassment, etc.)

Reluctantly leaving because of work friction (dealing with an inept or abrasive boss, being unable to advance professionally, a shift in the company's morals one can't support, etc.)

Being replaced by someone more skilled, less expensive, or with more availability

MINOR COMPLICATIONS

Difficulty finding another job

Leaving valued co-workers who shared a history with the character

The character having to explain the job loss to others

Being escorted off the premises in an embarrassing or public fashion

Dealing with the inconveniences that accompany a job change (losing access to an email account, having to find new insurance coverage, one's schedule being disrupted, etc.)

Having to deal with work associates after the termination notification (to fill out paperwork, to bring someone up to speed on a work project, etc.)

Being contacted by a client who doesn't know about the termination and having to rehash everything after the fact

Lack of organization resulting in a drawn-out termination process

POTENTIALLY DISASTROUS RESULTS

Angrily saying or doing things during the termination process that make a positive recommendation less likely

Threatening to sue, then being blackballed

Having to take a job one doesn't want or is overqualified for, resulting in a lack of fulfillment

Taking a pay cut because of a bad economy or limited job market

Seeking vengeance against the party responsible for one's departure

A lack of support from one's spouse or children (if the character chose to leave)

Not telling a spouse about being fired and them finding out anyway

Lying about the reason one was let go and the truth being revealed

The family struggling to adjust to less income (having to downsize, cut back on expenses, etc.)

Being rejected by former co-workers, friends, and colleagues

Floundering in the aftermath; being paralyzed with indecision or too stunned to move forward

Attempting to strike out on one's own and struggling to succeed

RESULTING EMOTIONS: Anger, Betrayed, Bitterness, Denial, Devastation, Disbelief, Disillusionment, Emasculation, Embarrassment, Fear, Hurt, Indignation, Panic, Powerlessness, Rage, Resentment, Resignation, Self-Pity, Shock, Unappreciated, Vengefulness, Worthlessness

POSSIBLE INTERNAL STRUGGLES
Feeling bitterness or resentment from being forced out of a beloved job
Embarrassment over the termination; worrying what other people are saying or thinking
Internalizing any unfair accusations or claims that caused the termination
Second-guessing the decision to leave
Losing one's sense of identity
Getting stuck at a certain point in the grieving process and lacking the motivation to move on
Being angry at being let go despite knowing one is partly to blame
Wanting to say certain things about the firing but thinking it's probably best to keep quiet
Fantasizing about ways to get even while knowing those thoughts are keeping the character from moving on

NEGATIVE TRAITS THAT MAY WORSEN THE SITUATION: Abrasive, Childish, Confrontational, Disrespectful, Insecure, Melodramatic, Resentful, Uncooperative, Violent

IMPACT ON BASIC NEEDS
Self-Actualization: Losing a job is a setback, but if the occupation was needed for the character to achieve a specific outcome or make a difference in a key area, it may feel like a door has permanently closed.

Esteem and Recognition: No one wants to admit they were fired. If the character's family tends to be judgmental or critical, this can cause even more difficulties with self-esteem.

Love and Belonging: The stress of a job loss, decline in self-esteem, and financial hardship may cause the character to lash out. If they introduce more friction to already fragile relationships, they could break things beyond repair.

Physiological Needs: If the character is unable to find a replacement job, their basic physiological needs could be threatened.

POSITIVE TRAITS TO HELP THE CHARACTER COPE: Calm, Diplomatic, Disciplined, Industrious, Mature, Organized, Proactive, Resourceful, Simple, Tolerant

POSITIVE OUTCOMES
Being able to pivot into a new career that is more fulfilling and rewarding
Having the freedom to relocate to a better place for one's family
Choosing to fight back against an illegitimate termination, thereby righting a wrong
Hindsight providing clues that a company may be planning to downsize and the character being able to prepare for it in the future
Adopting a positive, forward-looking mindset instead of one focused on the past
Accepting the part one played in being fired and resolving to do better
A scandal coming to light after the character's departure that would have stained their reputation had they still been employed

LOSING A SOURCE OF TRANSPORTATION

EXAMPLES
The character's carpool buddy pulling out of the arrangement
Public transportation maintenance, cuts, or closures limiting the character's options
The character's car being totaled in an accident
The character's motorcycle needing repair
Being unable to pay public transportation fees
Losing one's bus pass
An inability to pay for gas or tolls
The character's vehicle being impounded or repossessed
A bike being stolen
The character moving and having to wait for their vehicle to arrive
Having to share a vehicle with others in the family

MINOR COMPLICATIONS
Time lost having to repair the car or buy another one
Financial strain from having to retrieve the car from being impounded
Having to come up with a backup plan
The hassle of filing a police report
Being unable to bring one's child to school or other activities
Insurance going up due to the accident
Dealing with adjustments to one's schedule (if switching to ride share or public transportation, for example)
Having to ask for help from a friend, neighbor, or family member
Having to rent a car
Having to trust others to transport family members to school or work
Discomfort from sharing transportation with strangers
Having to figure out a new bus or train schedule

POTENTIALLY DISASTROUS RESULTS
Having to find a new job closer to home
Missing important meetings, classes, appointments, or events
Having to relocate to be closer to public transportation
Being stranded on the side of the road
The character being fired because they were late or absent too many times
Accepting a ride from an unknown person
Trauma associated with being a victim of an accident or theft
The character going into debt to replace their mode of transportation
Experiencing financial difficulties from new, unforeseen expenditures
Need pushing the character to steal a car and them being caught and arrested for it

RESULTING EMOTIONS: Anger, Anxiety, Bitterness, Despair, Desperation, Discouragement, Embarrassment, Frustration, Guilt, Humbled, Irritation, Overwhelmed, Powerlessness, Reluctance, Resignation, Self-Pity, Uncertainty, Unease, Vulnerability, Worry

POSSIBLE INTERNAL STRUGGLES
Being tempted to accept a ride from an unknown person
Shame at being unable to pay for expensive repairs or replace transportation
Being forced to choose between securing transportation and paying for other needs
Anxiety over using public transportation
Guilt over decision making that led to the loss of transportation
Guilt over inconveniencing others
Feeling a loss of control
Experiencing an ego hit from having to ask for help or trust in a mode of transport the character has always scorned

NEGATIVE TRAITS THAT MAY WORSEN THE SITUATION: Cocky, Controlling, Cynical, Disorganized, Flaky, Inflexible, Lazy, Materialistic, Nervous, Possessive, Pretentious, Spoiled, Stubborn, Whiny, Workaholic

IMPACT ON BASIC NEEDS
  Self-Actualization: The character's inability to get to and from specific locations may disrupt hobbies, schooling, and the ability to do valued charitable work.
  Esteem and Recognition: A loss of independence may make them feel self-conscious, especially if the lack is noticed by judgmental peers.
  Love and Belonging: The character's inability to attend familial engagements may cause problems with inflexible, demanding relatives.
  Safety and Security: A character who fails to replace their transportation quickly may lose their job, creating financial hardship and an inability to pay their bills.

POSITIVE TRAITS TO HELP THE CHARACTER COPE: Adaptable, Adventurous, Ambitious, Appreciative, Courteous, Disciplined, Easygoing, Friendly, Humble, Mature, Optimistic, Organized, Persuasive, Proactive, Resourceful, Responsible, Spontaneous, Wise

POSITIVE OUTCOMES
The carpool replacement becoming a friend, romantic interest, or new professional contact
The character planning better financially so they can be prepared for unforeseen events
Having more time to read, listen, work, or communicate (if the character is taking public transportation)
Changing to an eco-friendly option and feeling good about the choice
The public transportation schedule forcing the character to learn better time management
A forced relocation providing a shorter commute or better local schools
Saving time or money with the new transportation method

NEEDING TO DISOBEY AN ORDER

EXAMPLES
The character defying a ruler's illegal order or immoral decree
Refusing to comply with an order that violates the character's rights or religious beliefs
Defying an order to stay away from an abused or neglected person or animal
Breaking a restraining order to intervene in a dangerous situation
Ignoring a gag order to expose a cover-up
Refusing to reveal personal or incriminating information under threat of punishment
Defying a parent's attempts to arrange a marriage
Overstaying a visa to preserve one's safety
Lying to police or other authorities to protect someone
Defying court-ordered child custody arrangements
Refusing to comply with prejudicial or biased systems at work
A teacher or social worker disregarding a parent's orders when they're detrimental to their child
In the case of an emergency, refusing to stop driving when told to do so by a police officer
A soldier going AWOL (Absent Without Leave) to preserve their mental or physical well-being

MINOR COMPLICATIONS
Being threatened with repercussions
Angering the people who issued the order
Being reprimanded
Letting others down
The character having to explain their choice to others
Being maligned by those who don't know the reasons behind the character's actions
The character always looking over their shoulder, worrying their disobedience will be discovered

POTENTIALLY DISASTROUS RESULTS
Becoming the target of retribution
Being fired
Facing criminal charges or a lawsuit
The character's moral courage being tested
Making the wrong call, leading to a worse outcome than if the order had been followed
The character's reputation being ruined
Uninvolved family members sharing in the consequences
Losing the trust of others
The character's parental or basic rights being jeopardized
Being disowned by one's family for defying their orders
Being excommunicated
Acting on information that turns out to be incorrect (defying the order for nothing)
Giving up anonymity to go public with information and being put at risk

RESULTING EMOTIONS: Anguish, Anxiety, Apprehension, Conflicted, Denial, Desperation, Determination, Disillusionment, Doubt, Dread, Eagerness, Fear, Guilt, Impatience, Intimidation, Nervousness, Regret, Resentment, Self-Pity, Tormented, Uncertainty, Vulnerability

POSSIBLE INTERNAL STRUGGLES

Having to choose between protecting oneself or protecting others
Feeling as though one must choose between loyalties
Being tempted to lie about the circumstances
Feeling as though one's moral code is being compromised
Struggling to make an on-the-fly decision
Feeling disloyal
Dealing with the guilt of knowingly breaking a rule
Questioning one's judgment
Trying to not think about the consequences and just do what must be done

NEGATIVE TRAITS THAT MAY WORSEN THE SITUATION: Confrontational, Disloyal, Fanatical, Frivolous, Fussy, Impulsive, Indecisive, Inhibited, Mischievous, Nervous, Perfectionist, Selfish, Subservient, Worrywart

IMPACT ON BASIC NEEDS

Self-Actualization: Defying orders will almost always result in repercussions. A character who is seen as a troublemaker may struggle to succeed at work or be accepted in the circles that would enable them to reach their full potential.

Esteem and Recognition: If the character's situation is one others won't fully know about or understand, his reputation could be damaged even if it isn't deserved.

Love and Belonging: Disobeying an order can result in friction with loved ones who disagree with the decision or are worried about the fallout.

Safety and Security: A character who defies an order may oppose someone who's in a position to take things away, such as their job, home, protection, or other resources.

Physiological Needs: If the person in charge is powerful or corrupt, defying their orders could cost the character their life.

POSITIVE TRAITS TO HELP THE CHARACTER COPE: Bold, Cautious, Confident, Courageous, Decisive, Honorable, Idealistic, Inspirational, Objective, Passionate, Persistent, Protective, Socially Aware, Uninhibited

POSITIVE OUTCOMES

Shining a light on injustice or oppression
Being awarded and honored for the courage needed to defy the order
Saving someone's life
Earning the respect of others for taking a known risk
Inspiring others to tap into their moral courage

RECEIVING A BAD PERFORMANCE REVIEW

EXAMPLES
The character's business receiving a one-star review from a disgruntled customer
Having an uncomfortable conversation with a manager about one's lackluster sales
One's play being torn apart by critics in the media
The character receiving a painful review of their book that attacks their storytelling abilities
A bad review of the character's just-released video game citing numerous bugs and poor design
A homeowner pointing out imperfections in the character's remodeling work
A sports broadcaster running down a player's performance during a televised event
A reporter running an exposé on an ethics or privacy breach in the character's business
Being yelled at by the coach in the dressing room after a difficult loss
A date telling people that a sexual interlude with the character was disappointing

MINOR COMPLICATIONS
Feeling embarrassed over receiving negative judgment
Being placed on an action plan for improvement
Having to attend further training
Being ridiculed by colleagues
Feeling misunderstood
Being unhappy with work
Needing to attend retraining or upgrade one's education in a specific area
Having to take on extra practices or workouts
Having to work longer hours to make up for lost time
Loss of income from not getting promotions or bonuses

POTENTIALLY DISASTROUS RESULTS
Having to face a panel that will decide the character's professional fate
Being assigned a work schedule that clashes with the rest of the family's needs
Feeling like a failure
Being fired
The character's professional reputation being permanently tarnished
Being transferred or reassigned to another position or location
Not taking responsibility; blaming others
Feeling unsafe and insecure from being unfairly targeted and judged
Having to meet unreasonable expectations to redeem oneself
Reacting violently to the news
Experiencing depression and the sense of a loss of control
Becoming creatively blocked
Venting on social media or confiding in the wrong person
Falling back on destructive habits and addictions

RESULTING EMOTIONS: Anger, Annoyance, Anxiety, Betrayed, Confusion, Contempt, Defensiveness, Determination, Devastation, Disappointment, Disbelief, Discouragement, Emasculation, Envy, Frustration, Guilt, Humiliation, Inadequacy, Unappreciated, Worthlessness

POSSIBLE INTERNAL STRUGGLES

Questioning whether to accept the criticism or to speak against it
Being tempted to seek retribution
Struggling with feelings of low self-worth and inadequacy
Difficulty finding a balance between work and their personal life
Struggling to maintain optimism in a hostile work environment
Feeling forced to compromise one's values in order to do the job well
Being tempted to throw a co-worker under the bus
Wanting to quit but being ashamed; feeling like that would be running away or conceding defeat
Debating whether or not to share private, personal matters with one's boss

NEGATIVE TRAITS THAT MAY WORSEN THE SITUATION: Abrasive, Apathetic, Confrontational, Controlling, Cynical, Disrespectful, Impulsive, Irresponsible, Know-It-All, Melodramatic, Perfectionist, Rebellious, Uncooperative, Volatile

IMPACT ON BASIC NEEDS

Self-Actualization: A character who has received poor performance reviews is unlikely to be promoted or given coveted accounts. If their professional dreams include advancement, this could keep them from being fulfilled at work.

Esteem and Recognition: Being criticized for performance (fairly or not) can create deep insecurities that affect other areas of the character's life.

Love and Belonging: If the character's acceptance within an organization or community is dependent on specific achievements and accolades, a bad review could damage their standing or even cause them to be cast out.

Safety and Security: Losing a job based on a poor review (or more than one) can put the character in dire financial straits.

POSITIVE TRAITS TO HELP THE CHARACTER COPE: Ambitious, Centered, Charming, Confident, Cooperative, Patient, Persistent, Persuasive, Proactive, Professional, Responsible

POSITIVE OUTCOMES

Improving and finding satisfaction in a job well done
Finding a more suitable or satisfying job
Learning to ask for help from colleagues and management
Initiating a conversation that results in an overhaul of the company's review process
Realizing the current arrangement is a bad fit and finding a new one that aligns better with the character's skills and ethics
Using the criticism as fuel to prove everyone wrong and achieving enviable success as a result
Cutting ties with a toxic workplace, relationship, or environment that is eroding one's self-worth

WORK-LIFE BALANCE BEING THREATENED

EXAMPLES
A divorce making it hard for the character to concentrate at work
Having to plan a funeral for a loved one during a peak sale season
A co-worker quitting, leaving the character with double the workload
Employers hinting that the character should postpone maternity leave
Having to leave an important meeting to bail an adult sibling out of lockup
An injury or chronic illness that limits one's ability to work (prolonged sitting becoming painful, the character having limited mobility or suffering migraines when staring at a screen, etc.)
Bills piling up and forcing the character to take a second or third job
Starting a new job just as a home sells and the character needs to move
Being called at work because an elderly loved one has fallen at the care home
One's work-from-home situation being threatened by a child's suspension or a partner also working from home
Living with an addiction or battling a mental health condition
An important deadline being moved to coincide with a spouse's due date
Having to step in to coach little league while working weekends
Travel becoming a regular part of the job, adding friction to an already stressed marital relationship

MINOR COMPLICATIONS
Having to readjust and needing time to do that
Other people being negatively affected
Friction with loved ones
One's schedule being turned upside down
Being preoccupied with work and not being present with family
Needing to cancel or rearrange commitments
Having to give up leisure or personal care activities
Not receiving empathy from others
Being reprimanded at work or missing out on promising professional opportunities
Becoming the target of office gossip

POTENTIALLY DISASTROUS RESULTS
Losing one's job or business
Missing an important family event
A temporary difficulty turning into a permanent one
Trying to continue to balance everything without making adjustments
Losing track of critical needs at work or at home
The character's addiction affecting their work performance
Falling apart emotionally
Experiencing stress-related health issues
Missing critical deadlines

Trying to handle personal matters during working hours
Circumstances changing again while the character is already struggling to adjust

RESULTING EMOTIONS: Annoyance, Anxiety, Apprehension, Bitterness, Defeat, Depressed, Devastation, Discouragement, Fear, Frustration, Guilt, Inadequacy, Insecurity, Nervousness, Overwhelmed, Panic, Self-Pity, Worry

POSSIBLE INTERNAL STRUGGLES
Feeling pressured to perform in one's roles
Feeling guilty about being unable to perform better at work or at home
Pretending everything is under control when it's not
Feeling torn between the demands
Struggling with anxiety, stress, and feelings of inadequacy
Resenting others for having an easier time
Regretting previously-made choices and feeling stuck
Fantasizing about escaping all responsibility and starting over

NEGATIVE TRAITS THAT MAY WORSEN THE SITUATION: Addictive, Apathetic, Compulsive, Controlling, Disorganized, Foolish, Inattentive, Inflexible, Insecure, Melodramatic, Perfectionist, Resentful, Stubborn, Workaholic

IMPACT ON BASIC NEEDS
　　Self-Actualization: Tapping into one's full potential in the workplace or in family life may be impossible for a character who is trying to do it all.
　　Esteem and Recognition: A character struggling to meet everyone's needs may feel like a failure at home, at work, or both.
　　Love and Belonging: Loved ones or colleagues may view the character as unreliable and incompetent for not being fully present, leaving the character feeling unfairly judged.
　　Safety and Security: A character who loses his job or works himself to exhaustion trying to keep all the balls in the air may find his physical or mental health compromised.

POSITIVE TRAITS TO HELP THE CHARACTER COPE: Adaptable, Calm, Centered, Decisive, Efficient, Industrious, Organized, Proactive, Professional, Resourceful, Responsible

POSITIVE OUTCOMES
Prioritizing the important aspects of one's life
The character's efforts to advocate for herself being understood and appreciated
Pursuing a different career path that is more compatible with one's personal life
Learning to accept help from others
The character admitting they're in over their head and learning how to say no
Recognizing someone else's struggle (having experienced it personally)
Learning positive coping mechanisms, such as meditation, prayer, rest, setting boundaries, exercise, etc.

Increased Pressure and Ticking Clocks

A DEADLINE BEING MOVED UP

EXAMPLES

The timeline to fulfill a promise being bumped up

Needing to have important paperwork completed earlier than planned because of a clerical error

Needing to have materials prepped for a meeting that is taking place sooner than expected

The date being changed for a rally or event that the character is responsible for, making them hurry to complete their plans

A student being "asked" by a professor to swap presentation dates for a school assignment, resulting in an earlier deadline

Needing to secure resources sooner than expected (for a battle, to prepare for imminent danger, etc.)

Learning a window of opportunity is closing faster than anticipated (to escape, to overcome an obstacle, to impress the right people, to prove one's innocence, to save someone's life, etc.)

MINOR COMPLICATIONS

One's schedule and personal plans being disrupted

Having to inconvenience other people whose support is needed to complete a task

Losing sleep

Having to sacrifice quality for efficiency

Disappointing loved ones by placing their needs last

The character having to ask for help when they don't want to (because it makes them look weak, there's a quid pro quo involved, or the other person is a rival or enemy)

Being forced to change one's plan to fit the new timeline (cutting back on the scope of the project, changing the venue, having to pay more to obtain what one needs, etc.)

Other people perceiving the character as being unprepared or a poor planner

Going over a manager's head to get something done on time and angering them

POTENTIALLY DISASTROUS RESULTS

Rushing that leads to safety issues (and someone being injured)

Having to make a deal that carries a high personal cost, such as sacrificing a cherished goal, returning an expensive favor, or placing oneself in harm's way, etc.

Being blamed for a poor turnout or sloppy end result

Failing because the timeline was impossible to meet

The character's reputation being destroyed because their end result was subpar

Being held accountable for a completely blown budget

Being stressed and treating someone poorly, damaging the relationship beyond repair

Getting caught cutting corners or breaking the law to meet the deadline

RESULTING EMOTIONS: Anger, Apprehension, Defeat, Desperation, Determination, Dread, Emasculation, Embarrassment, Flustered, Frustration, Inadequacy, Overwhelmed, Panic, Resentment, Resignation, Skepticism, Stunned, Unappreciated, Worry

POSSIBLE INTERNAL STRUGGLES
Anxiety over how to meet the deadline; suffering a crisis of faith in one's abilities
The character knowing they weren't to blame but feeling bad for putting others in a difficult position
Anger (about the deadline being changed) that wars with feelings of duty and responsibility
Being tempted to break the law or lie to get what one needs
Having to choose between meeting the deadline or creating a product that will make one proud
Facing an immediate choice between the good of the many and the good of the few when friends or loved ones may become collateral damage
Wanting to quit because it's the easier thing to do
Facing the temptation to fabricate an excuse (a death in the family, being ill, etc.) that will give the character more time

NEGATIVE TRAITS THAT MAY WORSEN THE SITUATION: Abrasive, Cocky, Disorganized, Extravagant, Forgetful, Inattentive, Indecisive, Irresponsible, Martyr, Melodramatic, Needy, Perfectionist, Scatterbrained, Weak-willed, Whiny, Worrywart

IMPACT ON BASIC NEEDS
Self-Actualization: The character may do things to meet the deadline they didn't think they were capable of, leading to an identity crisis.
Esteem and Recognition: If the character is used as a scapegoat, their reputation may be damaged, hurting their prospects moving forward.
Love and Belonging: When fixing a situation requires sacrifice (canceling a vacation to work, forcing the family to move to fulfill a duty, etc.), loved ones aren't always understanding.
Safety and Security: Tight deadlines can force a character to take risks they might normally not take. If something goes wrong, the character or those they care about could be injured, placed in danger, or suffer hardship from unexpected fallout.

POSITIVE TRAITS TO HELP THE CHARACTER COPE: Adaptable, Adventurous, Calm, Decisive, Efficient, Focused, Obedient, Organized, Persistent, Persuasive, Resourceful, Sensible, Wise

POSITIVE OUTCOMES
Becoming better at time management
Being able to hone one's organizational and planning skills
Becoming more adaptable when things go sideways
A chance to lead and gain valuable experience
Becoming better at working with others
Discovering who one's friends truly are by seeing who sticks around to help and who does not
The character learning they're far more capable than anyone believed
Meeting the deadline, thereby earning the gratitude and respect or teammates or co-workers

A DELAY THAT MAKES ONE LATE

EXAMPLES
The character oversleeping (due to an alarm not going off, a hangover, etc.)
A diaper explosion as the character is getting ready to leave
The dog escaping and having to be chased down
Facilities issues, such as a pipe breaking or the fire alarm going off
A transportation breakdown (the car won't start, one's bike being stolen, etc.)
Forgetting an important item (a wallet, passport, phone, etc.) and having to go back for it
Getting stuck in traffic, behind a school bus, or at a drawbridge
Taking a wrong turn
Getting a ticket
Getting into a car accident
Having to take an important call (from the kids' school, the boss, a doctor, etc.)
Having to wait on someone else, such as a carpool driver, late school bus, or babysitter
Poor planning—due to being overwhelmed by other things or a flaw in the character's personality

MINOR COMPLICATIONS
Friction with others who are inconvenienced
One's credibility being damaged
Forgetting something important because one is in a hurry
Something falling through the cracks because it was impossible to get everything done
Being short-tempered with others due to the stress
Losing valuable prep time (before a class, a presentation, a meeting, etc.)
Minor health implications (increased hypertension, aggravating an ulcer, etc.)
Missing a meal and becoming cranky

POTENTIALLY DISASTROUS RESULTS
Being late to an interview and not getting the job
Missing a flight
Ruining a last chance at romance
Getting into an accident due to rushing
Giving in to road rage
Forgetting to take medication and suffering a medical episode (going into diabetic shock, having a seizure, etc.)
Forgetting a promise (to pick up a neighbor's child from daycare, to take an elderly relative to their doctor's appointment, etc.)
Missing a mandatory court appearance
Being triggered into a panic attack or mental meltdown
Losing one's temper and berating someone who isn't to blame and the tantrum being recorded and shared online

RESULTING EMOTIONS: Anger, Defensiveness, Desperation, Determination, Dread, Embarrassment, Flustered, Guilt, Impatience, Overwhelmed, Panic, Powerlessness, Regret

POSSIBLE INTERNAL STRUGGLES

Being tempted to lie about the cause of lateness to avoid looking inept

The character being a stickler for punctuality and chafing about being late

Feeling as if the world is conspiring against the character, yet knowing the idea is preposterous

Self-directed anger for one's lack of organization but also feeling helpless to change

An inability to forgive oneself for a human mistake (because of perfectionistic tendencies)

Struggling with defeatist thoughts (if the impact of the tardiness is dire)

NEGATIVE TRAITS THAT MAY WORSEN THE SITUATION: Confrontational, Defensive, Disorganized, Flaky, Foolish, Forgetful, Fussy, Impatient, Irresponsible, Martyr, Melodramatic, Nervous, Obsessive, Oversensitive, Perfectionist, Scatterbrained, Worrywart

IMPACT ON BASIC NEEDS

Esteem and Recognition: Missing a once-in-a-lifetime opportunity may greatly impact the character's self-esteem, especially if they are to blame.

Love and Belonging: Dropping the ball one too many times might be the straw that breaks the character's relationships with family or loved ones.

Safety and Security: A character rushing because they're late or distracted increases their chances of getting into an accident or being injured.

Physiological Needs: A delay could cause the character to fail to secure something life-saving in time: a boat transport to escape an assassin, shelter from a tsunami, a much-needed vaccine, etc.

POSITIVE TRAITS TO HELP THE CHARACTER COPE: Adaptable, Appreciative, Calm, Confident, Disciplined, Friendly, Innocent, Kind, Optimistic, Persistent, Resourceful, Witty

POSITIVE OUTCOMES

A chance encounter that wouldn't have happened had the character been on time

Learning a valuable lesson to plan better in the future

Taking responsibility for one's mistake and being forgiven

Recognizing one is overcommitted and taking steps to keep it from happening again

Missing one's final destination and realizing it was for the best

Avoiding a terrible fate, such as a gas explosion at work or a train derailment with no survivors, because of the delay

Being in the right place at the right time (and saving someone else's life, taking the same elevator as a talent scout and being discovered, or noticing danger and preventing an accident)

BEING BLACKMAILED

NOTES: Blackmail occurs when one party demands some kind of compensation in return for not revealing potentially damaging (true or false) information about the victim. The possibilities for a blackmail scenario are virtually limitless when you consider the many secrets a victim may not want revealed combined with the demands the blackmailer could make.

EXAMPLES
A character's secrets the blackmailer could threaten to reveal:
An affair
Proof of a crime (the character's hit and run accident, a murder, sexual inappropriateness, etc.)
Evidence of a crime committed by the character's child
Damaging correspondence between the character and another party
Information about a loved one that would be considered taboo in that time period or setting (a mental health condition, their sexual orientation, attending Communist meetings in the 1940s, etc.)
Recordings of racist comments or behavior
Accusations that were silenced or covered up
Nepotism in high places
Proof of lies, fraud, or espionage

In return for the character's silence, the blackmailer may demand:
Money or items of value (jewelry, paintings from an art collection, a patent in the works, etc.)
Sexual favors
Verbal support for them or their cause
The character's help punishing the blackmailer's competitor or enemy
Security credentials that will provide access to a person, facility, or sensitive materials
That certain legislation, permits, or paperwork be pushed through
That the victim turn a blind eye to the blackmailer's criminal behavior
The victim remove him or herself from an influential position

MINOR COMPLICATIONS
Lost sleep from worrying the secret will get out
An inability to focus on work or school
Not being able to talk to anyone about the situation; having to go through it alone
Lying to many people and losing track of what has been said to whom
Having to come up with cover stories (for who the blackmailer is, where the character disappeared to for the past three hours, why money is being withdrawn, etc.)
Disagreeing with a confidante about what course of action should be taken

POTENTIALLY DISASTROUS RESULTS
The secret (real or fabricated) getting out
The blackmailer returning afterwards and demanding more
Giving in to a demand that requires the victim to break the law or become complicit in some way

Damaged relationships with loved ones when they discover the secret

The blackmailer reminding the character of his reach by threatening or hurting loved ones

Bankrupting oneself to pay off the blackmailer

Not giving in to demands because the accusation isn't true and not being believed by others when the story breaks

Becoming involved in a criminal investigation because of one's involvement with the blackmailer

Sacrificing a career, marriage, or other valuable commodity to keep the secret private

RESULTING EMOTIONS: Anger, Anguish, Anxiety, Denial, Despair, Desperation, Dread, Fear, Guilt, Horror, Panic, Powerlessness, Remorse, Self-Loathing, Tormented, Vulnerability

POSSIBLE INTERNAL STRUGGLES

Being paralyzed with indecision about what to do

Imagining other people know or suspect what's going on

Wanting to confide in loved ones but needing to lie to protect them

Feeling shame or self-loathing over the past transgressions one is being blackmailed for

Half-wanting the secret to be known to end the agony of keeping it

Moral questions over how far to go to ensure the blackmailer stays silent

NEGATIVE TRAITS THAT MAY WORSEN THE SITUATION: Defensive, Impulsive, Nervous, Paranoid, Reckless, Self-Destructive, Uncooperative, Vindictive, Worrywart

IMPACT ON BASIC NEEDS

Self-Actualization: Someone being blackmailed will often try to fly under the radar and avoid the notice of others. Characters in this position aren't likely to take risks and will likely fall short of their ultimate dreams and goals.

Esteem and Recognition: It would be easy for a blackmailing victim to feel a lowered sense of esteem as they wonder how they managed to become a victim or get into this situation to begin with.

Love and Belonging: A victim keeping secrets from loved ones may find those important relationships strained. The same can be true if the loved ones know about the blackmailing and resent the victim for putting them all in this situation in the first place.

Safety and Security: Often, a threat of violence is used to keep the victim in line. By nature, most blackmailers are happy to follow through, meaning the danger is real for the character and their loved ones.

POSITIVE TRAITS TO HELP THE CHARACTER COPE: Calm, Cautious, Disciplined, Obedient, Persuasive, Proactive, Protective, Resourceful, Tolerant, Wise

POSITIVE OUTCOMES

Coming clean about something that has been weighing on the victim's mind for years

Finally taking responsibility for one's actions

Confiding in someone and seeing the relationship grow stronger through the trial

Taking charge of the situation instead of letting others dictate the character's choices

The victim growing in confidence when they realize they have done the right thing

BEING GIVEN AN ULTIMATUM

NOTES: "Ultimatum" is a Latin word meaning "last one." It's a final demand that, if not met, will result in serious consequences for the character—they will lose something they care about or action will be taken against them. The one making the demand may have good reasons for issuing an ultimatum or they might just want to be in control, but they will be someone close to the character or have leverage or authority over them. Some examples of what the character may be asked to do are as follows.

EXAMPLES
Give up a relationship (end a toxic friendship, stop seeing someone, commit to one partner, etc.)
Get help in the form of starting rehab, seeing a doctor, or talking to a teacher or police officer
Quit a bad habit (drinking, drug use, spying on people, behaving recklessly, etc.)
Stop doing something (interfering with parenting a child, going behind someone's back, meddling in a couple's marriage, lying, cheating, flouting the law, manipulating people, etc.)
Start doing something, such as taking medication, exercising, eating better, or attending couple's counseling
Obey the person giving the ultimatum. Not all demands are reasonable or can be explained, and some people simply wish to assert control. The situation could be for the other person's benefit (a parent giving a child an ultimatum if they don't get into the car right now) or malevolently motivated (an unhinged person threatening violence if their demands are not met).

MINOR COMPLICATIONS
The situation keeping the character up at night
Being called out for one's difficulty focusing at school or work
Other relationships suffering (because the character is keeping secrets, taking out the stress on their kids, etc.)
Minor health issues, such as weight loss, stomach upset, headaches, or fatigue
Dragging things out and prolonging the agony (through stalling, avoidance, denial, etc.)
Having to avoid the person who made the ultimatum

POTENTIALLY DISASTROUS RESULTS
Not taking the other person seriously
Choosing the path that allows the character to continue in hurtful or destructive behavior
Giving in to an unreasonable ultimatum
Refusing to comply with a healthy ultimatum and losing an important relationship with a friend, spouse, or child
Listening to foolish advisors and making the wrong choice
Making a decision that results in the character living with dissatisfaction, insecurity, or regret
The character giving up something they truly love and value

RESULTING EMOTIONS: Anger, Anguish, Betrayed, Bitterness, Conflicted, Defensiveness, Defiance, Denial, Desperation, Determination, Dread, Fear, Panic, Powerlessness, Resentment, Resignation, Self-Loathing, Self-Pity, Shame, Uncertainty, Vulnerability, Worry, Worthlessness

POSSIBLE INTERNAL STRUGGLES

Being plagued with indecision; not knowing what to do

Resenting the person making the ultimatum despite knowing it comes from a place of caring

The character wanting to be left alone but also knowing they need help

Feeling enslaved to a behavior or addiction but fearing the pain that comes with letting go of it

Struggling with feelings of shame or self-loathing for allowing oneself to get into this situation or be pushed around by others

Anger at the sacrifice being demanded when others are not asked to do the same

The character doubting their instincts or discernment

Facing two terrible options, both of which result in a lose-lose scenario

Anguish over making a decision that will impact others

Loving someone but knowing their irrational ultimatum indicates deeply-rooted problems

NEGATIVE TRAITS THAT MAY WORSEN THE SITUATION: Addictive, Antisocial, Apathetic, Confrontational, Defensive, Dishonest, Irrational, Melodramatic, Needy, Oversensitive, Paranoid, Stubborn, Subservient, Uncooperative, Vindictive, Weak-Willed

IMPACT ON BASIC NEEDS

Self-Actualization: If the character chooses to give up something valuable or stay with someone who makes unreasonable demands, they could easily reach a point of feeling dissatisfied with the turn their life has taken.

Esteem and Recognition: Whether the character realizes their actions have brought them to this point or they recognize that the person making the ultimatum is trying to take advantage, their self-esteem can be diminished. Their reputation can also be impacted if others think they caved to an unreasonable demand instead of standing up to the other party.

Love and Belonging: If the character's response creates distance in their relationships, they may begin to feel isolated.

Safety and Security: A character who gives in to an unhealthy ultimatum may end up in an unsafe relationship that threatens their physical or emotional well-being.

POSITIVE TRAITS TO HELP THE CHARACTER COPE: Bold, Cooperative, Courageous, Gentle, Just, Kind, Loyal, Mature, Objective, Persuasive, Resourceful, Sensible

POSITIVE OUTCOMES

Recognizing the need for change (in the case of a well-meant ultimatum)

Recognizing in the aftermath of an ultimatum that it was a good thing; being grateful for it

Reevaluating priorities and getting a clear idea of what's important

Using the ultimatum to bring about positive change (letting go of something destructive or realizing the one making the demand is toxic, mentally ill, or needs help)

Increased confidence over having made the right decision in a difficult situation

BEING HUNTED

EXAMPLES
The character being pursued by police or other law enforcement agencies
Someone in a position of authority putting a bounty out on the character
Becoming a target for a serial killer or stalker
Being hunted by a dangerous individual because of what the character knows or has seen
Being trapped in a closed environment (an island, spaceship, or scientific research facility) where a predatory creature is on the loose
Being literally hunted by others as part of a demented sporting activity

MINOR COMPLICATIONS
Living with anxiety or stress, which may cause impulsive decision making
The character not knowing they're being hunted and doing things that make them easier to track (using credit cards, checking in on social media, telling friends where they will be, etc.)
Time wasted trying to find one's way out
The character having to rely on others for help
Conflict with friends or loved ones who withhold help
Having to make decisions quickly and those decisions compounding the problem
Having to lie (and keep track of those lies)
Dealing with minor inconveniences (having to sleep in a car, being short on cash, etc.)
Being innocent, yet having to commit crimes to evade capture and secure what one needs (stealing food, breaking into an unoccupied home to have a safe place to sleep, etc.)
Sustaining a minor injury while evading capture (pulling a muscle, spraining an ankle, etc.)

POTENTIALLY DISASTROUS RESULTS
Being unable to evade the police or bounty hunter and being arrested
Being turned in by someone close to the character, such as a spouse or sibling
Being captured by someone who lacks remorse or other hallmarks of humanity
Running out of vital supplies or defensive measures, such as food or ammunition
A bystander getting caught in the crossfire and being injured or killed
The hunter using loved ones or friends as leverage
Resorting to unsavory methods of earning money, such as theft or prostitution
Developing PTSD because of the traumatic experience
Experiencing paranoia (imagining danger around every corner)
Suffering serious injury or death

RESULTING EMOTIONS: Anguish, Anxiety, Defiance, Depressed, Desperation, Determination, Doubt, Dread, Fear, Guilt, Horror, Hysteria, Loneliness, Overwhelmed, Panic, Paranoia, Powerlessness, Rage, Resignation, Shock, Terror, Tormented, Vulnerability

POSSIBLE INTERNAL STRUGGLES
Being torn between wanting to find help and needing to stay hidden
Struggling to think clearly in the midst of panic and desperate circumstances

Trying to figure out if they're to blame; struggling with feelings of guilt, culpability, and existential concepts (like fate)

Conflict between wanting to end the battle and wanting to stay alive

Needing help but not knowing who to trust

Being faced with the decision to cross certain moral lines in order to survive

Knowing loved ones are worried about the character and feeling guilty about that

Wanting to reach out to loved ones and make sure they're okay but being afraid to involve them

NEGATIVE TRAITS THAT MAY WORSEN THE SITUATION: Controlling, Foolish, Fussy, Gullible, Ignorant, Impulsive, Inattentive, Lazy, Martyr, Morbid, Reckless, Scatterbrained, Ungrateful

IMPACT ON BASIC NEEDS

Self-Actualization: A character in a survival situation would not be able to focus on self-actualization—meaning, this need would go unmet until the more immediate need was stabilized.

Esteem and Recognition: For a character who sees herself as tough, strong, or dominant, being hunted would severely affect the way she views herself.

Love and Belonging: A character on the run will quickly become disconnected from loved ones and family—especially if the character is purposely distancing herself from them to keep them safe.

Safety and Security: This character's sense of emotional and physical safety will be threatened by the simple act of them being hunted.

Physiological Needs: If the hunters are intent on killing, the character is in very real danger of losing their life.

POSITIVE TRAITS TO HELP THE CHARACTER COPE: Analytical, Bold, Calm, Confident, Creative, Curious, Decisive, Independent, Meticulous, Observant, Patient, Persistent, Resourceful, Spunky, Uninhibited

POSITIVE OUTCOMES

The character is able to resolve the issue and neutralize the threat

Discovery of inner resilience that carries them through future trials

The character being vindicated when charges are dismissed

Forging stronger bonds with the people who help them

The character learning an important set of survival skills

The character discovering damning evidence against the hunter, which allows her to gain her freedom

A killer being captured, offering the character closure so they can move on from the ordeal

BEING MADE TO WAIT

EXAMPLES

The character being placed on hold during a phone call

Arriving on time to an appointment with a professional (doctor, lawyer, beauty services, etc.) and having to wait

Standing in line to purchase goods, receive services, or utilize a facility

Waiting to hear whether an adoption has gone through

Awaiting the return of a loved one (from college, a business trip, deployment, etc.)

Waiting to receive test results (for medical care, an academic assessment, etc.)

Anticipating an update on an injured or sick loved one

Anticipating the arrival or departure of a visitor

Awaiting the arrival of transportation (a train, a car service, etc.)

Missing a window for career advancement and having to wait for the next opportunity

Waiting for a paycheck or financial settlement

Experiencing travel delays due to traffic, construction, route changes, or an accident

Waiting for news from law enforcement regarding a criminal investigation

Waiting for a jury to return a verdict

Being impatient to reach legal age and enjoy certain privileges (drinking, voting, gambling, etc.)

Having to wait on personal milestones, such as getting married or starting a family

Waiting for someone to wake up from a coma

Dealing with quarantine requirements

MINOR COMPLICATIONS

Losing time

Experiencing schedule disruptions or delays

Having to seek out alternative options that might be available sooner

Feeling frustration, anxiety, impatience, uncertainty, and stress

Loss of money (if the character is missing work, quarantining, paying expediting fees, etc.)

Anxiety over possibly missing a phone call, email, or other form of communication

Difficulty focusing on day-to-day tasks

The character driving others crazy with their constant requests for information

Not being able to secure a gift for a loved one

Lowered morale in the workplace

Resenting the person responsible for the wait

Becoming crabby or irritable

POTENTIALLY DISASTROUS RESULTS

Having to wait a long time for a critical medical appointment or procedure

Getting caught trying to bribe one's way to the front of a line

Making a rash or impulsive decision that worsens the situation

Taking out a loan to make ends meet

Counting on a raise or bonus that doesn't materialize

A temporary wait turning into a permanent one (police fail to catch a suspect, a loved one slips into a coma interminably, a family member doesn't seek the addiction help they need, etc.)
The character passing up employment or educational opportunities because they're waiting on a certain situation to resolve
Dealing with a boss or client who doesn't cope well with waiting
Not having what one needs and losing an opportunity that may never come again
Resorting to substances or other unhealthy coping mechanisms
A relationship ending because a partner is tired of waiting for the other to follow through

RESULTING EMOTIONS: Agitation, Anger, Annoyance, Anxiety, Concern, Contempt, Despair, Desperation, Discouragement, Disillusionment, Dread, Eagerness, Frustration, Hopefulness, Impatience, Moodiness, Nervousness, Powerlessness, Rage, Unappreciated

POSSIBLE INTERNAL STRUGGLES
Trying to stay resilient in the face of a seemingly unending situation
Constantly fighting the urge to press people for updates
Being tempted to engage in unethical behavior (bribery, cheating, etc.) to hurry the outcome
The character knowing they're being difficult to live with but not knowing how to change
Seeking for ways to take charge of the situation and hurry the process along

NEGATIVE TRAITS THAT MAY WORSEN THE SITUATION: Abrasive, Catty, Childish, Confrontational, Disrespectful, Grumpy, Impatient, Impulsive, Nagging, Obsessive, Oversensitive, Spoiled, Whiny

IMPACT ON BASIC NEEDS
Self-Actualization: Situations where the character is waiting for an important decision or ruling to be made could put their personal goals in limbo, too.
Esteem and Recognition: An impatient or impulsive character may show their true colors during a waiting period, changing the way others view her.
Love and Belonging: A character who is having to wait to be reunited with loved ones may begin to feel lonely and deserted.
Safety and Security: The stress from waiting on a life-changing decision may cause anxiety, sleeplessness, weight loss, and other physical and emotional difficulties.

POSITIVE TRAITS TO HELP THE CHARACTER COPE: Adaptable, Appreciative, Calm, Confident, Cooperative, Easygoing, Empathetic, Happy, Mature, Patient, Wise

POSITIVE OUTCOMES
Learning patience and other positive ways to cope with uncertainty
Learning the importance of having a backup plan (not putting all the eggs in one basket)
Strengthening relationships within one's support network
Being given the gift of time to consider if the character truly wants the thing they're waiting for

BEING SADDLED WITH UNEXPECTED RESPONSIBILITY

EXAMPLES

An elderly parent suddenly declining to the point that the character must care for them
A parent dying and leaving the character in charge of their estate
The character becoming a legal guardian when the parents of her godchild are killed
The character getting pregnant unexpectedly
A man discovering he has fathered a child and now needs to be a parent
A working parent unexpectedly having to homeschool or supervise their child's virtual learning
An accident rendering the character's child physically or mentally disabled
Downsizing at work that results in more responsibility for the character
The character's job description changing, resulting in added duties
A boost in clients or customers that results in more work for employees
Committee members quitting, leaving those who remain to pick up the pieces
A natural or manmade disaster (a terrorist attack, civil unrest, a typhoon, etc.) that creates additional responsibilities for the character

MINOR COMPLICATIONS

Needing extra training to complete new responsibilities
Feeling overwhelmed
Having to work longer hours
Having to change jobs to accommodate a new schedule
Conflict with colleagues or teammates
Lowered morale at work or with a volunteer organization
Having to take time off work
Conflict with family members about the character's increased workload
Making mistakes due to stress, lack of experience, or time-management difficulties
Strained finances (from raising an additional child or paying medical bills for an elderly parent)
Having no time for fun or leisure activities
Having less time to spend with friends
Fearing they won't be able to manage or care for the person needing their help
Resenting the people responsible

POTENTIALLY DISASTROUS RESULTS

Balls being dropped that create a disaster (a child being removed from the character's custody, being demoted due to a far-reaching mistake, etc.)
The character losing their job from taking off too many days or calling in sick too often
More people quitting, creating an impossible workload for those who remain
Suffering a mental breakdown from the stress
Hurrying to bring on help (at work, for childcare, etc.) and learning too late the person they hired was wrong for the job
The stress being the final straw that ends a tenuous marriage

Friendships being strained or broken because the character has no time for them
Physical ailments arising from a lack of self-care (malnutrition, hypertension, sleep deprivation)

RESULTING EMOTIONS: Anger, Anguish, Annoyance, Anxiety, Depressed, Despair, Determination, Disbelief, Dread, Fear, Frustration, Inadequacy, Neglected, Overwhelmed, Panic, Resentment, Resignation, Self-Pity, Shock, Unappreciated, Worry, Worthlessness

POSSIBLE INTERNAL STRUGGLES
Putting on an air of positivity despite being overwhelmed or panic-stricken
Wanting to do the job and be viewed as capable but knowing the extra responsibility is too much
Struggling to decide what to do (if the character has a choice about taking on the responsibility)
Wanting to do the right thing but not wanting to complicate one's current lifestyle
Resenting the person in one's care and being overwhelmed with shame for feeling that way

NEGATIVE TRAITS THAT MAY WORSEN THE SITUATION: Addictive, Apathetic, Disorganized, Extravagant, Flaky, Frivolous, Irresponsible, Lazy, Nervous, Perfectionist, Pessimistic, Resentful, Selfish, Temperamental, Volatile, Workaholic, Worrywart

IMPACT ON BASIC NEEDS
Self-Actualization: A character overwhelmed with life responsibilities would be forced to set their dreams and desires aside, making self-actualization an impossibility.
Esteem and Recognition: An overwhelmed character's performance is going to suffer—at work, in the home, and in relationships—resulting in the additional burdens of insecurity, inadequacy, and self-doubt.
Love and Belonging: A character in this situation will have to reprioritize, likely putting imperative responsibilities above relationships. This can cause friction and stress within the character's support system.

POSITIVE TRAITS TO HELP THE CHARACTER COPE: Adaptable, Ambitious, Analytical, Appreciative, Calm, Cautious, Confident, Cooperative, Disciplined, Easygoing, Efficient, Focused, Happy, Honorable, Industrious, Nurturing, Optimistic, Organized

POSITIVE OUTCOMES
Being able to provide valuable care and attention for someone in need
Being rewarded for one's hard work with a raise or promotion
The character being recognized with awards or praise for their contributions
One's life becoming deeper and more meaningful thanks to the unexpected responsibility
Learning to balance family and work life
Learning to be efficient, thereby being able to do more than the character thought possible
The character learning it's okay to say no to a situation that's beyond their capabilities

BEING THRUST INTO THE SPOTLIGHT

EXAMPLES
A reluctant understudy suddenly having to play the leading role
A video or social post going viral and turning the character into a phenomenon
The character's product (a book, movie, song, etc.) becoming an instant hit
The character's spouse achieving fame overnight
Winning a high-profile competition or contest
The character's superpowers or magical abilities being revealed
Making news headlines for doing something heroic or inspirational
Witnessing an infamous crime and becoming a star witness in the trial
Being discovered by a talent scout while doing something mundane
The character discovering they're closely related to a celebrity or government leader
Dating someone famous
Being accused of a high-profile or particularly heinous crime
Saving someone's life in an unusual circumstance

MINOR COMPLICATIONS
Dealing with the loss of anonymity and privacy
The character always having to think about how they look, what they say, etc.
Receiving hate mail or being trolled on social media
Conflict with friends who are jealous of the character's sudden fame
Existing relationships shifting because of increased scrutiny for the character and everyone around them
Arguments with family or roommates about a lack of privacy
The character fearing that incriminating moments from their past will be discovered
Having to keep working and innovating to stay on top
Being overwhelmed with new opportunities that must be examined and sorted through
Hobbies and interests shifting for the character, causing them to drift away from old friends

POTENTIALLY DISASTROUS RESULTS
Being physically harmed or seeing their loved ones harmed, because of their sudden fame
Their reputation being trashed publicly
Skeletons being dragged from the character's closet and paraded for the world to see
Developing addictions or mental health issues as coping mechanisms
Being stalked or receiving death threats
Becoming fake; the character not being true to who they really are
The character changing their values and morals to fit with the people around them
Becoming obsessed with—and constantly worrying about—what the public thinks
The character abandoning lifelong friendships in favor of new ones that serve her better
The character being intimidated or bullied into staying in the spotlight
Becoming violent with a reporter or photographer
The character going on the run to avoid being arrested for something they didn't do

RESULTING EMOTIONS: Acceptance, Adoration, Amusement, Annoyance, Anxiety, Conflicted, Disbelief, Dissatisfaction, Eagerness, Elation, Excitement, Flustered, Frustration, Insecurity, Intimidation, Irritation, Overwhelmed, Panic, Pleased, Reluctance, Resentment

POSSIBLE INTERNAL STRUGGLES

The character wanting to express who they truly are while staying in the public's good graces
The character recognizing the new popularity is destroying their relationships but not wanting to give it up
Being tempted to cross moral lines to stay in the spotlight
The character having to cross moral lines to prove innocence of wrongdoing
Feeling abandoned and betrayed by those who believe the bad things the media is saying
Wanting to give up the spotlight but knowing the decision will upset certain loved ones
Struggling to know if new friends are real or are only drawn to the character's fame
The character feeling the fame is unwarranted, that they don't deserve it

NEGATIVE TRAITS THAT MAY WORSEN THE SITUATION: Abrasive, Addictive, Compulsive, Confrontational, Disloyal, Disrespectful, Foolish, Gullible, Impulsive, Inhibited, Insecure, Materialistic, Paranoid, Reckless, Tactless, Uncouth, Verbose

IMPACT ON BASIC NEEDS

Self-Actualization: A character who is dropped into the spotlight may feel the need to keep up appearances or maintain their fame, leading to an erosion of who they are at their core.

Esteem and Recognition: A character with a negative spotlight fixed on them will struggle with self-worth, especially if those closest to them also believe what's being said about them.

Love and Belonging: A character can be surrounded by people and still be completely isolated due to him losing contact with the grounding people in his life or not being able to truly be himself.

Safety and Security: Mental health issues arising from the constant barrage of unwarranted criticism is a real concern for people in the spotlight, as are physical threats from unhinged individuals who would harm them.

POSITIVE TRAITS TO HELP THE CHARACTER COPE: Adaptable, Ambitious, Appreciative, Centered, Confident, Diplomatic, Discreet, Easygoing, Enthusiastic, Extroverted, Humble, Inspirational, Intelligent, Loyal, Objective, Pensive, Perceptive, Sensible

POSITIVE OUTCOMES

The character using their newfound influence to benefit others
Benefiting financially from the fame
Learning to navigate a new world through networking and socializing
Forging stronger relationships with friends and loved ones after passing through the trials of sudden fame
The character recognizing what's really important and choosing to step out of the spotlight
The character learning how to live a public life without sacrificing himself
Being vindicated as evidence is revealed that supports the character's innocence

GETTING LOST

EXAMPLES
The character getting lost in a busy urban area while trying to reach a destination
Getting lost in the wild, far from help
A child or vulnerable adult being separated from their caregiver
A tourist losing their tour guide or group
Fleeing to a safe rendezvous point but being unable to find it
Having to escape an area by a certain time and not being able to find the way out

MINOR COMPLICATIONS
Being late for a meeting or appointment
Being stuck with someone who is needy, argumentative, verbose, or annoying in some way
The character's phone dying, taking their only map with it
Needing to be rescued
Running into trouble for being in the wrong part of town
Needing to repeatedly stop and ask for directions
Anxiety or panic setting in, making it harder to think clearly
Looking foolish in front of others
Being blamed by one's companions
Getting caught out after curfew
Causing worry for others who are wondering where the character is
Having to care for others while leading the attempt to find the way
Taking frustrations out on others; yelling, insulting, or snapping at them

POTENTIALLY DISASTROUS RESULTS
The character sustaining an injury
Wandering unknowingly into dangerous territory
Being attacked by unsavory characters
Accepting help from someone who means the character harm
Having to find one's way while also fleeing from danger
Getting caught in severe weather conditions
Underestimating the danger and using up necessary supplies too quickly
Snapping under the pressure of being responsible for the rest of the group
An altercation causing the character to leave the group, putting them more at risk
Someone in the party disappearing
Discovering after a long period of time that the character has been going in circles
A new development that adds a critical deadline to reaching the destination (a critically injured party member, nightfall bringing on a new threat, etc.)
Death from exposure, exhaustion, or dangerous animals

RESULTING EMOTIONS: Agitation, Anger, Annoyance, Anxiety, Apprehension, Concern, Defensiveness, Desperation, Determination, Embarrassment, Fear, Flustered, Frustration, Guilt, Inadequacy, Insecurity, Loneliness, Overwhelmed, Panic, Surprise, Uncertainty, Wariness

POSSIBLE INTERNAL STRUGGLES
Needing to seek help but not wanting to leave an injured person behind to do so
Deflecting blame instead of accepting responsibility and moving on
Coming to a crossroads and not knowing which way to go
Having to act calm and controlled to avoid upsetting others in the group
Disagreeing with the group leader but being uncertain and not wanting to speak up
Harboring resentment or anger for the person who got the group lost
Showing calmness and optimism to others but being a panicky mess on the inside

NEGATIVE TRAITS THAT MAY WORSEN THE SITUATION: Abrasive, Apathetic, Controlling, Devious, Forgetful, Grumpy, Impulsive, Inattentive, Needy, Reckless, Scatter-brained, Stubborn, Timid, Worrywart

IMPACT ON BASIC NEEDS
Esteem and Recognition: If a character wants to be seen as capable and reliable, getting lost can contradict that projected identity and affect their sense of self-worth.
Love and Belonging: A character who is separated from loved ones or human beings in general for a long period of time will miss that community and fellowship with others.
Safety and Security: Getting lost in an unsafe environment can put the character in immediate physical danger.
Physiological Needs: There are many possible complications to getting lost in a remote area, such as being physically injured with no possibility of help, running out of critical supplies, or falling ill. Any of these could realistically result in the character's death.

POSITIVE TRAITS TO HELP THE CHARACTER COPE: Adaptable, Adventurous, Alert, Analytical, Calm, Cautious, Courageous, Curious, Disciplined, Industrious, Nature-Focused, Observant, Organized, Persistent, Thrifty

POSITIVE OUTCOMES
Ending up somewhere more interesting than the character had intended to go
Discovering abilities and strengths the character didn't know they had
Becoming a more proactive person who prepares better in the future
The character developing the ability to think on their feet
Meeting new people they would not have otherwise encountered

HAVING TO BEAT THE CLOCK

EXAMPLES
The character falling ill or being injured and having less time to complete a task
A deadline being bumped up
A client adding to the scope of work in the middle of a project
Needing to gather evidence or find witnesses before a trial date
Having to get somewhere by a certain time and running into traffic, construction, a parade, etc.
Missing a bus, ferry, or other mode of transport
Being given an ultimatum by a loved one to shape up or else
Only having a short period of time to divert a disaster (a bomb going off, an asteroid strike, etc.)

MINOR COMPLICATIONS
Loss of sleep due to working long nights
Decreased productivity in other areas of life
Making mistakes due to rushing
Foregoing fun and relaxing activities in favor of getting the job done
Having to learn on the job
Becoming scatterbrained and forgetful because there's just too much going on
Losing patience (snapping at people, being discourteous, etc.)
The character falling behind and the boss or client losing confidence in them
Sacrificing quality for completion; settling for "good enough"
Friction with family members over personal sacrifices needing to be made to meet the deadline
Blaming other people instead of taking responsibility for one's actions

POTENTIALLY DISASTROUS RESULTS
Hiring stopgap helpers who turn out to be a liability rather than a benefit
Reckless and erratic driving that causes an accident
Becoming addicted to stimulants
Physical ailments brought on by stress (migraines, digestive issues, hypertension, ulcers, etc.)
Failing and being fired, kicked out of college, removed from a project, etc.
Losing the competition or contest
Poor service or performance that results in the loss of an important client
Disappointing a benefactor or sponsor and losing their financial support
Public humiliation over failing to accomplish the goal in time
Large-scale devastation (if the deadline is related to a natural disaster, terrorist attack, etc.)
Failure wrecking the character's reputation
Falling into financial ruin from being fired, receiving less work, or being blackballed

RESULTING EMOTIONS: Anxiety, Apprehension, Concern, Determination, Doubt, Dread, Excitement, Fear, Irritation, Overwhelmed, Panic, Shock, Uncertainty, Unease, Worry

POSSIBLE INTERNAL STRUGGLES

Being tempted to pay someone else to do the work

Guilt or shame over realizing the character is responsible for the mess

Struggling to reconcile work and family responsibilities

Self-sabotaging through procrastination because the character believes the situation is hopeless

The character struggling with feelings of inferiority when comparing their progress with that of a rival

Battling a martyr complex (if the character feels they were treated unfairly)

Wanting to bridge the gap with angry family members but not knowing how to do so

Feeling resentful toward those who never seem to face shifting deadlines or who have ample resources to navigate changes

NEGATIVE TRAITS THAT MAY WORSEN THE SITUATION: Apathetic, Compulsive, Disorganized, Indecisive, Lazy, Perfectionist, Scatterbrained, Uncooperative

IMPACT ON BASIC NEEDS

Self-Actualization: The need to meet a deadline could remove flexibility, creativity, and spontaneity from the character's world, keeping them from being able to work on self-improvement at their own speed.

Esteem and Recognition: For characters whose self-esteem and identity are tied to their jobs, missing a deadline can change the way they view themselves (for the worse).

Love and Belonging: Some relationship deadlines are bigger than others, especially when there's friction between the parties. For example, if the character can't find a way to fix a rift with his daughter before she leaves for university, he might find this relationship growing more strained and distant as time passes.

Physiological Needs: If the need to beat the clock is tied to impending disaster, the lives of others may hang in the balance.

POSITIVE TRAITS TO HELP THE CHARACTER COPE: Adaptable, Adventurous, Ambitious, Confident, Decisive, Efficient, Focused, Industrious, Spontaneous

POSITIVE OUTCOMES

Learning to manage time much better

Being reminded of the importance of priorities

Discovering how to balance their workload so they can avoid last-minute rushes

Becoming a more conscientious person

Developing the ability to "think on their feet"

Realizing the importance of family

Using the experience to become better organized and plan for the "what if" scenario

Realizing that not every goal is worth the cost and finding balance by stepping away from the challenge

HAVING TO PROVE ONE'S INNOCENCE

EXAMPLES

The character being accused of something they didn't do

The character being framed for someone else's crime

A case of mistaken identity leading to an unfair accusation

Being in the wrong place at the wrong time, making the character appear guilty by association or involved in some way

The character getting caught doing something harmless that looks suspicious—such as forgetting where they parked their car and trying to unlock the wrong one

An innocent character being suspected because they were guilty of a similar act in the past

MINOR COMPLICATIONS

Awkward conversations with the accuser as the character pleads their case

Time taken from other activities to prove innocence

Having to take time off work to make statements or meet with people

Feelings of frustration or anger about the false accusation

Anxiety about whether they will be able to clear their name

Not knowing where to start in gathering evidence

Having no alibi for the incriminating event

Conflict with other characters who are intent on finding the character guilty

Having to answer difficult questions under duress

Shouldering the burden of people thinking the character is guilty

Losing friends who can't accept the character's innocence

Struggling to fully clear their name, even after proving their innocence

POTENTIALLY DISASTROUS RESULTS

The character responding impulsively and reinforcing the accuser's negative ideas about them

Being abandoned by loved ones who believe the character to be guilty

Loved ones being incriminated by their association with the character

Having to endure a lengthy trial process

Not being able to afford proper legal representation; being unable to mount a convincing defense

Victims seeking vengeance against the character

Suffering a catastrophic loss of reputation as a result of the false allegation

The character losing a job or suffering a divorce because of the allegations

Being forced to undergo a lengthy and unnecessary rehabilitation program

Being convicted and thrown into jail

Stress and anxiety making the character look guilty—when they fail a polygraph test, for instance

Damning evidence from the character's past coming to light, making them look more guilty

RESULTING EMOTIONS: Agitation, Anger, Anxiety, Bitterness, Concern, Defensiveness, Despair, Desperation, Determination, Dread, Embarrassment, Fear, Flustered, Frustration, Intimidation, Irritation, Nervousness, Overwhelmed, Rage, Self-Pity, Shame, Skepticism

POSSIBLE INTERNAL STRUGGLES
Wanting to prove their own innocence but having no idea how
Struggling with feelings of isolation and insecurity
Wanting to tell the truth but doing so would implicate a loved one
Feeling guilty, even though they've done nothing wrong
Fighting back the desire to seek vengeance against the accuser
Stifling feelings of anger, rage, or bitterness in an effort to get back to normal
Reliving the interaction or event as the character scours for clues to better understand how it happened

NEGATIVE TRAITS THAT MAY WORSEN THE SITUATION: Abrasive, Apathetic, Confrontational, Dishonest, Disorganized, Disrespectful, Forgetful, Impatient, Impulsive, Inhibited, Nervous, Uncommunicative, Uncooperative, Unethical

IMPACT ON BASIC NEEDS
Self-Actualization: If a character is convicted of a crime but is later exonerated, that conviction may still damage their ability to pursue meaningful life goals. A high-profile crime will be remembered—meaning, the character's name will always be tied to it.
Esteem and Recognition: Reputation damage starts with an accusation. Even if the character is proven innocent, some people will lose respect for them simply because they were mixed up in the situation in the first place.
Love and Belonging: Others might abandon a character they believe is guilty, isolating the afflicted party at a time when they most need support.
Safety and Security: If the accusation results in jail time for the character, the likelihood of experiencing unsafe situations in prison is almost guaranteed.
Physiological Needs: A character convicted of a serious crime may end up receiving the ultimate punishment and being sentenced to death.

POSITIVE TRAITS TO HELP THE CHARACTER COPE: Analytical, Bold, Calm, Charming, Confident, Cooperative, Courteous, Discreet, Efficient, Honest, Industrious, Observant, Optimistic, Organized, Persistent, Persuasive, Resourceful

POSITIVE OUTCOMES
The character being able to prove their innocence and clear their name
Finding a new lease on life after a brush with the law and choosing a new path
Making the world a safer place by providing evidence to indict the guilty party
The character emerging on the other side of the situation and seeing who their true friends are
Being able to offer forgiveness to the accuser
Bringing awareness to a flaw in the justice system and fighting to change it
The character realizing that if they succeeded in this situation, they can endure anything

INCURRING AN UNEXPECTED EXPENSE

EXAMPLES
A natural disaster damaging the character's home
A loved one's injury or sudden illness producing hefty medical fees
The death of a loved one generating travel expenses and other bereavement costs
Changes in travel plans producing fees and loss of deposits
Having to pay for a traffic ticket
Paying a fine for breaking a community bylaw
Having to hire a lawyer
Getting stuck with hidden fees
A health hazard in the home requiring the character to relocate to a hotel
Having to hire a tutor for one's child
A car accident that totals the character's car, forcing them to buy a new one
The character's pet falling ill and needing extensive medical treatment
Having to financially support a friend or family member
Being sued and having to pay a settlement

MINOR COMPLICATIONS
Having to make budget cuts in other areas to accommodate unexpected expenses
Having to take on side jobs to make up the cost, sacrificing personal time
Feeling put upon (especially if several unexpected expenses hit in a row)
The character feeling shame or embarrassment over their limited financial means
Trying to save money by fixing the problem oneself and only making it worse
Having to give up a treasured hobby or pastime to cut costs
Walking to work to save gas money
Having to explain to kids why they can't have that new item or go for ice cream
Avoiding socializing to avoid the associated costs (paying for drinks out, a babysitter, etc.)
Loved ones having to make financial sacrifices to make ends meet
Having to ask family members for a loan, causing embarrassment

POTENTIALLY DISASTROUS RESULTS
Incurring damages to one's credit rating
Being unable to attend a loved one's wedding, graduation, or other important event
Having to file bankruptcy
Becoming homeless because the character couldn't make it to work or pay the bills
Losing one's license or business privileges
Getting money from a loan shark and creating an entirely new (and worse) problem
Relationships being strained (from money being lent, having to move in with extended family, a spouse discovering the character hid the financial details, etc.)
Foregoing expensive but critical expenses (such as a medical procedure) to save money
Getting a second (or third) job to earn money to cover the costs

RESULTING EMOTIONS: Anger, Anguish, Annoyance, Anxiety, Bitterness, Concern, Defeat, Desperation, Determination, Devastation, Disbelief, Dread, Fear, Frustration, Guilt, Overwhelmed, Powerlessness, Self-Pity, Shock, Vulnerability, Worry

POSSIBLE INTERNAL STRUGGLES

Having to make difficult choices about where money can now be spent
Being tempted to get money in an unethical or unlawful way
Having to choose between one's wants and needs
Dealing with regret over not making better financial decisions and being better prepared
Hating that one's spouse or children are having to go without and being tempted to alleviate the guilt in unwise ways (by spending money on gifts, letting the kids get away with everything, etc.)
Undeserved feelings of inadequacy for not having more or being able to provide better

NEGATIVE TRAITS THAT MAY WORSEN THE SITUATION: Compulsive, Defensive, Extravagant, Foolish, Greedy, Inflexible, Irresponsible, Jealous, Materialistic, Pretentious, Self-Indulgent, Selfish, Stubborn, Uncommunicative

IMPACT ON BASIC NEEDS

Esteem and Recognition: A character whose self-esteem is tied to their possessions will struggle if they suddenly can't keep up with their materialistic, spend-happy peers.

Love and Belonging: Money is a common area of friction between family members; if the character's loved ones are unwilling to change their habits or blame the character for the new financial situation, fissures may develop in those important relationships.

Safety and Security: Financial difficulties that threaten necessary resources, like medical care, a healthy home, and the ability to hold a job, can quickly undermine the character's sense of security.

POSITIVE TRAITS TO HELP THE CHARACTER COPE: Analytical, Appreciative, Creative, Decisive, Disciplined, Efficient, Industrious, Meticulous, Organized, Patient, Proactive, Protective, Resourceful, Responsible, Sensible, Thrifty, Unselfish

POSITIVE OUTCOMES

Learning to budget for unexpected financial expenses
Through savvy financial planning, getting to a place where the character is able to financially help others
The expense leading to repairs that make the character's life safer—e.g., by removing mold from the home or fixing a car that was headed for a breakdown
Learning to ask for help and rely on others
The character being able to share their successful response plan with others who are struggling monetarily
Examining expenditures and deciding what's necessary and what isn't, helping the character to streamline their bills and allocate money for the important things

MISSING AN IMPORTANT MEETING OR DEADLINE

EXAMPLES
The character confusing the date or time of the important event
Falling ill or being injured and being unable to deliver on a favor
Members bailing on a group project, leaving the character to carry the bulk of the workload
Procrastinating and running out of time
Oversleeping and missing a meeting with one's social worker, lawyer, or parole officer
An emergency at home stealing the character's time and making them miss their deadline
Discovering a promising opportunity (such as a contest or job interview) but learning about it after the deadline has passed
Missing the birth of one's child because the character's phone was on silent during a golf round with business clients

MINOR COMPLICATIONS
Disgruntled team members having to cover for the character
Experiencing minor health problems, such as insomnia or headaches
Looking unprofessional in front of colleagues or managers
Having to share incomplete work that makes the character appear incompetent to others
The character's work reputation being tarnished
Family members being frustrated by the character's lack of commitment
A friend being angry because the character didn't do what they said they would
The meeting having to be rescheduled, inconveniencing others
The deadline being pushed back, disappointing the client and angering co-workers
Getting the silent treatment from one's spouse
The character making excuses rather than taking responsibility
Avoiding the people associated with the missed appointment

POTENTIALLY DISASTROUS RESULTS
Having to endure academic consequences (failing a class, losing a scholarship, etc.)
Lying to a spouse about what happened and being caught, further eroding their trust
Missing the chance to interview for one's dream job
Failure or poor performance wrecking the character's reputation
Throwing others under the bus, ruining relationships with them
The loss of a large client generating a financial setback for the company
Being removed from a profitable account at work
Being demoted
Trying to cover for one's lack of preparation (calling in sick the day of the meeting, for example) and getting caught
Calling someone out for missing an important event, then losing credibility by doing the same thing
Losing a custody battle because of the character's inability to get to required meetings

An overwhelmed character flying off the handle at being criticized, worsening the situation
A romantic partner getting fed up with the character's unreliability and ending the relationship

RESULTING EMOTIONS: Agitation, Anger, Anguish, Anxiety, Defensiveness, Disappointment, Embarrassment, Frustration, Guilt, Inadequacy, Nervousness, Overwhelmed, Panic, Remorse, Stunned, Unease, Worry

POSSIBLE INTERNAL STRUGGLES
The character struggling with guilt or shame because they created the problem
Being in denial over the reasons for the procrastination (being unhappy with the job, feeling incapable, etc.)
Being tempted to manufacture a lie to avoid consequences
Convincing oneself the missed opportunity wasn't a big deal
Distressing thoughts about finding a way out that reveal just how overwhelmed the character is and how much they need help

NEGATIVE TRAITS THAT MAY WORSEN THE SITUATION: Apathetic, Defensive, Dishonest, Disloyal, Evasive, Irresponsible, Perfectionist, Spoiled, Stubborn, Temperamental, Uncooperative

IMPACT ON BASIC NEEDS
   Self-Actualization: Important meetings and deadlines are established for a reason; the consequences for missing them can have ramifications across all areas of a character's life, greatly limiting their ability to be all they can be.
   Esteem and Recognition: A character who becomes known by others as unreliable, irresponsible, or selfish may begin to see himself the same way.
   Safety and Security: If the missed deadline means losing a window of time to escape, the character's troubles will escalate as their safety declines.

POSITIVE TRAITS TO HELP THE CHARACTER COPE: Ambitious, Charming, Confident, Cooperative, Diplomatic, Honest, Honorable, Mature, Passionate, Persuasive, Professional, Unselfish

POSITIVE OUTCOMES
Learning to track deadlines and plan workloads accordingly
The character recognizing and acknowledging their own weaknesses
Realizing the missed opportunity wasn't the best one for the character anyway
The character taking ownership of their mistake and being given a second chance
Being more misunderstanding when others default on their obligations
The character working twice as hard with family in the future to prove their dedication, thereby winning back their trust

REALIZING ONE IS AT A DISADVANTAGE

NOTES: In any society, people exist with different qualities, talents, experiences, and backgrounds. While differences make people unique and interesting, an unfortunate reality is that society tends to cater to a specific type of person, putting those outside of that type at a disadvantage. Differences in education, skills, mobility level, cognitive abilities, popularity, etc. can create an inequity in opportunity and may mean those people will be treated differently. In addition to this, perceived differences cause biases and discrimination, creating further inequities. As a result, a disadvantaged character will have additional challenges and face specific types of conflict.

EXAMPLES
The character discovering that a perceived difference (skin color, sexuality, lack of magical powers, etc.) is the reason they are being ostracized, marginalized, or limited in opportunity
The character realizing their dreams are unattainable because they lack the necessary finances
Lacking the skills or training necessary to achieve a goal
Lacking the measure of talent needed to prevail
Recognizing a trait the character thought was beneficial is actually a flaw and responsible for many of their troubles
Being associated with someone who puts the character at a disadvantage (because they're unpopular, a criminal, a racist, etc.)
The character realizing certain events from their past, should they be made public, will make it difficult for them to succeed
Having a mental health condition (such as a panic disorder, PTSD, or a mood disorder) that others do not
Losing one of the five senses
Receiving a medical diagnosis for a degenerative or terminal condition, such as cancer, arthritis, Parkinson's disease, or multiple sclerosis
Being injured in a way that will lead to lifelong memory issues or cognitive struggles
Being labeled with a hurtful stereotype that is unfair and limiting
Having a belief system others can't accept (practicing witchcraft, being openly agnostic in a faith-based society, being part of a group marriage, etc.) and being ostracized for it

MINOR COMPLICATIONS
Feelings of anger or despair at not being able to change the disadvantage
Anger for being targeted for reasons outside of one's control
Having to find new ways of working to accommodate for the situation
Dealing with pity, bias, and small-mindedness
The character constantly having to affirm their value to others and fight for equality
Adjusting to new routines, such as remembering to take medications on a specific schedule
Having to work twice as hard to be respected or achieve desired results
Experiencing losses because of the disadvantage (losing a competition, not getting into college, not making a sports team, missing out on promising opportunities at work, etc.)
Trying to hide the (real or perceived) disadvantage to make things easier

POTENTIALLY DISASTROUS RESULTS

Experiencing judgment, reprisals, or violence from those who are intolerant or fearful of differences

Being dumped when the disadvantage is discovered

Resorting to expensive, dangerous, or experimental treatments to improve one's situation

Refusing to acknowledge a personal challenge, resulting in the character's inability to learn coping mechanisms or receive treatment to offset some of their struggles

Giving up too soon on attempts to gain new skills that will allow the character to achieve a competitive dream

RESULTING EMOTIONS: Anger, Anguish, Bitterness, Defensiveness, Denial, Depressed, Determination, Embarrassment, Frustration, Insecurity, Powerlessness, Self-Pity, Shame

POSSIBLE INTERNAL STRUGGLES

Realizing they need help but being too proud to ask for it

Anguish over being stymied for reasons outside of their control

Rage toward people who are small-minded and judgmental

Resentment toward an uncaring society that could make life easier but refuses to

Wishing they could change something about their identity, then feeling guilty about it

NEGATIVE TRAITS THAT MAY WORSEN THE SITUATION: Impatient, Insecure, Macho, Oversensitive, Perfectionist, Prejudiced, Resentful, Self-Destructive, Uncooperative

IMPACT ON BASIC NEEDS

Self-Actualization: Developing a condition or disorder that limits the character's ability to achieve a cherished goal may require them to shift their focus to something new (but just as meaningful).

Esteem and Recognition: A character who believes an underlying condition diminishes their value will have to overcome that thinking to achieve self-acceptance.

Love and Belonging: Being treated differently for things outside the character's control can leave them feeling bitter and disconnected unless they can find people who accept and love them for who they are.

Safety and Security: If the character is in contact with someone who persecutes those who are different, they may end up in an unsafe situation.

POSITIVE TRAITS TO HELP THE CHARACTER COPE: Adaptable, Ambitious, Appreciative, Intelligent, Passionate, Patient, Persistent, Proactive, Resourceful, Spunky

POSITIVE OUTCOMES

Finding common ground with others and forming bonds with them

Learning to thrive in spite of the challenge

Helping others redefine their ideas around differences or perceived differences

Gaining a deeper understanding of identity and one's inner strength

Shining a light on unfair practices toward people with the character's difference

UNWANTED SCRUTINY

EXAMPLES
The character drawing unwanted attention (accidentally dropping something, making noise, talking too loudly) while trying to stay under the radar
Being assigned an overseer to watch one's every move
Mistakenly doing something that raises the suspicions of others
A lapse in judgment that causes others to be wary of the character
The stakes being raised in a way that everyone's attention is focused on the outcome
A loss of trust that causes someone to closely monitor the character's activities
Being followed or investigated
The character having their performance (decisions, judgments, etc.) evaluated in a test
Their loyalty being questioned, resulting in less freedom and autonomy
An increase in security measures that makes it harder to circumvent them
Being caught up in something by accident (wrong place, wrong time) that leads to being monitored for further "transgressions"
Being placed under a microscope because of racism, prejudice, or a bias
Celebrity-like status that results in the character's activities being publicized

MINOR COMPLICATIONS
Having very little privacy
Having to deal with more red tape
The character needing to report their activities or actions in a way that wasn't necessary before
Delays caused by increased security or new processes that have been implemented
Being assigned a partner or a team instead of being allowed to work independently
Having to adhere to new protocols that require someone to sign off on the character's work
Being forced to put off certain objectives until the scrutiny passes
Losing out on an opportunity
The character having to be careful about what they say and to whom

POTENTIALLY DISASTROUS RESULTS
Cracking under the pressure and making a big mistake
The character being caught in a lie or doing something they weren't supposed to do
Being unable to achieve a vital goal because of the scrutiny
Trust issues growing to the point where a relationship becomes irrevocably damaged
An enemy using the scrutiny to seed further suspicions about the character's motives
The character being forced into a corner, requiring them to break the law or become the opposition (but for the right reasons)
Being limited because of prejudice or an unfair bias
Trying to evade scrutiny and failing
The character being observed and recorded, then blackmailed
The character discovering a GPS tracker on their vehicle
Finding hidden cameras in places the character believed were private

RESULTING EMOTIONS: Agitation, Anger, Annoyance, Betrayed, Bitterness, Contempt, Defensiveness, Defiance, Determination, Disappointment, Disbelief, Disillusionment, Frustration, Indignation, Panic, Paranoia, Resentment, Shock, Unappreciated, Uncertainty, Worry

POSSIBLE INTERNAL STRUGGLES
Trying to forgive those who now mistrust the character
Being angry for making the mistake or misstep that led to the scrutiny
The character losing faith in himself or others at a critical time
Knowing there's a leak in the group and trying to figure out who is being disloyal
Resenting the constant scrutiny even though the character knew it was part of the deal (as a celebrity, CIA operative, cult member, criminal, etc.)

NEGATIVE TRAITS THAT MAY WORSEN THE SITUATION: Abrasive, Cocky, Confrontational, Disorganized, Impatient, Impulsive, Judgmental, Macho, Melodramatic, Mischievous, Obsessive, Rebellious, Reckless, Self-Destructive, Verbose, Vindictive, Volatile

IMPACT ON BASIC NEEDS
   Self-Actualization: A character may discover their dream career comes with chains that restrict their freedom and autonomy, which sours their fulfillment.
   Esteem and Recognition: A higher level of scrutiny is often born from a lack of trust—meaning, the people surrounding the character think poorly of him (believing him to be incapable, unethical, unreliable, etc.). This can bring the character down, particularly if he agrees with their assessment of his character.
   Love and Belonging: The character's close relationships may not be able to withstand the ongoing unwanted attention, leaving him isolated and forced to deal with the situation alone.

POSITIVE TRAITS TO HELP THE CHARACTER COPE: Cautious, Confident, Cooperative, Disciplined, Honest, Honorable, Humble, Intelligent, Introverted, Loyal, Obedient, Observant, Private, Resourceful, Sensible, Simple, Studious, Talented, Wholesome, Witty

POSITIVE OUTCOMES
The character being forced to slow down and think things through, thereby improving their success
The character learning who their friends really are
The character learning self-reliance and gaining confidence in their capabilities
The character discovering a knack for creatively coming up with ways to thwart observers and gain much-needed privacy

No-Win Scenarios

BEING CAUGHT IN THE MIDDLE

EXAMPLES
The character disagreeing with a spouse's parenting decision
Having a significant other who doesn't get along with the character's family
Being a mid-level manager, caught between the workers and upper management
Being good friends with two people who were in a relationship but have broken up
Being a child of divorced parents who are always talking badly about each other
Playing peacemaker in a family feud
A political figure trying to meet the needs of people with opposing views
Being a confidant to two parties who are in conflict with one another
Loving (and investing in) a pastime that one's significant other hates
Being accountable to co-founders who have preferred ways of doing things
Being asked to keep a secret that really should be revealed
The character being asked for an opinion when they know the truth will upset the other person
Being blackmailed to do or say things that hurt someone else

MINOR COMPLICATIONS
Experiencing frustration or feelings of helplessness
Being pressured to take a side
Struggling to remain neutral
Awkward conversations and encounters
Feeling overlooked or voiceless
Lying by omission and telling half-truths to keep the peace
Being honest with a wrongdoer and being castigated for it
Being used by the involved parties (via a bid for power, to get back at each other, etc.)
Being pressured by one party for information about the other
Having to reprimand an employee or co-worker
The character never feeling like they can be truly honest
Trying to please both parties and ending up pleasing no one

POTENTIALLY DISASTROUS RESULTS
Revealing information the character had been entrusted with
Feeling unwanted or unseen
Getting involved in a physical confrontation that causes injury to the character
Having to confront loved ones about the uncomfortable situation
Being coerced by the parties to do things that violate the character's moral code
Being disowned or cut off by friends or family
Having to uphold the law despite personal feelings
Needing to lay off or fire someone
Angering the wrong person
The situation getting so bad the character must cut ties with the people putting them in the position
Struggling to identify or embrace one's own identity

RESULTING EMOTIONS: Agitation, Anger, Anguish, Annoyance, Anxiety, Betrayed, Conflicted, Discouragement, Dread, Frustration, Intimidation, Irritation, Neglected, Nervousness, Resentment, Sadness, Unappreciated, Uncertainty, Worry

POSSIBLE INTERNAL STRUGGLES
Questioning one's own priorities
Debating whether to get involved, stay neutral, or exit the situation
Knowing one is being manipulated but not know how to stop it
Wanting to extricate oneself from the situation but also wanting to help
Feeling as though love and acceptance come with a price

NEGATIVE TRAITS THAT MAY WORSEN THE SITUATION: Catty, Controlling, Cowardly, Flaky, Gossipy, Gullible, Ignorant, Indecisive, Insecure, Jealous, Needy, Nervous, Subservient, Timid, Weak-Willed, Worrywart

IMPACT ON BASIC NEEDS
Self-Actualization: A character who is stuck in the middle of other people's problems may not have the time or energy to pursue their own desires.
Esteem and Recognition: If the character is being used, manipulated, or guilted into playing her part, she could likely begin to despise herself for not being stronger or more assertive.
Love and Belonging: The character in this situation may feel as though her place among friends or family has strings attached, making her believe one wrong move will oust her from those important relationships.

POSITIVE TRAITS TO HELP THE CHARACTER COPE: Bold, Centered, Confident, Creative, Diplomatic, Discreet, Honest, Independent, Objective, Observant, Persuasive, Sensible, Spunky, Uninhibited

POSITIVE OUTCOMES
Serving as a mediator in a way that yields a positive outcome
Protecting the parties from unnecessary hassle, hurt, or danger
Being able to stop a conflict from escalating
Improving one's communication skills
Being a confidant to someone in need
Learning to set healthy boundaries
An increased capacity to see situations from more than one perspective

BEING SET UP TO FAIL

EXAMPLES

The character being assigned a job where the negative outcome is already suspected or known

Being deprived of basic needs, such as food, water, or sleep, in order to be broken down

Being provided with insufficient financial resources

Being assigned a job that is beyond one's skill set

Being denied the materials needed to complete a task

Being assigned an impossible deadline

A highly moral character being placed in a situation that will require them to compromise their beliefs to win their freedom

Entering a rigged competition or contest

The character being put in a situation tailored to her weakness so a failure can be used against her

A young or new character being pitted against a seasoned competitor they cannot beat

A student being given an assignment that is too advanced for them

Being tested on material that hasn't been covered

Being set up in a romantic relationship with someone who has ulterior motives or goals that oppose the character's

Being used as a scapegoat so others can avoid the fallout tied to their bad decisions

MINOR COMPLICATIONS

Having to be creative in obtaining resources

Needing to ask for help from others

Having to deal with unreasonable or difficult people (any port in a storm)

Finding the time to make up for deficiencies

Maintaining a positive attitude

Being in an uncomfortable situation

Appearing ungrateful or negative

Needing to trade or bargain to obtain what one needs

Feeling duped

Finding the courage to remove oneself from the situation once it's clear what's going on

Speaking out against the unfairness and being labeled as paranoid or a troublemaker

POTENTIALLY DISASTROUS RESULTS

Making a critical mistake due to stress, exhaustion, and the pressure to succeed

Overspending one's personal finances

The character being perceived as a failure, despite how little control they have over circumstances

Feeling overwhelmed by the task at hand

Having to admit failure

Being fired

Receiving a poor performance or public review

Staffing shortages or equipment deficiencies creating dangerous circumstances

Feeling used or taken advantage of
Being threatened for not adhering to corrupt practices
Becoming trapped in the situation
Seeing no way out and deciding to "go along to get along"
Becoming blinded by anger and revenge and going too far to win

RESULTING EMOTIONS: Anger, Anguish, Appalled, Betrayed, Bitterness, Confusion, Contempt, Defiance, Depressed, Despair, Determination, Disillusionment, Emasculation, Fear, Frustration, Hatred, Hurt, Inadequacy, Powerlessness, Rage, Self-Pity, Shame, Shock

POSSIBLE INTERNAL STRUGGLES
Second-guessing the intentions of others
Being tempted to hold a grudge toward those who created the unfair conditions
Struggling to accept things that are beyond the character's control
Wanting to get out of the situation but not knowing how
Second-guessing one's efficacy and purpose
Feeling torn between seeing something through versus quitting
Being tempted to avoid failure by unlawful means
Questioning whether or not to be a whistleblower

NEGATIVE TRAITS THAT MAY WORSEN THE SITUATION: Confrontational, Controlling, Fussy, Gullible, Inattentive, Indecisive, Insecure, Macho, Martyr, Perfectionist, Stubborn, Subservient, Unethical, Vindictive

IMPACT ON BASIC NEEDS
   Self-Actualization: A character who fails in a bid to achieve a dream (even if it's not their fault) may be wary of trying again in the future, finding it easier to give up and settle for less.
   Esteem and Recognition: Failing at a task or relationship may cause others to think less of the character, even if conditions were beyond their control.
   Love and Belonging: A character who was victimized this way may have a hard time trusting others; this reluctance could make it harder to pursue and maintain deep and meaningful relationships.

POSITIVE TRAITS TO HELP THE CHARACTER COPE: Ambitious, Analytical, Bold, Confident, Creative, Decisive, Focused, Humble, Perceptive, Persistent, Resourceful, Responsible, Studious, Talented

POSITIVE OUTCOMES
Easily recognizing similar situations and manipulations in the future
The character going public with their experience to bring the guilty parties to justice
Finding innovative methods and new allies that enable the character, against all odds, to succeed
The character refusing to internalize the situation; recognizing their failure has nothing to do with their abilities

BEING UNABLE TO SAVE EVERYONE

EXAMPLES
The character rescuing people who are drowning in the aftermath of a boat accident
Trying to liberate people being held captive but being unable to free everyone
Trying to rescue family members from a burning building
Arriving on the scene of a train derailment where multiple people have critical injuries and being unable to get to them all
Leading an escape attempt in which some of the captives were too scared to take the opportunity and were left behind
Having a transport that can save people from an imminent threat but it has limited seating
Supporting ground troops by sniping from a distance but being unable to take out every enemy
Facing two simultaneous threats and only being able to respond to one (two bombs to be diffused, synchronized attacks happening on different battle fronts, etc.)
Needing to treat multiple people suffering from the same illness or condition and not having enough medication for them all

MINOR COMPLICATIONS
Not knowing how to prioritize one's attention
Having to choose between multiple loved ones who are suffering
Becoming paralyzed, causing further challenges or risks
Struggling to organize other survivors or bystanders to maximize the number of people who can be saved
Arguments with others over who to save and why
Seeing the clear path forward but being unable to take action (because the character is injured, someone else is in charge, etc.)
Working in an environment that becomes increasingly dangerous as time goes on

POTENTIALLY DISASTROUS RESULTS
Making a stress-induced mistake that costs lives
Relationships being ruined because of the choices one made
Being injured or falling victim to the same condition (being captured while trying to liberate others, inhaling toxic fumes while helping others escape, contracting a disease, etc.)
Being held criminally responsible despite doing everything right—a doctor being sued by the family of someone who didn't make it, for example
Being blamed or used as a scapegoat by someone using the tragedy to their advantage
Being cast out or shunned (by one's family, community, etc.) for choosing to save certain people over others
Developing Post-Traumatic Stress Disorder (PTSD) in the aftermath

RESULTING EMOTIONS: Anguish, Conflicted, Defeat, Depressed, Despair, Desperation, Determination, Devastation, Flustered, Grief, Guilt, Horror, Inadequacy, Panic, Powerlessness, Rage, Regret, Self-Loathing, Shame, Terror, Tormented, Worthlessness

POSSIBLE INTERNAL STRUGGLES

The character knowing they did their best but feeling guilty over being unable to save everyone

Beating oneself up for split-second choices made in the moment of crisis

Knowing they made the right choices about who to save but being unable to voice this to others for fear of repercussions

Questioning one's prioritization decisions that may have been based in bias

Blaming oneself for a lack of foresight (not being better prepared, lacking proper training for the crisis, not preventing the event from happening in the first place, etc.)

Guilt and shame over accidentally contributing to the event's occurrence—e.g., a security guard saving some tenants from a shooter that he later realizes he let into the building

Suffering from survivor's guilt in the aftermath; the character questioning why they survived when others who were more capable did not

NEGATIVE TRAITS THAT MAY WORSEN THE SITUATION: Cowardly, Disorganized, Indecisive, Perfectionist, Selfish, Unintelligent, Weak-Willed

IMPACT ON BASIC NEEDS

Self-Actualization: A character caught up in this situation may avoid scenarios where they are directly responsible for the welfare of others. If that role of responsibility (being a mother or father, for instance) is part of their identity, they may reject it out of fear and never feel fully actualized.

Esteem and Recognition: If grief causes others to attack the character and blame them for their decisions and actions, it might trigger the character's insecurities, crumbling their self-worth.

Love and Belonging: If a victim was a loved one, this could cause friction with existing family members.

POSITIVE TRAITS TO HELP THE CHARACTER COPE: Bold, Calm, Courageous, Decisive, Focused, Honorable, Intelligent, Objective, Observant, Persistent, Protective

POSITIVE OUTCOMES

A greater appreciation for life and reprioritizing what's truly important

The brush with tragedy causing the character to reevaluate their own relationships

Choosing to let go of grudges because life is too short

Realizing life is precious; deciding to live it free of regret

Becoming better able to share emotion with others, ceasing to hold back

Gaining perspective about one's place in the world and what one really wants, leading to a stronger focus on achieving meaningful goals

The character being prompted to become more skilled or better prepared in the future

CONFLICTING INTERNAL NEEDS OR DESIRES

NOTES: By definition, conflict forces characters to choose between competing needs or desires. The most powerful conflicts involve choices whereby the outcomes both have value. While this entry explores some examples of this kind of conflict, you can find many more in the MORAL DILEMMAS AND TEMPTATIONS section of this book.

EXAMPLES
The character wanting children when their partner does not
Struggling with peer pressure
The character wanting to leave a job that a friend helped secure
Wanting to stay in a location while a significant other wants to move
Wanting to end a marriage but needing to stay for the children's sake
The character struggling with their faith and considering leaving their religion
Yearning to have both a career and a family but not being able to do both
Deciding between a less-satisfying job that pays well and lower-paying, fulfilling work
Objecting to war but wanting to serve one's country
Defending a guilty defendant during a trial
Deciding whether or not to serve as a witness to a violent crime
A character who values privacy craving a career that would put them in the spotlight
Unburdening one's guilt by sharing an uncomfortable truth
Not knowing what to do when one's personal desires conflict with a loved one's
A character wanting to be accepted by others while staying true to himself
The character being tempted to do something they know they shouldn't

MINOR COMPLICATIONS
Dealing with criticism from others who don't know the whole story
Making a decision that disappoints friends, family, an employer, or mentor
Having to convince loved ones to come around to the character's way of thinking
Making the right decision but doing it in a way that hurts others
Resenting the people on the other side of the issue, even if they're not deliberately trying to make the character's life difficult
Choosing to compromise on something really important
Being afraid to make the wrong decision
Difficulty weighing the pros and cons of the decision
Having to listen to other people tell the character what they would do in his situation

POTENTIALLY DISASTROUS RESULTS
Losing an important ally, job, or opportunity as a result of the decision
Seeking advice from the wrong person (someone foolish, inexperienced, or with ulterior motives)
Others being harmed or set back by the character's decision
Being disowned by one's family
Making a decision that will benefit others and having to live an unfulfilled life because of it

Making a decision that will benefit the character and being vilified for doing so

Creating a situation where someone else must make the decision (because the character is too afraid to), then having to live with it

The character changing their moral beliefs to make it easier to make the decision they want

RESULTING EMOTIONS: Agitation, Anguish, Anxiety, Conflicted, Confusion, Defensiveness, Discouragement, Doubt, Dread, Embarrassment, Flustered, Inadequacy, Obsession, Overwhelmed, Reluctance, Resignation, Uncertainty, Worry

POSSIBLE INTERNAL STRUGGLES

The character wanting to please herself but also wanting approval from others

Being paralyzed by the ongoing inability to make a decision

The character questioning their moral code—wondering if they're being closed-minded, old-fashioned, or too fixed in their thinking

Being tempted to maintain the status quo versus making a decision that would cause change

Looking to compromise in a situation where there is a clear right and wrong

Struggling to separate emotion from judgment, especially when facing questions of right vs. wrong

The character changing who they are or giving up on their dreams

Making a decision, then obsessing over it and second-guessing it

NEGATIVE TRAITS THAT MAY WORSEN THE SITUATION: Childish, Cowardly, Flaky, Foolish, Gullible, Impatient, Indecisive, Nervous, Obsessive, Selfish, Superstitious, Weak-Willed, Worrywart

IMPACT ON BASIC NEEDS

Self-Actualization: A character struggling to make this choice may become wary of facing difficult decisions in the future; this risk aversion can keep them from making the changes needed to achieve personal and professional growth.

Esteem and Recognition: The longer this inner turmoil goes on, the more the character may question their instincts and their ability to make the right choices under pressure.

Love and Belonging: A character struggling internally may pull away from loved ones to hide their indecision and insecurity, creating distance in those relationships.

POSITIVE TRAITS TO HELP THE CHARACTER COPE: Analytical, Centered, Decisive, Efficient, Honest, Just, Objective, Patient, Responsible, Unselfish, Wise

POSITIVE OUTCOMES

The character being at peace with the decision they made

Earning the respect of and support from others for navigating a difficult situation

The character's ideas about right and wrong being solidified through the process

Discovering unexpected satisfaction in meeting a loved one's needs

Talking things through with a trusted friend and avoiding endless loops of doubt and indecision

HAVING TO HURT SOMEONE TO SAVE THEM FROM A WORSE FATE

NOTES: This thorny situation has no simple solution and can birth a lot of conflict for a character. For specific examples, see HAVING TO DECIDE TO HELP OR DO NOTHING, LEAVING SOMEONE TO THE CONSEQUENCES OF THEIR ACTIONS, BEING THE BEARER OF BAD NEWS, HAVING TO BREAK A PROMISE, and HAVING TO PUNISH SOMEONE.

EXAMPLES
The character having to confront someone about unhealthy attitudes or habits
Breaking up with someone because the character knows it won't work out in the long run
Turning down an unqualified or inexperienced job candidate
Turning someone in for committing a crime
Evicting a loved one so they can learn to stand on their own feet
The character having to hold a student back in school
Forbidding a relationship between a loved one and someone who would be bad for them
Turning someone down for a loan they won't be able to repay
Reporting someone who is experiencing a mental health crisis, abuse, or neglect so they can be helped
Holding an intervention for a loved one with an addiction problem
The character surrendering their parental rights because they can't care for their child
Cutting off contact with a loved one before they're hurt by an upcoming decision
Issuing a consequence so a child can learn from their mistakes
Intervening to remove bad influences from a teen's life
Sharing a friend's secret about abuse, an unhealthy relationship, or a harmful habit
Choosing to give bad news to a friend so they won't hear it from a stranger

MINOR COMPLICATIONS
Procrastinating over doing the difficult thing
Trying to find the right words to explain one's actions
Doing the deed without sufficient preparation
Taking a get-it-over-with approach and one's lack of tact causing more pain
Having good intentions but lacking all the necessary information or details
The other party not appreciating the character's choice or method of delivery
Developing a reputation for meddling in the affairs of others
Friends and loved ones disagreeing with the character's decision
The character having to make the difficult decision on their own (due to privacy issues)

POTENTIALLY DISASTROUS RESULTS
The other person physically or verbally attacking the character
The other party responding in a dysfunctional way (relapsing into an addiction, denying the situation, becoming suicidal, etc.)

Saving the other person but losing their friendship
Being forced to make a decision where none of the outcomes are good
Unintentionally making the situation worse
Being unable to help the person in the aftermath because the relationship has been damaged
The offended party trashing the character's reputation with others

RESULTING EMOTIONS: Anguish, Anxiety, Appalled, Bitterness, Conflicted, Despair, Determination, Devastation, Doubt, Dread, Fear, Guilt, Hopefulness, Intimidation, Love, Nervousness, Regret, Resignation, Unappreciated, Uncertainty, Unease, Worry

POSSIBLE INTERNAL STRUGGLES
Seeing all the different perspectives, making it harder to choose the right course of action
Second-guessing whether the right decision is being made
Feeling ashamed for being tempted to take the easier road and let nature take its course
The character knowing someone else's life is in their hands and struggling to bear the weight
The character blaming herself for the part she played (even if there was no real choice)
Questioning how much or how little to tell the people involved
Insurmountable guilt causing the character to withdraw into herself

NEGATIVE TRAITS THAT MAY WORSEN THE SITUATION: Addictive, Apathetic, Callous, Cowardly, Cruel, Flaky, Gossipy, Impulsive, Indecisive, Judgmental, Melodramatic, Pushy, Tactless, Verbose, Vindictive, Weak-Willed

IMPACT ON BASIC NEEDS
   Esteem and Recognition: The character's struggle to identify the best course of action may leave them feeling inadequate and undependable.
   Love and Belonging: A friend or family member who is turned in or exposed for their misdeeds will very likely feel betrayed. So while the character is trying to prevent them from continuing down a dark path, it's unlikely that relationship will survive.
   Safety and Security: Someone who doesn't react well to bad news could hurt the character or make threats that cause them to feel unsafe.

POSITIVE TRAITS TO HELP THE CHARACTER COPE: Analytical, Bold, Cooperative, Diplomatic, Empathetic, Friendly, Honorable, Nurturing, Objective, Observant, Persuasive, Protective, Sensible, Supportive, Wise

POSITIVE OUTCOMES
Averting a disaster for a loved one
Building trust in a relationship
Being seen as someone who can make difficult but sensible choices
The character gaining satisfaction from having put the needs of others before their own
Preventing someone from suffering
Being assured the right decision was made even if it wasn't well-received

HAVING TO PICK THE LESSER OF TWO EVILS

EXAMPLES
Injuring or killing someone in self-defense
Having an abortion or facing pregnancy-related medical risks
Seeking a medical solution that will have severe side effects or letting a serious illness go untreated
Allowing parents to choose one's marriage or career (thereby maintaining the relationship) or defying them to pursue personal happiness (and risking alienation)
Making financial sacrifices now so one can obtain something in the future or getting what one wants now and having to go without in the future
Making the choice to succumb to blackmail rather than be exposed
Ending a close but toxic relationship
Choosing a high-paying job that compromises the character's morals or a financially dissatisfying job that allows them to be true to their values
Having to lay off employees to save a business or hold onto them, causing the company to go under
Going public with a scandal and becoming a target (instead of turning a blind eye and remaining safe)
Surrendering a dream to meet someone else's basic needs (by taking in an ailing parent or allocating finances to help an underserved portion of the population) or fulfilling one's ambition and living with uncertainty or guilt
Having to choose between putting a critically ill pet to sleep or going into debt to secure an expensive treatment

MINOR COMPLICATIONS
Knowing a decision must be made and none of the results will be satisfying
A relationship being damaged
The character being criticized by others for their impossible choice
Making the best decision and still having to live with unpleasant results
Mental distress from being in the situation
In the wake of the character's indecision, someone else stepping in and choosing the option the character is most opposed to
Feeling misunderstood by others
Having to justify the choice to those who have something at stake

POTENTIALLY DISASTROUS RESULTS
Making the wrong decision
After action has been taken, new information coming to light that reshapes the situation
Facing criminal charges for the part the character played
Being rejected by family
Becoming the target of violence
An unhappy party talking badly about the character on social media
Relationships ending as a result of the decision

Having no allies; having to go through the situation alone
Procrastinating to the point that something awful happens
Choosing the lesser of two evils and still being unable to save or help the other party

RESULTING EMOTIONS: Anger, Anguish, Anxiety, Appalled, Bitterness, Conflicted, Depressed, Despair, Determination, Devastation, Doubt, Dread, Fear, Guilt, Hysteria, Intimidation, Nervousness, Regret, Resignation, Unappreciated, Uncertainty, Unease, Worry

POSSIBLE INTERNAL STRUGGLES
Questioning why one has been put in this position
Feeling inadequate for not being able to spot an option that avoids painful fallout
Weighing the various options and not seeing a clear path forward
The character being unable to forgive himself for the decision, leading to depression
Maintaining a long-range view in the face of short-term impacts
Knowing what's right but being reluctant to put people through pain and agony
Living with perpetual unhappiness caused by regret

NEGATIVE TRAITS THAT MAY WORSEN THE SITUATION: Cowardly, Cynical, Foolish, Frivolous, Indecisive, Insecure, Needy, Nervous, Prejudiced, Pushy, Selfish, Tactless, Unintelligent, Weak-Willed, Worrywart

IMPACT ON BASIC NEEDS
   Self-Actualization: A character who is consumed by guilt or haunted by this no-win situation will need to forgive themselves if they are to pursue satisfying personal goals.
   Esteem and Recognition: The character in this situation is sure to be criticized; if they don't go into it with a strong sense of self, they may emerge doubting their decision and believing the bad things others say about them.
   Love and Belonging: This kind of scenario can generate strong opinions from those outside the situation, meaning the character is likely to lose friends or supporters no matter what choice they make.
   Safety and Security: A character facing this dilemma is almost certain to feel less than safe if either option will produce difficult fallout and backlash.

POSITIVE TRAITS TO HELP THE CHARACTER COPE: Analytical, Calm, Cautious, Confident, Courageous, Decisive, Diplomatic, Easygoing, Honorable, Idealistic, Just, Kind, Mature, Objective, Persuasive, Responsible, Wise

POSITIVE OUTCOMES
The character making the decision and putting it behind them, confident they did their best
Taking action that greatly improves someone else's life
Finding a sense of pride and self-worth for making the hard decision
The character's values and ideals being affirmed
Being recognized for having good judgment
Avoiding a disaster in exchange for accepting a manageable loss
Others looking up to the character because they didn't let fear sway them

NEEDING TO SACRIFICE ONE
FOR THE GOOD OF MANY

EXAMPLES

The character limiting their intake of basic needs so loved ones can have them

Sending someone to near-certain death so they can find help in the aftermath of a disaster or accident

Leaving someone behind to act as a rear guard so the rest of the group can escape

Sending someone into a dangerous situation so people can be rescued

Assigning someone to sample a community's food supply that's suspected of being poisoned

The character choosing to be a whistleblower, knowing it will put a target on their back

Giving up one's life to save others

Participating in clinical trials or an experimental medical treatment

Firing a high-paid employee to keep others on payroll

Medical resources in an apocalyptic situation being reserved for those who are most likely to survive

Sending a spy into enemy territory to gain much-needed information

Assassinating a despot to save millions of lives

Culling a sick animal from the herd to keep the others from falling ill

MINOR COMPLICATIONS

Having to choose who will be sacrificed

Being criticized for selectively choosing the sacrificial person so it's not one of the character's friends or loved ones

Having to listen to biased, hysterical, or otherwise unhelpful advice

Having to explain one's decision to others

Having to persuade others that this is for the best

Being viewed as heartless for one's decision

Being replaced as the leader in the wake of one's decision

Being pressured by powerful people to do what they want

POTENTIALLY DISASTROUS RESULTS

Failing to make the right choice

Being unable to live with the outcome

Developing PTSD

Facing criminal charges for the decision

The sacrifice being unsuccessful or ineffective

The person risking themselves suffering serious injury or death

Having to watch the person suffer and carry the burden of their sacrifice

Having to interact with the person's left-behind family members

Watching the person die

Missing an alternative solution that would have made the sacrifice unnecessary

Being hated by others for one's decision, even though there was no good choice

Facing a mutiny in one's group
Becoming hardened in the aftermath to the point of apathy

RESULTING EMOTIONS: Anger, Anguish, Anxiety, Defiance, Depressed, Despair, Determination, Devastation, Disgust, Doubt, Dread, Fear, Grief, Guilt, Hopefulness, Horror, Inadequacy, Loneliness, Panic, Powerlessness, Rage, Remorse, Self-Loathing, Shame, Tormented

POSSIBLE INTERNAL STRUGGLES
Second-guessing one's ability to choose the right person to act as sacrifice
Vacillating between various options
Being tempted to pass the responsibility to someone else
Finding the courage to sacrifice oneself
Relying on bias to make the decision (choosing a competitor or enemy, for instance) and struggling with guilt for not being more objective
Reliving painful moments from the situation (the conversation informing the person they would be left behind, the last glimpse of the person, the moment of their death, etc.)
Being overwhelmed by shame and self-loathing for not finding a way to save everyone
Knowing the decision was systematic and objective but still experiencing turmoil over it

NEGATIVE TRAITS THAT MAY WORSEN THE SITUATION: Apathetic, Catty, Controlling, Cowardly, Cruel, Gullible, Ignorant, Impulsive, Manipulative, Morbid, Prejudiced, Selfish, Stubborn, Subservient, Tactless, Vindictive, Weak-Willed, Worrywart

IMPACT ON BASIC NEEDS
Esteem and Recognition: The character's self-esteem or reputation may be permanently damaged as a result of having to make such an impossible decision.
Love and Belonging: A character who is unable to forgive himself or move past the decision may push people away and isolate himself, either as a form of punishment or to keep from getting close to people he will maybe one day have to sacrifice.
Safety and Security: In a situation where the group is critical to survival, any decision that puts the character at risk with that group will inherently threaten both his safety and security.
Physiological Needs: In a volatile, post-apocalyptic scenario where people are desperate and willing to do anything to survive, the character may encounter lethal resistance by the chosen one's family and friends.

POSITIVE TRAITS TO HELP THE CHARACTER COPE: Analytical, Bold, Calm, Centered, Confident, Courageous, Decisive, Diplomatic, Independent, Just, Meticulous, Objective, Optimistic, Persuasive, Sensible, Wise

POSITIVE OUTCOMES
Being able to save the lives of many people
Obtaining help or securing safety for a group
Being rewarded instead of damned for doing well in an impossible situation
The character finding forgiveness though they didn't expect it
Finding worthiness in being responsible for these decisions so others aren't burdened with them

APPENDIX A: HOW WILL YOUR CHARACTER RESPOND TO CONFLICT?

Conflict can come in many forms and will hit your characters again and again in the story. Our goal is to think of meaningful conflict scenarios that do more than push them to work harder to succeed—it challenges their perceptions and forces them to choose: Will they be controlled by the fear of what may happen or will they act in spite of it?

Below is a chart of generalized paths to success or failure to keep in mind. Many external factors will influence the outcome, and we want our characters to fail at times so they dig even deeper. But for a character on a change arc, no matter how they might resist at first, an internal transformation will become necessary for them to eventually win.

PATH TO SUCCESS	POSSIBLE CONFLICT SCENARIOS	PATH TO FAILURE
NEED Feels held back or unfulfilled	OBSTACLES CHALLENGES ROADBLOCKS	**NEED** Feels held back or unfulfilled
OPPORTUNITY Possible solution to a problem or path to something better	CLASHING BELIEFS TRAPS	**OPPORTUNITY** Possible solution to a problem or path to something better
CONFLICT A challenge that forces them outside their comfort zone	COMPETITION PROBLEMS OPPOSITION TIME LIMITS	**CONFLICT** A challenge that forces them outside their comfort zone
FEAR Remembers painful past experiences but pushes through	TEMPTATION RELATIONSHIP FRICTION	**FEAR** Becomes paralyzed from believing that past experiences will reoccur
GROWTH Adopts new methods, behaviors & ideas	COMPETING GOALS PRESSURE LIMITATIONS	**ANTI-GROWTH** Retreats to old methods & flawed thinking
ACHIEVEMENT Fulfilled & ready for the next challenge	INNER STRUGGLE OBLIGATIONS	**FAILURE** Unfulfilled but reluctant to pursue a better life

APPENDIX B: IDENTIFYING YOUR CHARACTER'S INTERNAL CONFLICT

A character traversing a change arc will have one overarching internal struggle that will plague them throughout the story. Because they'll have to acknowledge and settle this inner conflict to achieve success, it's vital for you to know what it is. It can stem from various sources, so use this tool to brainstorm options.

Before you can identify the character's main internal conflict, you'll need to establish a few important pieces of their arc:

> **Emotional Wound**: What traumatic event from the past still haunts your character?
> **Outer Motivation**: What is your character's main story goal?
> **Inner Motivation**: What missing need will be met by achieving that goal?

Once you've figured these out, use them to discover what inner conflict your character will struggle with throughout the story. Keep in mind that this conflict will 1) directly block their inner motivation, and 2) relate to their self-esteem or fulfillment. Below are a few examples to illustrate how the pieces fit together. For a refresher on which missing needs could be the cause of your character's inner motivation, see the Unmet Human Needs portion of the INTERNAL CONFLICT AT THE STORY LEVEL section of this book.

Zack Mayo (*An Officer and a Gentleman*)			
Emotional Wound(s)	**Outer Motivation**	**Inner Motivation**	**Inner Conflict**
His mother's suicide; being raised by his carousing, self-indulgent father and having to fend for himself	*Become an officer in the Navy*	*Become an officer and be part of a group (Love and Belonging)*	*Life has taught Zack that he can only count on himself. His self-serving mindset keeps him from developing the deep and meaningful relationships that will allow him to truly belong.*
Cheryl Strayed (*Wild*)			
Emotional Wound(s)	**Outer Motivation**	**Inner Motivation**	**Inner Conflict**
Her mother's death	*Hike the 1100-mile-long Pacific Crest Trail*	*Find peace for herself (Self-Actualization)*	*Cheryl's inability to let go of the grief and anger surrounding her mother's death makes healing difficult.*
Erin Brockovich (*Erin Brockovich*)			
Emotional Wound(s)	**Outer Motivation**	**Inner Motivation**	**Inner Conflict**
Growing up poor with a learning disability	*Win the court case for her underdog clients*	*Accomplish something important that will garner the respect of others (Esteem and Recognition)*	*Erin's brusque communication skills, defensiveness, and confrontational nature make it difficult for her to gain the respect of others and achieve her goal*

APPENDIX B: IDENTIFYING YOUR CHARACTER'S INTERNAL CONFLICT

Gather the following information to identify the main source of inner conflict for your characters. If you'd like to deepen the story, look for places where these factors might clash, driving the members of your story's cast apart, or alternatively, create common ground, bringing them together.

Character 1			
Emotional Wound	**Outer Motivation**	**Inner Motivation**	**Inner Conflict**

Character 2			
Emotional Wound	**Outer Motivation**	**Inner Motivation**	**Inner Conflict**

Character 3			
Emotional Wound	**Outer Motivation**	**Inner Motivation**	**Inner Conflict**

Character 4			
Emotional Wound	**Outer Motivation**	**Inner Motivation**	**Inner Conflict**

Download additional copies of this template at https://writershelpingwriters.net/writing-tools/.

CREATE A PAGE-TURNER WITH VOLUME 2 OF THE CONFLICT THESAURUS

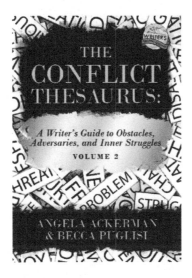

With so many conflict scenarios to explore, this topic just couldn't be contained in one book. Enter the second half of *The Conflict Thesaurus*. This volume continues the exploration of conflict and how it will shape the plot and challenge your characters. You'll also find information on character agency, writing the all-important climax scene, methods for ramping up your conflict, and how to resolve it in ways that satisfy readers.

The entry portion of the second volume is similar to the first but contains different categories. This will provide you with more ways to craft psychological and physical struggles that will force your characters to dig deep to overcome them:. For your convenience, we've provided the following list of conflict scenarios that can be found in this book, along with a sample entry. For more information on all our publications, please visit the Writers Helping Writers' bookstore page (https://writershelpingwriters.net/bookstore/).

LOSS OF CONTROL

A Break-In
A Family Member Dying
A Partner Racking up Debt
A Recession or Economy Crash
An Unexpected Pregnancy
Bad Weather
Being Captured
Being Evicted
Being Framed
Being Given Bad News
Being Injured

Being Orphaned
Being Pushed Toward a Specific Destiny
Being Scammed
Being Stranded
Being Taken in for Questioning
Discovering One Has a Child
Getting in a Car Accident
Having a Miscarriage
Having a Panic Attack
Having to Leave Someone Behind
Having to Move
Losing a Child in a Public Place

Not Achieving a Coveted Goal
Rent Being Raised
The Death of a Pet

POWER STRUGGLES
Being Arrested
Being Bullied
Being Falsely Accused
Being Pressured by Family
Being Pressured to Conform
Being Sabotaged
Being Sued
Clashing Beliefs
Experiencing Discrimination
Experiencing Harassment
Forced Attendance
Misaligned Goals
Nepotism or Favoritism

LOSING AN ADVANTAGE
A Competitor Showing Up
A Place of Safety Being Compromised
Being Cast Out of a Group
Having to Leave One's Home or Homeland
Lacking an Important Resource
Losing a Key Witness
Losing a Vital Item
Losing Access to Someone Important
Losing Access to Something Important
Losing an Ally
Losing One's Funding
Rules Changing to One's Disadvantage
Running out of Critical Supplies
Something Important Being Stolen

EGO-RELATED CONFLICTS
An Unexpected Loss of Prestige or Wealth
Being Cut from a Team
Being Discredited
Being Excluded
Being Lied To
Being Micromanaged
Being Physically Marred Before an Important
Event
Experiencing a Crisis of Self-Doubt

Facing a Challenge Beyond One's Skill or
Knowledge
Having to Rely on Others
Having to Stay Behind
Learning That One Was Adopted
Needing to Borrow Money
Not Being Taken Seriously
One's Authority Being Threatened
Public Humiliation
Telling the Truth but Not Being Believed

DANGERS AND THREATS
A Dangerous Crossing
A House Fire
A Loved One Being Put in Harm's Way
A Mechanical Malfunction
A Natural Disaster
A Threatening Criminal Being Set Free
A Way of Life Being Threatened
Being Assaulted by a Stranger
Being Assigned a Dangerous Task
Being Cut off from Help
Being Exposed to an Allergen
Being Poisoned
Being Recognized
Being Targeted by a Monster or Supernatural
Force
Being Targeted for Revenge
Being Trapped
Facing a Threat While Unarmed
Having To Hide or Escape Detection
Having to Make a Final Stand
Having to Split up for Safety
War Breaking Out
Witness Intimidation

MISCELLANEOUS CHALLENGES
A Fear or Phobia Rearing Its Head
A Health Issue Cropping Up
A Repressed Memory Resurfacing
An Anticipated Event Being Canceled
An Unexpected Change of Plans
An Unwanted Intrusion
Being Cursed
Being Forced to Lead

Being in the Wrong Place at the Wrong Time
Being Mistaken for Someone Else
Being Placed Under a Spell
Being Unable to Forgive Oneself
Contemplating Suicide
Discovering a Dead Body
Experiencing Memory Loss
Having a Crisis of Faith
Having to Blindly Trust Someone
Having Unwanted Powers
Needing to Circumvent Security
Needing to Infiltrate a Group
Needing to Lie Convincingly
Not Knowing What One Wants
Physical Exhaustion

SAMPLE ENTRY: BEING INJURED

EXAMPLES
Slipping on a wet floor
Falling down a flight of stairs
Misusing a tool and sustaining an injury
Overexerting while working out
Being injured while playing a sport
Being attacked by an animal or another person
Getting hurt while under the influence
Sustaining an injury because a safety protocol wasn't followed
Being hurt in a car accident

MINOR COMPLICATIONS
Feeling foolish (if the character is at fault)
Attending multiple doctor or physical therapist appointments
Missing work or school while healing
Having to file medical insurance or legal documentation
Having to rely on others while recuperating
Complications resulting in a longer than usual recovery time
Needing to learn about the injury and the options for treating it
Having to arrange for childcare
Finding affordable medical care
Being questioned by police (if foul play was involved) or safety inspectors and human resources (if the injury happened at work)
Missing out on previously made plans
Not being able to care for family while recovering
Having to go to the hospital

POTENTIALLY DISASTROUS RESULTS
Being blamed despite someone else being at fault
Facing legal charges for criminal activity related to the injury
Needing care and having no one to help
Becoming injured in an isolated location
Needing to relocate closer to loved ones or medical care
The character being unable to continue their job because of the injury
Not having access to adequate medical care
Incurring insurmountable medical bills
Becoming disfigured or disabled in a life-altering way
The injury leading to life-threatening medical complications
Miscarrying a baby
Suffering chronic pain
Becoming addicted to pain pills
A family member being injured or killed in the same situation that wounded the character

RESULTING EMOTIONS: Anxiety, Bitterness, Defeat, Denial, Depressed, Devastation, Disbelief, Emasculation, Embarrassment, Fear, Frustration, Grief, Guilt, Humbled, Impatience, Inadequacy, Insecurity, Powerlessness, Regret, Self-Pity, Shock, Uncertainty, Worthlessness

POSSIBLE INTERNAL STRUGGLES
Experiencing guilt for having to depend on others
Struggling with trauma associated with the circumstances of the injury
Feeling shame for choices that led to the situation
Struggling with the loss of independence and self-reliance
The character questioning their self-worth
Hating that people treat them differently after the injury
Accident-related anxiety affecting the character's performance
Developing a fear or phobia around being injured
Having difficulty accepting the injury's impact on their life
Experiencing survivor's guilt

NEGATIVE TRAITS THAT MAY WORSEN THE SITUATION: Addictive, Controlling, Cowardly, Impatient, Impulsive, Inflexible, Insecure, Macho, Melodramatic, Morbid, Needy, Perfectionist, Pessimistic, Reckless, Resentful, Self-Destructive, Vain, Weak-Willed, Withdrawn

IMPACT ON BASIC NEEDS
Self-Actualization: An injury will likely move the character's focus away from higher-level needs, especially if it directly impairs an activity they previously enjoyed. They may also become pessimistic and bitter if the injury forces them to give up a dream.
Esteem and Recognition: A character's self-image will suffer if an injury lessens their ability to function as they once did.
Safety and Security: A character's injury and an inability to care for themselves or loved ones can threaten their sense of security.
Physiological Needs: Under specific circumstances, an injury in an isolated location could become life-threatening.

POSITIVE TRAITS TO HELP THE CHARACTER COPE: Adaptable, Ambitious, Analytical, Appreciative, Centered, Courageous, Disciplined, Industrious, Inspirational, Objective, Optimistic, Patient, Persistent, Proactive, Resourceful, Responsible, Sensible, Spiritual

POSITIVE OUTCOMES
Learning to persevere and overcome obstacles
Finding a better career path because of the injury
Becoming inspired to help others or taking up a philanthropic cause
Educating others about the injury or circumstances surrounding it
Learning to accept help from others
Becoming more cautious and responsible
Finding faith in life's difficult circumstances
Discovering a community of survivors
Acquiring a renewed perspective on life

RECOMMENDED RESOURCES

Like oil in an engine, conflict keeps your story chugging along. If you're looking to add to your knowledge of conflict and how it can contribute to character development and a strong story structure, consider the following writing guides.

Conflict & Suspense is packed with everything you need to know to spice up your story, move your plot forward, and keep your readers turning pages. (James Scott Bell)

Understanding Conflict (and What it Really Means) is an easy-to-use guide filled with ideas on how to build and amplify conflict. (Janice Hardy)

Save the Cat: The Last Book on Screenwriting You'll Ever Need isn't just for screenwriters. This best-selling guide is a primer on storytelling in any form, packed with information on making your ideas more marketable and your story more satisfying. (Blake Snyder)

The Conflict Thesaurus at One Stop for Writers contains the entire collection of entries in one database, expanded to include even more information to make your story's conflict as powerful and dramatic as possible.

The One Stop for Writers' Conflict Tutorial is a quick and dirty manual on conflict and what it can do for your story and characters. It's a handy reference when you need a refresher on this important storytelling element.

Formal and Informal Scene Maps at One Stop for Writers allow you to plan and organize the scenes in your story to make sure they're doing what they need to do. With formal and informal maps at your disposal, you'll be able to record the conflict scenarios, stakes, character motivation, and emotions that will play a part in each scene.

ADD WRITERS HELPING WRITERS®
TO YOUR TOOLKIT!

Over a decade of articles are waiting to help you grow your writing skills, navigate publishing and marketing, and assist you on your career path. Sign up for blog updates to get expert craft advice from resident writing coaches delivered weekly to your inbox, stay informed about forthcoming books, and discover unique resources. You can access even more practical writing tips by signing up for our Writers Helping Writers newsletter (https://writershelpingwriters. net/subscribe-to-our-newsletter/).

PRAISE FOR...

THE EMOTION THESAURUS

"One of the challenges a fiction writer faces, especially when prolific, is coming up with fresh ways to describe emotions. This handy compendium fills that need. It is both a reference and a brainstorming tool, and one of the resources I'll be turning to most often as I write my own books."

~ **James Scott Bell, best-selling author of** *Deceived* **and** *Plot & Structure*

THE POSITIVE AND NEGATIVE TRAIT THESAURUSES

"In these brilliantly conceived, superbly organized and astonishingly thorough volumes, Angela Ackerman and Becca Puglisi have created an invaluable resource for writers and storytellers. Whether you are searching for new and unique ways to add and define characters, or brainstorming methods for revealing those characters without resorting to clichés, it is hard to imagine two more powerful tools for adding depth and dimension to your screenplays, novels or plays."

~ **Michael Hauge, Hollywood script consultant and author of** *Writing Screenplays That Sell*

THE URBAN AND RURAL SETTING THESAURUSES

"The one thing I always appreciate about Ackerman and Puglisi's Thesauri series is how comprehensive they are. They never stop at just the obvious, and they always over-deliver. Their Setting Thesauri are no different, offering not just the obvious notes of the various settings they've covered but going into easy-to-miss details like smells and tastes. They even offer to jumpstart the brainstorming with categories on potential sources of conflict."

~ **K.M. Weiland, best-selling author of** *Creating Character Arcs* **and** *Structuring Your Novel*

THE EMOTIONAL WOUND THESAURUS

"This is far more than a brilliant, thorough, insightful, and unique thesaurus. This is the best primer on story—and what *really* hooks and holds readers—that I have ever read."

~ **Lisa Cron, TEDx Speaker and best-selling author of**
Wired for Story* and *Story Genius

THE OCCUPATION THESAURUS

"Each and every thesaurus these authors produce is spectacular. *The Occupation Thesaurus* is no different. Full of inspiration, teachings, and knowledge that are guaranteed to take your writing to the next level, it's a must. You need this book on your craft shelf."

~**Sacha Black, best-selling author of fantasy and the *Better Writing* series**

THE CONFLICT THESAURUS, VOLUMES 1 & 2

"If characters drive the story, then conflict operates as the engine to every tale. Keeping this tenet in mind, writing experts Angela Ackerman and Becca Puglisi return with their most ambitious, hefty thesaurus yet, examining conflict in multiple dimensions and on multiple levels. Every writer should keep this volume handy as they work."

~ **Ekta R. Garg, editor and author of *The Truth About Elves***

Curious about our books? Download samples of all the volumes in our special **Show-Don't-Tell Pro Pack**, available at Writers Helping Writers®. (https://writershelpingwriters.net/writers-helping-writers-descriptive-thesaurus-sampler-2/).

EVERYTHING YOU NEED TO CREATE
IN ONE PLACE

ONE STOP
F O R
WRITERS

Ready for a game-changer?

In today's crowded market, only exceptional fiction gets noticed. So the authors of this book created One Stop for Writers—a go-to web app that will activate your imagination and provide the story support you need to create stronger, fresher stories. It contains:

- The largest show-don't-tell descriptive database available anywhere
- A hyper-intelligent Character Builder tool
- Custom Character Arc Blueprints
- Story Maps, Scene Maps, and Timeline tools
- Idea generators
- Templates, worksheets, tip sheets, and checklists that demystify a variety of storytelling elements
- Craft tutorials and terminology glossaries
- The Storyteller's Roadmap, a step-by-step system for planning, writing, and revising a story or novel

If you've been searching for a resource to shorten the learning curve and help you create authentic characters who are part of well-structured, engaging plots … well, One Stop for Writers will change the way you create fiction. No more staring at the screen, wondering what to write. No more wishing you had an expert to help you navigate story craft. Get ready to write stronger fiction faster.

Visit One Stop for Writers (https://onestopforwriters.com) and test-drive our 2-week FREE TRIAL. If you choose to subscribe, use the **ONESTOPFORWRITERS** code for a one-time discount of 25% off any plan.

See you at One Stop!

Made in United States
North Haven, CT
25 March 2024

50471678R00167